Elements of the Law of Agency

Elements of the Law of Agency

By

Ernest W. Huffcut

Professor of Law in Cornell University School of Law

BeardBooks

Washington, DC

Reprinted 1999 Beard Books, Washington, D.C.

Printed in the United States of America

ISBN 1-893122-23-9

TO

HARRY B. HUTCHINS, FRANCIS M. BURDICK,
AND CHARLES A. COLLIN,

WHO, TOGETHER WITH THE LAMENTED DOUGLASS BOARDMAN,
CONSTITUTED THE FIRST FACULTY OF THE CORNELL
UNIVERSITY SCHOOL OF LAW,

THIS VOLUME IS GRATEFULLY INSCRIBED BY THEIR
PUPIL AND CO-WORKER,

THE AUTHOR.

PREFACE.

The primary purpose of this volume is to set forth the manner in which obligations are incurred through the acts of an agent, and to do this as a natural sequence to a study of the manner in which like obligations are incurred by one's own acts. The obligations here dealt with are mainly contract obligations, or tort obligations springing from contract; the tort obligations of a master for the acts of his servant are discussed only so far as the two fields overlap. Parts I. and II. will serve, however, as an introduction to the latter subject, since they are mainly concerned with the contract of employment.

A volume of selected cases to accompany the text is in preparation, and will shortly appear.

The desire to keep the volume within as small a compass as possible made it inexpedient to give references to parallel series of reports in the foot-notes, but this defect has been in part remedied by printing such references in the table of cases.

It were ungrateful not to acknowledge the debt owing to previous writers on this subject. The works of Mr. Justice Story, Mr. Wharton, Mr. Evans and his American editor, Mr. Ewell, and the more recent work of Mr. Mechem, have been of the greatest assistance, and are among the permanent treasures of our legal literature. It is hoped that this little volume may serve to introduce the student to an important branch of the law of obligation which he will pursue further in these works of the masters.

E. W. H.

Cornell University School of Law,
October, 1895.

TABLE OF CONTENTS.

INTRODUCTION.

CHAPTER I.

PRELIMINARY TOPICS.

PART I.

FORMATION OF THE RELATION OF PRINCIPAL AND AGENT.

CHAPTER II.

FORMATION OF THE RELATION BY AGREEMENT.

1. *Agency by Contract.*

1. *By Bilateral Act.*

2. *By Unilateral Act.*

3. *By Operation of Law.*

4. *Irrevocable Agencies.*

PART II.

LEGAL EFFECT OF THE RELATION AS BETWEEN PRINCIPAL AND AGENT.

CHAPTER VII.

OBLIGATIONS OF PRINCIPAL TO AGENT.

CHAPTER VIII.

OBLIGATIONS OF AGENT TO PRINCIPAL.

1. *Agents by Contract.*

PART III.

LEGAL EFFECT OF THE RELATION AS BETWEEN THE PRINCIPAL AND THIRD PARTIES.

CHAPTER IX.

CONTRACT OF AGENT IN BEHALF OF A DISCLOSED PRINCIPAL.

CHAPTER X.

CONTRACT OF AGENT IN BEHALF OF UNDISCLOSED PRINCIPAL.

1. *The Doctrine of Privity of Contract.*

2. *Liability of an Undisclosed Principal.*

3. *Rights of an Undisclosed Principal.*

CHAPTER XI.

ADMISSIONS AND DECLARATIONS OF AGENT.

CHAPTER XII.

NOTICE TO AGENT.

CHAPTER XIII.

LIABILITY OF PRINCIPAL FOR TORTS OF AGENT.

1. *Liability for Torts Generally.*

2. *Liability for Fraud of Agent.*

3. *Liability for Statutory Torts and Crimes.*

4. *Liability for Torts of Sub-Agent.*

5. *Public Principals and Charities.*

CHAPTER XIV.

LIABILITY OF THIRD PERSON TO PRINCIPAL.

1. *Contract Obligations.*

2. *Quasi-Contract Obligations*

3. *Tort Obligations.*

4. *Trust Obligations.*

PART IV.

LEGAL EFFECT OF THE RELATION AS BETWEEN THE AGENT AND THIRD PARTIES.

CHAPTER XV.

CONTRACT RELATIONS BETWEEN AGENT AND THIRD PARTY.

1. *Where Principal alone is Bound.*

2. *Where Agent alone is Bound.*

3. *Where both Principal and Agent are Bound.*

4. *Where neither Principal nor Agent is Bound.*

5. *Special Case of Public Agents.*

6. *Liability of Agent in Quasi-Contract.*

7. *Liability of Third Person to Agent.*

CHAPTER XVI.

TORTS BETWEEN AGENT AND THIRD PARTY.

APPENDIX.

TABLE OF CASES.

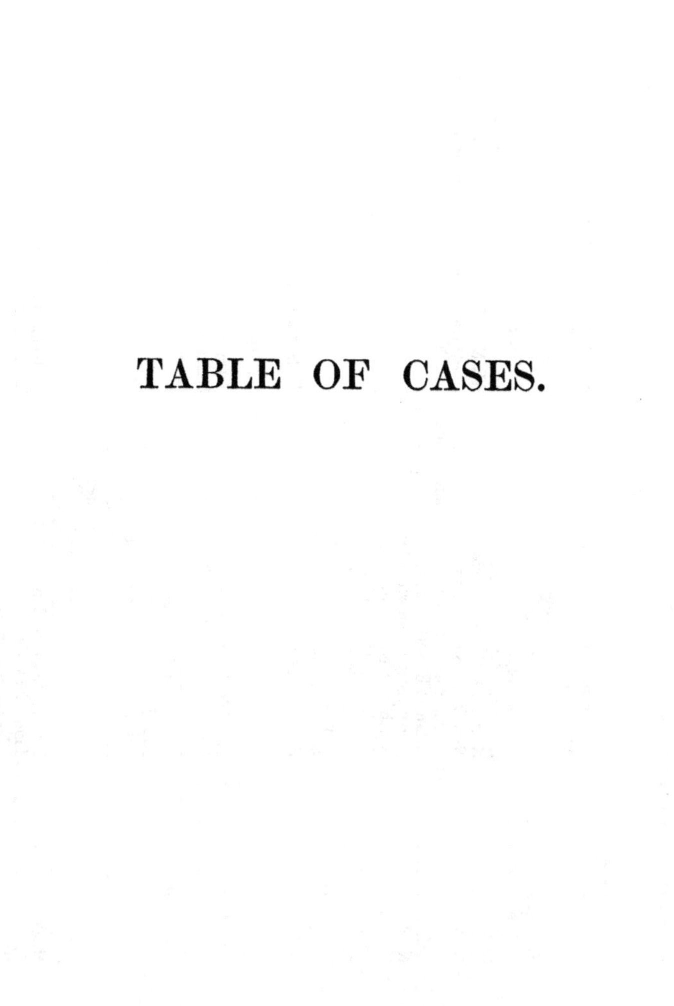

EXPLANATORY NOTE.

In the foot-notes to the text, the jurisdiction from which the citation is taken usually appears by the name of the report itself, or, where the report bears the name of the reporter, in parentheses. Where no jurisdiction is indicated, the citation is from an English report.

In the following table reference is given not only to the report cited in the text, but also to parallel reports, periodicals, and reprints. These are indicated by the following abbreviations: —

AMERICAN REPORTS.

ABBREVIATION.	FULL TITLE.	JURISDICTION.	PERIOD COVERED.
A. D.	American Decisions	Selected State Decisions	1700–1869
A. R.	American Reports	Selected State Decisions	1869–1887
A. S. R.	American State Reports	Selected State Decisions	1887–
Fed. Cas.	Federal Cases	All U. S. District and Circuit Courts	1789–1880
Fed. Rep.	Federal Reports	All U. S. District and Circuit Courts	1880–
L. R. A.	Lawyers' Reports Annotated	Selected Federal and State Decisions	1888–
N. Y. St. R.	New York State Reporter	All New York Courts	1886–
N. Y. Supp.	New York Supplement	Intermediate and Lower New York Courts	1888–
	(National Reporter System. Includes also Fed. Rep., N. Y. Supp., and S. C. R.)		
Atl.	Atlantic Reporter (1885–)	All State and Territorial Decisions in Courts of last resort	1879–
N. E.	Northeastern Reporter (1885–)		
N. W.	Northwestern Reporter (1879–)		
Pac.	Pacific Reporter (1883–)		
So.	Southern Reporter (1887–)		
S. E.	Southeastern Reporter 1887–)		
S. W.	Southwestern Reporter (1886–)		
S. C. R.	Supreme Court Reporter	U. S. Supreme Court Decisions	1881–

ENGLISH REPORTS.

ABBREVIATION.	FULL TITLE.	JURISDICTION.	PERIOD COVERED.
Eng. C. L.[1]	English Common Law Reports	(American Reprint of English Cases)	1813–1865
Eng. L. & Eq.	English Law and Equity Reports	(American Reprint of English Cases)	1850–1857
Jur.	The Jurist		1837–1854
Jur. N. S.	The Jurist, New Series		1854–1866
L. J. Bk.	Law Journal Reports, Bankruptcy		1832–
L. J. Ch.	Law Journal Reports, Chancery		
L. J. C. P.	Law Journal Reports, Common Pleas		
L. J. Ex.	Law Journal Reports, Exchequer		
L. J. Q. B.	Law Journal Reports, Queen's Bench		
L. T.	Law Times Reports		1860–
Moak	Moak's English Reports	(Selected English Cases)	1871–1887
T. L.	Times Law Reports		1884–
W. R.	Weekly Reporter		1852–

[1] As these volumes have sub-labels indicating the original English report, it has not been thought profitable to give parallel references to this series.

TABLE OF CASES.

THE LAW OF AGENCY

AS RELATED TO CONTRACT.

PRINCIPAL AND AGENT.

THE LAW OF AGENCY.

INTRODUCTION.

CHAPTER I.

PRELIMINARY TOPICS.

§ 1. Representation in the Law of Obligation.

THE doctrine of representation is of the highest importance in the law of obligation. A man is obligated either (1) because he has consented to be, or (2) because the law on considerations of public policy or utility thinks it best he should be. And these fundamental principles of obligation extend not only to the relations established by the individual in person, but also to the relations established by him through the instrumentality of one to whom he, or the law acting for him, has delegated authority. Representation therefore creates a secondary range of obligations differing from the primary range only in the fact that the one obliged acts not in person but through a representative.

The problem reduced to its simplest terms is to discover when, and under what circumstances, a man is obligated by the act of his representative. This problem would be a comparatively easy one were it true that a man is obliged by the act of his representative only when he has in fact authorized the representative to do or not to do that which results in obligation. Agency is a compendious term signifying the instrumentality through which a result is accomplished; in its normal sense it means the instrumentality through which the will of an individual is accomplished. If therefore a man chooses to employ a particular agency to carry out his pre-determined purpose he is of course responsible for the result determined upon and reached, as fully as if he had acted immediately instead of mediately. In such a case we should be concerned only with the result, and not with the means through which it was accomplished. But the doctrine is much more sweeping in its application. In the employment of a human agency the principal must take account, not only of his own will but also of the will of the agent. This second will may prove either incompetent, or careless, or perverse, and from this incompetence, carelessness, or perversity may flow consequences never intended by the principal, but for which the law holds him accountable. Thus it follows that a man may be obligated by the act of a representative which he has not only not authorized but which he has in terms forbidden. Further, he may be obligated by the act of one whom he never made his representative, or he may be obligated retroactively by the adoption of the act of one who was not his representative at the time the act was done.

The study of the law of obligation, — whether in contract or in tort, — requires, therefore, for its completion, a study of the law of representation.

§ 2. Basis of the Doctrines of Representation.

Historically the basis of the doctrines of representation or agency is to be sought in the fiction of identity.[1] This

[1] O. W. Holmes, Jr., 4 Harv. L. Rev. 345; 5 Ib. 1. See 2 Pollock and Maitland, Hist. of Eng. Law, 225–227, 530, where the learned authors

notion is familiar in the law applicable to husband and wife, where the fiction of unity or identity has been pushed to its extreme limit. It re-appears in the curious modern doctrine of the identification of a child with its parent or guardian in cases of negligence.[1] It is, in fact, founded on the primitive notion of the family relationship, a relationship which included as one of its titles the relation of master and servant.

The progress from status to contract has, however, rendered agreement rather than family relationship the starting point of the doctrines of representation. A man is now generally a representative, not because he has been born such, but because he has agreed to be such. A man is now generally bound as principal, not because of his status toward some representative, but because he has agreed to be responsible for the acts of his representative, or at least has agreed that some person shall represent him with the like effect as if he acted in person. Yet the agency of a wife in the purchase of necessaries is a distinct remnant of the older doctrine based on status. And in many particulars, the modern law of agency is profoundly influenced by the old notion of the identity of the principal and agent, — as in the doctrines applicable to notice or to the rights and liabilities of undisclosed principals.[2]

The maxim "*Qui facit per alium facit per se*" embodies the general doctrine on which the law of principal and agent rests.[3] "He who acts through another acts in person," is the general proposition. The inquiry is, when is one acting through another, and when is that other acting for himself?

doubt this, and query whether the basis is not the greater ability of the master to pay; and see to the same effect 7 Harv. L. Rev. 107.

[1] Hartfield *v.* Roper, 21 Wend. (N. Y.) 615.

[2] 5 Harv. L. Rev. 1–6.

[3] 4 Harv. L. Rev. 347.

§ 3. Constituent and Representative.

Representation involves two persons, the one represented and the one representing. To avoid confusion between the different kinds of representation the one represented may, in a general way, be termed the constituent, and the one representing may be termed the representative. The subject then divides itself into two main branches, the law of master and servant, and the law of principal and agent; the constitutent may be either (*a*) a master, or (*b*) a principal; the representative may be either (*a*) a servant, or (*b*) an agent.

This distinction is of comparatively recent origin and is not even yet always clearly observed. Blackstone treats agents as a "species of servants."[1] Very recent writers have contended that the two are essentially identical.[2] But since the time of Lord Mansfield who settled the principles of the mercantile law, and in view of the extraordinary development of commercial enterprises in the present century, the distinction has become, if not absolutely essential, at least highly convenient. While, as will be pointed out hereafter, it is not always easy to draw a sharp line of distinction between the two classes of representatives, yet it is possible to do so in the great majority of instances, and it will conduce to clearer conceptions of the doctrines peculiar to representation if the distinction is observed. The law of contract and tort often overlap, yet no one would contend that for that reason we should treat the law of obligation as a whole without observing the distinction between the two.

While there are various classes of agents, the distinctions among the classes are based either on the degree of the authority or on the nature of the service. But of

[1] 1 Comm. 427.

[2] O. W. Holmes, Jr., 4 Harv. L. Rev. 345; 5 Ib. 1; Charles Claflin Allen, 28 Am. L. Rev. 9.

servants there are two classes, which differ in kind so far as the relation to the master is involved. This difference is material, however, only where the master is sought to be obligated by one servant for the negligent act of another. In such a case it is essential to inquire whether the two servants are fellow-servants, for if so, one cannot recover against the master for an injury caused by the negligent act of another.[1] Accordingly the courts have made a distinction between servants who are fellow-servants and those who are not, one class of cases resting the distinction on the rank of the servants, a distinction known as the "superior officer doctrine,"[2] and another class of cases resting the distinction on the nature of the act performed, a distinction known as the "vice-principal doctrine,"[3] but which, to avoid confusion in nomenclature, might better be termed the "vice-master doctrine." These distinctions belong to a treatise on the law of master and servant, and are introduced here only for the purpose of completing a classification and explaining a nomenclature which are fundamental in the law of representation.

The results of this classification may be tabulated as follows: —

I. Obligation arises from the act of the one obliged, or from the act of his representative.

II. Obligation through representation involves, (1) the constituent, (2) the representative, (3) the one in whose favor the obligation arises.

III. Constituent and representative are general terms which may be divided into, —

[1] Farwell *v.* Boston, &c. R., 4 Met. (Mass.) 49.

[2] Chicago, &c. R. *v.* Ross. 112 U. S. 377. Cf. Baltimore, &c. R. *v.* Baugh, 149 U. S. 368.

[3] Loughlin *v.* State of New York, 105 N. Y. 159; Crispin *v.* Babbitt, 81 N. Y. 516.

(1) Master and servant, the servant being either, (*a*) an ordinary or fellow servant, (*b*) not an ordinary or fellow servant, known variantly as (*α*) a superior officer or (*β*) a vice-master;

(2) Principal and agent, the agent having various special names, not, however, indicating differences in kind.

§ 4. Distinction between Agent and Servant.

The fundamental distinction between an agent and a servant lies in the nature of the act which each is authorized to perform. An agent represents the principal in the performance of an act resulting in a contractual obligation, or an obligation springing from contract relations. A servant represents the master in the performance of an act not resulting in contractual obligation. The law governing the one belongs therefore to that branch of the law of obligation having to do with contracts, or torts springing from contracts, as deceit. The law governing the other belongs to that branch of the law of obligation having to do with torts generally. And so we find the subject treated in the books on contract and tort respectively. The same reasons that lead to a separate treatment of contract and tort lead to a separate treatment of agents and servants.

Since it is the nature of the act to be performed that constitutes the essential difference between the two classes of representatives, it follows that the same representative may be both an agent and a servant, and herein lies the source of much of the confusion that prevails in the discussion of the law of representation. It is often said that the distinction lies in the fact that an agent is vested with discretion, while a servant is not.[1] But this is obviously

[1] 28 Am. L. Rev. 9, 22, *citing* Chicago, &c. R. Co. *v.* Ross, 112 U. S. 377, 390.

incorrect. A railway conductor is not an agent merely because he is vested with a wide discretion as to the management of his train; he may or may not be a vice-master, but he is a servant so long as his authority is to do an act not resulting in contractual obligation; if vested with authority to engage employees then for that purpose he is an agent and not a servant, since his act results in the creation of a contractual obligation. So a representative authorized to sell a horse to a specified person at a specified price for cash is not a servant merely because he has no discretion as to the terms of the sale; his act results in a contractual obligation, and he is therefore an agent; if, however, he is vested with authority to drive the horse to a designated place he is a servant in the performance of that duty, for if he drive the horse negligently to the injury of A. the constituent becomes liable in tort for the damage.[1]

§ 5. Definition of Agent.

An agent may be defined as a representative vested with authority to bring or aid to bring his constituent, called a principal, into contractual relations with third persons.

"Vested with authority" includes authority acquired either through the will of the principal or by operation of law, and authority acquired either prior or subsequent to the performance of the representative act.

[1] "The great and fundamental distinction between a servant and an agent is, that the former is principally employed to do an act for the employer, not resulting in a contract between the master and a third person, while the main office of an agent is to make such contracts. Servants may make contracts incidentally, while agents may in the same way render acts of service. The principal distinction between them, however, is as above stated." — Dwight, Persons and Pers. Prop. p. 323. See Singer Mfg. Co. *v.* Rahn, 132 U. S. 518; Hand *v.* Cole, 88 Tenn. 400; Jones *v.* Avery, 50 Mich. 326.

"Contractual relations" includes all the topics usually treated in works on contracts, as the formation of contract, the discharge of contract, rights of action, judgments, admissions, notice, etc.

§ 6. Distinction between Agency and other Contractual Relations.

It is often difficult to determine whether a contract between A. and B. results in the creation of the relation of principal and agent or of a relation of a different character. Yet on the solution of this question depends the liability of the parties to each other and to third persons.

(1) *Agency or Sale.* Whether the relation between the parties is that of principal and agent or vendor and vendee must depend upon the construction of the contract. A. agrees to dispose of goods placed in his hands by B., and at periodical intervals return an account to B. of the sales made, and turn over to B. the value of the goods sold, at a fixed price, keeping himself the difference between this price and the price at which he has sold them. This might be a *del credere* agency,[1] or a sale as between A. and B. The construction to be placed on the contract will vary in accordance with the terms and the evident intention of the parties.[2] The refinements are too nice to be discussed here, but will be disclosed by an examination of the cases.

(2) *Agency or Lease.* In like manner it becomes a matter of construction whether a party to a contract is an agent or a lessee. Although the party may be acting under a formal power of attorney authorizing him to

[1] *Post,* § 96.

[2] *Ex parte* White, L. R. 6 Ch. App. 397; *Ex parte* Bright, L. R. 10 Ch. D. 566; National Cordage Co. *v.* Sims, (Nebraska) 62 N. W. Rep. 514; Willcox, &c. Co. *v.* Ewing, 141 U. S. 627; Chezum *v.* Kreighbaum, 4 Wash. 680; Singer Mfg. Co. *v.* Rahn, 132 U. S. 518.

represent the other party in the management of certain property, yet this, in connection with the conduct of the parties, may be construed as a lease of the property so as to make the lessee liable for rent as the assignee of the term.[1]

(3) *Agent or Independent Contractor.* If A. engages B. to do a certain work, B. may be the agent or servant of A., or he may be an independent contractor. The test usually applied is whether A. retains any control over the means or methods by which the work is to be accomplished. If he does, B. is an agent or servant;[2] if he does not, B. is an independent contractor.[3] The question whether A. is liable for the unsafe condition of his premises, or of a public street over which he has been given control, involves other considerations having to do with the high degree of responsibility placed upon occupiers of premises.[4]

(4) *Agency or Partnership.* It is sometimes difficult to determine whether a contract creates the ordinary relation of principal and agent or the special relation of partnership. Even where parties unite in a joint enterprise and agree to share the profits, a partnership does not necessarily result; the participation in profits is an element in the problem, but is not decisive. It is a question of construction upon the whole agreement, the intention of the parties being the controlling consideration.[5]

[1] Ragsdale *v.* Land Co., 71 Miss. 284, 303–7.

[2] Linnehan *v.* Rollins, 137 Mass. 123; Lawrence *v.* Shipman, 39 Conn. 586. But the owner may approve or disapprove the work daily without retaining control. Casement *v.* Brown, 148 U. S., 615.

[3] Bailey *v.* Troy, &c. Co., 57 Vt. 252; Harrison *v.* Collins, 86 Pa. St. 153; King *v.* New York Central, &c. R., 66 N. Y. 181.

[4] Gorham *v.* Gross, 125 Mass. 232; Woodman *v.* Metropolitan R. Co., 149 Mass. 335.

[5] Grinton *v.* Strong, 148 Ill. 587; Wright *v.* Davidson, 13 Minn. 449.

(5) *Transfer of Service.* A principal or master may transfer temporarily the service of the agent or servant to another, so as to make the latter the representative of the transferee. Thus A. rents a machine to B. with a man to operate it. If, in the operation of the machine, the man is under the control of B., he becomes B.'s servant as to the operation, though not perhaps as to the inspection and repair, of the machine.[1] But otherwise, if the man remains under the control of A., who stands somewhat in the relation of an independent contractor.[2] The master cannot transfer the control over a servant without the latter's consent.[3]

§ 7. Classification of Agents.

Agents are often divided into general agents and special agents, and many refinements as to the liability of the principal have been built upon this classification. The distinction is a vague one, and often leads to more confusion than it cures. To begin with, writers do not agree as to the distinction itself, much less as to its legal effects. One writer makes the distinction to consist in the extent of the representation ; that is, if the agent represents the principal in a single transaction, he is a special agent, while if he represents him in all business dealings of a particular kind, he is a general agent.[4] Another writer finds the distinction in the source of the discretionary power. If the agent's powers are fixed by the terms of his appointment, he is a special agent, while if his powers are fixed by custom and usage, he is a general agent.[5]

1 Donovan *v.* Laing, (1893) 1 Q. B. 629.

2 Quinn *v.* Complete Electric Const. Co., 46 Fed. Rep. 506 ; Huff *v.* Ford, 126 Mass. 24.

3 *Post*, § 86.

4 Mechem on Agency, § 6 ; Story on Agency, § 17 ; Butler *v.* Maples, 9 Wall. (U. S.) 766.

5 Holland, Jurisp. (5th ed.) p. 234 ; Dwight, 1 Col. Law T. 81.

Clearly it would be of the first importance to know which of these views is correct if anything depended upon the distinction, for they are irreconcilable. If a principal entrusted a cargo of wheat to a factor to sell, the agent would be a special agent under the first view, but a general agent under the second. If a principal's liability depends upon the solution of the question whether the agent is special or general, the conclusions reached would be exactly opposed to each other. As we shall see later, the question of the principal's liability can be determined without involving it in the solution of this preliminary question.[1] The terms special agent and general agent may therefore be disregarded except as terms of convenience to indicate broadly the scope of the agency.

Agents are also divided into *del credere* agents, or those who guarantee their principals against the default of those with whom contracts are made, and agents not *del credere*, or those who do not guarantee credits.[2]

Special names are also applied to certain classes of agents, as, attorneys-at-law, auctioneers, brokers, factors or commission merchants, shipmasters, cashiers, etc.[3]

§ 8. Division of the Subject of Agency.

Agency may be treated from two quite distinct points of view. First, it may be treated as a contract between the principal and the agent, and inquiry may be directed to the ascertainment of the terms and legal effects of this contract. Second, it may be treated as a means to the formation of contractual relations between the principal and some third person, and inquiry may be directed to the ascertainment of the legal effects of the employment of such an instrumentality. The first view of the subject presents no special difficulties, since the contract obligations are created by the two parties in person, and the

[1] *Post*, § 104. [2] *Post*, § 96. [3] *Post*, § 110 *et seq.*

usual doctrines of contracts for personal service are applicable. The second view is the one which makes necessary a special treatment of the law of agency, — first, because an agency for the purpose indicated may be created otherwise than by contract between the principal and agent; and second, because a principal whose will is represented by a second will may be bound, though the second will prove careless, incompetent, or perverse, and though it act in direct opposition to his own will. A third view, subordinate to the second, is that of the relation of the agent to the third party with whom he deals in behalf of his principal, for an agent may, in consequence of his manner of dealing, incur legal obligations or acquire legal rights as to the third person.

The subject is therefore divided into four parts : —

1. The formation of the relation, either as to the obligations subsisting between the principal and agent, or between the principal and the third party.

2. The mutual rights and obligations of the principal and agent as to each other.

3. The mutual rights and obligations of the principal and any third person with whom the agent may have dealt.

4. The mutual rights and obligations of the third person and the agent.

PART I.

FORMATION OF THE RELATION OF PRINCIPAL AND AGENT.

§ 9. Introductory.

The inquiry whether the relation of principal and agent has been formed or exists may arise either in a controversy between the principal and agent, or between the principal and some third person with whom the agent has dealt, or between the agent and such third person. To avoid useless repetition, this part of the work will therefore discuss the formation of the relation as concerns any one or all of these possible cases. For the one or the other of these purposes the relation may be formed in any one of four ways: (1) by agreement; (2) by ratification; (3) by estoppel; (4) by necessity.

In addition to a consideration of the methods of forming the relation, this part will also discuss the methods by which the relation may be terminated.

CHAPTER II.

FORMATION OF THE RELATION BY AGREEMENT.

§ 10. Elements of Agreement.

Agreement implies offer and acceptance, or the meeting of the minds, or manifestation of the meeting of the minds, of the parties.[1] Accordingly an agency by agreement is one where the principal and agent mutually consent to the formation of the relation. Such agreement may amount to a contract, or it may fall short of contract. If it amount to a contract, it is binding as between the principal and agent, and when acted upon may bind the principal to third persons or third persons to the principal. If it fall short of contract, it will not be binding as between the principal and agent as a contractual obligation, but when acted upon by the agent as an authority to do or not to do certain things for the principal, may bind the principal to third parties and third parties to the principal, and may render the agent liable to the principal for misfeasance, or to third parties for excess of authority. We have therefore to consider the formation of the relation, (1) by contract, (2) by agreement falling short of contract.

1. *Agency by Contract.*

§ 11. Elements of Contract.

A contract of agency must possess all the essential elements of any enforceable contract, namely, true agreement, consideration, competent parties, legality of object,

[1] Anson on Cont. (8th ed.) p. 3.

and in some cases a particular form.[1] Most of these elements call for no special discussion, as they differ in the contract of agency in no essential particular from the like elements in any contract known to the law. Some special points of difficulty may be briefly noted.

§ 12. Agreement, Forms of.

The agreement between the principal and agent may take any one of three forms: (1) the offer of a promise for an act; (2) the offer of an act for a promise; (3) the offer of a promise for a promise.[2]

The first case is where the principal promises remuneration if the agent will render a service. The promise may be express, or it may be an implied promise to pay what the services are reasonably worth. An express agreement controls;[3] in its absence an implied agreement may be inferred. Strictly the promise would be offered for the act only when there was a request that the act be done.[4] And even in such a case the circumstances may negative any implication that the services were to be paid for.[5] Such is the result where the services are rendered by one member of a family at the request of another.[6]

The second case is where the agent offers a service which the principal accepts. The acceptance may be by express words, stating the terms, in which case the express promise would control; or it may be by conduct, in which case there is an implied promise to pay what the services are reasonably worth.[7] The test is as to whether a reason-

[1] Anson on Cont. (8th ed.) pp. 10 *et seq.*

[2] Anson on Cont. (8th ed.) Pt. VI. Ch. i.

[3] Wallace *v.* Floyd, 29 Pa. St. 184.

[4] Van Armen *v.* Byington, 38 Ill. 443.

[5] Scott *v.* Maier, 56 Mich. 554.

[6] Hall *v.* Finch, 29 Wis. 278.

[7] Muscott *v.* Stubbs, 24 Kans. 520; McCrary *v.* Ruddick, 33 Iowa, 521.

able man would understand that the agent expected to be paid for his services. It is because reasonable men understand that services rendered by one member of a family for another are generally gratuitous that an offer of an act by the one, accepted by the other, raises no promise to pay.[1] Of course if the offer of the act is not communicated to the principal until after it is performed, and he has therefore had no opportunity either to accept or reject it, he would not be bound.[2]

The third case is that of a promise for a promise, or where there is an express contract, the agent promising to perform the service, and the principal to pay for it. In this, and the other cases, it is necessary that the agreement be real, that is, free from mistake, misrepresentation, fraud or duress.

§ 13. Consideration.

Consideration consists in a benefit to the promisor or a detriment to the promisee. It is as necessary to the contract of agency as to contracts generally. The only case calling for special mention is where the services have been rendered gratuitously, and there is a subsequent promise to pay for them. Generally speaking there would be no consideration for the subsequent promise, since, there being no prior legal obligation, the case would be one of past consideration, which will not support a promise.[3] Cases which seem to hold to the contrary are those in which there was either a previous request, express or implied, or where the services were rendered under such circumstances as not to be deemed gratuitous, and the

[1] Hertzog *v.* Hertzog, 29 Pa. St. 465; Hall *v.* Finch, 29 Wis. 278.

[2] Bartholemew *v.* Jackson, 20 Johns. (N. Y.) 28; James *v.* O'Driscoll, 2 Bay (S. C.), 101.

[3] Allen *v.* Bryson, 67 Iowa, 591.

subsequent promise merely fixes expressly the value of the services.[1]

But while gratuitous services may raise no promise to compensate, a promise to perform a gratuitous service, followed by an actual performance, in whole or in part, may be enforceable to the extent of rendering the agent liable for negligence. But whether this is on the ground of contract or tort, is not clear.[2]

§ 14. Parties, — Competency of, generally.

Generally speaking, parties competent to make any contract are competent to make a contract of agency.[3] As between the principal and agent this rule is well enough, but as between the principal and third persons it calls for further examination and modification. On the one hand, we have to inquire whether an incompetent person, as a lunatic or an infant, can make a contract through a competent agent; on the other, whether a competent person can make a contract through an incompetent agent. This discussion is applicable to cases of gratuitous agency and of ratification as well as to cases of agency by contract.

§ 15. Parties. — Infant Principals.

It is sometimes said that all contracts of an infant are voidable except two, — the contract for necessaries, which is binding, and the contract for the appointment of an agent, which is void.[4] It is the last proposition which calls for special notice.

If an infant, by contract or otherwise, appoints an agent, and this agent makes a contract with X. in behalf of the

[1] Dearborn *v.* Bowman, 3 Metc. (Mass.) 155; Hicks *v.* Burhans, 10 Johns. (N. Y.) 243; Wilson *v.* Edmonds, 24 N. H. 517.

[2] Thorne *v.* Deas, 4 Johns. (N. Y.) 84. See *post*, § 29.

[3] See generally Anson on Cont. (8th ed.) Pt. II. Ch. iii.

[4] Fetrow *v.* Wiseman, 40 Ind. 148, 155.

infant principal, is the contract so made void or voidable? If the appointment of the agent is a void act, then obviously no legal results can flow from it, and the contract with X. must likewise be void. If void, it could not be ratified by any subsequent act of the principal.[1] There are many cases which make the sweeping statement of the law that the appointment of an agent by an infant is a void act, and that the acts done by the agent in behalf of the principal are likewise void.[2] But these authorities are in every case based upon the appointment of an attorney by formal warrant of attorney, and the rule to be deduced from them is that the formal power or warrant of attorney by an infant is void. The American cases show a decided tendency to confine the rule to this class of cases, and to hold that the appointment of agents by an infant generally, is a voidable and not a void act.[3] Yet there is authority for the broader rule that the appointment of any agent by an infant is void.[4] It is admitted that the exception, if it be one, is not founded on any intelligible principle, and the tendency to confine it within the narrow limits of formal powers of attorney is likely to prevail.[5]

§ 16. Parties. — Insane Principals.

The generally accepted rule in England as to the effect of insanity upon contracts is that "a defendant who seeks

[1] *Post*, § 41.

[2] Philpot *v.* Bingham, 55 Ala. 435; Knox *v.* Flack, 22 Pa. St. 337; Bennett *v.* Davis, 6 Cow. (N. Y.) 393.

[3] Patterson *v.* Lippincott, 47 N. J. L. 457; Towle *v.* Dresser, 73 Me. 252; Hardy *v.* Waters, 38 Me. 450; Hastings *v.* Dollarhide, 24 Cal. 195; Whitney *v.* Dutch, 14 Mass. 457.

[4] Trueblood *v.* Trueblood, 8 Ind. 195; Armitage *v.* Widoe, 36 Mich. 124.

[5] Cases *supra;* Moley *v.* Brine, 120 Mass. 324; Fairbanks *v.* Snow, 145 Mass. 153.

to avoid a contract on the ground of his insanity, must plead and prove, not merely his incapacity, but also the plaintiff's knowledge of that fact, and unless he proves these two things he cannot succeed."[1] In the United States the authorities are in confusion, but the following principles are supported by abundant and perhaps decisive authority: (1) Where the sane person does not know of the other party's insanity, and there has been no judicial determination of such insanity, and the contract is so far executed that the parties cannot be put *in statu quo*, the contract is binding on the lunatic.[2] (2) Conversely, the contract is voidable if the sane party knew of the other's insanity;[3] if the lunatic had in fact been adjudged insane, whether the sane party knew such fact or not;[4] if the contract is bilateral, or if the sane party can be put *in statu quo*.[5] (3) The contract is void if the statute provides that contracts by lunatics shall be void,[6] or if it provides that contracts by lunatics under guardianship shall be void;[7] and in some jurisdictions the doctrine of void contracts is pushed beyond statutory limits in case of deeds, and all deeds of insane persons under guardianship are held void;[8] there is also high authority to the

[1] Lopes, L. J., in Imperial Loan Co. *v.* Stone, 1892, 1 Q. B. 599; Drew *v.* Nunn, L. R. 4 Q. B. D. 661.

[2] Gribben *v.* Maxwell, 34 Kans. 8; Young *v.* Stevens, 48 N. H. 133; Mutual Life Ins. Co. *v.* Hunt, 79 N. Y. 541.

[3] Crawford *v.* Scovell, 94 Pa. St. 48.

[4] Inquisitions to ascertain facts of public interest are analogous to proceedings *in rem*, and so conclusive on all the world. Wadsworth *v.* Sharpsteen, 8 N. Y. 388, 392; Carter *v.* Beckwith, 128 N. Y. 312.

[5] Burnham *v.* Kidwell, 113 Ill. 425. See Wirebach *v.* First Nat. Bk., 97 Pa. St. 543.

[6] This is sometimes the case as to deeds. Ind. Rev. St. (1881), § 2917; Ga. Code, § 2735.

[7] Cal. Code, §§ 38–40; Dak. Civ. Code, §§ 2519–21.

[8] Van Deusen *v.* Sweet, 51 N. Y. 378; Gibson *v.* Soper, 6 Gray, (Mass.) 279; Rogers *v.* Blackwell, 49 Mich. 192; Hovey *v.* Hobson, 53 Me. 451.

effect that a power of attorney by a lunatic is absolutely void.[1]

The application of these principles to the contract of agency would support these propositions. As between the principal and agent the contract would be voidable if, when it was formed, the principal had been adjudged insane, or the agent knew he was in fact insane. It would be void if the statute declared contracts of insane persons void, and, it would seem, if it was created by power of attorney. It would be binding if the insane person had not been so adjudged and the agent made the contract in good faith ignorant of the insanity; at least it would be binding so far as acted upon by the agent.

As between the principal and third parties the same result would follow. Knowledge of the insanity, or the absolute notice arising from its judicial determination, would make the contract voidable. But absence of both knowledge and notice would make it binding, at least in all cases where the contract has been acted upon. But what of the case where the agent knows his principal is insane? If the principal is sane when the agent is appointed, but subsequently becomes insane to the knowledge of the agent, but unknown to the third party, the contract is binding.[2] This is put on the ground that the principal when sane represents the agent as having authority, and third persons may act on the representation until they have notice of its withdrawal. It is a case where one of two innocent parties must suffer by the wrongful act of the agent, and the loss should fall on the one whose representation is the proximate cause of the injury.

§ 17. Parties. — Married Women as Principals.

A married woman could make no binding contract at

[1] Dexter *v.* Hall, 15 Wall. (U. S.) 9.

[2] Drew *v.* Nunn, L. R. 4 Q. B. D. 661; Davis *v.* Lane, 10 N. H. 156; Matthiessen, &c. Co. *v.* McMahon's Adm'r, 38 N. J. L. 536.

common law. All her contracts were absolutely void. Modern statutes, however, have gone far to remove her common law disabilities, and she may now contract in some jurisdictions as freely as an unmarried woman. To the extent that she may contract in her own person she may contract through an agent,[1] but, of course, to no greater extent.[2]

§ 18. Parties. — Corporations as Principals.

A corporation has the powers expressly conferred by its charter or impliedly necessary to carry into effect the provisions of that instrument. The corporate charter usually confers an express power to appoint agents, but even in the absence of such provisions the power is implied, both as to the official agents through whom a corporation must act, and also as to the inferior agents who may be employed at the discretion of the managers.[3] But the appointment of an agent in excess of these powers would be a void act, not binding on the corporation so far as the agent is concerned, though if the corporation had had the benefit of his services he might recover in *quantum meruit*.[4] *Query* as to the result where the appointment of the agent was *ultra vires*, but the contract made by him with a third person was *intra vires*.

§ 19. Parties. — Partnerships as Principals.

In a partnership each member is usually a principal, and also an agent in the management of the partnership affairs. As agent each partner has the authority necessary

1 Weisbrod *v.* Chicago, &c. R., 18 Wis. 35.

2 Kenton Ins. Co. *v.* McClellan, 43 Mich. 564; Nash *v.* Mitchell, 71 N. Y. 199.

3 Protection Life Ins. Co. *v.* Foote, 79 Ill. 361; Hurlbut *v.* Marshall, 62 Wis. 590; Washburn *v.* Nashville, &c. R. R. Co., 3 Head, (Tenn.) 638; St. Andrew's Bay Land Co. *v.* Mitchell, 4 Fla. 192.

4 Slater Woollen Co. *v.* Lamb, 143 Mass. 420.

for carrying on the partnership,[1] and among other powers he has the power to appoint agents to carry out the purposes for which the partnership exists.[2] But if the appointment be to do an act which the partner could not do himself without special authorization from his co-partners, the appointment will not bind the firm.[3] And if the appointment requires to be made under seal it cannot be made except by the joint act of all the partners, but adding a seal to an instrument where none is necessary will not bring the appointment within this rule.[4]

§ 20. Parties. — Unincorporated Clubs, etc., as Principals.

Unincorporated clubs and other voluntary associations, as churches, political organizations, and the like, are not competent principals because they are not legal entities. But their members are competent joint principals, and may be held as such if they have acted jointly in the appointment of an agent.[5] Mere membership in the club does not make them principals as to contracts made by the officers or committees of the club.[6] It must be shown that they authorized the agent of the club to act as their agent and pledge their credit. But this is a question not of the competency of the principal, but of the fact and extent of the agency.[7]

§ 21. Parties. — Aliens as Principals.

Aliens are generally as competent to create an agency as citizens or subjects. But an alien enemy cannot,

[1] Leake on Contr. (3d ed.), p. 451 and cases cited.

[2] Tillier *v.* Whitehead, 1 Dall. (Pa.) 269; Lucas *v.* Bank, 2 Stew. (Ala.) 280.

[3] Charles *v.* Eshleman, 5 Colo. 107.

[4] Lucas *v.* Bank, *supra;* Edwards *v.* Dillon, 147 Ill. 14.

[5] Ray *v.* Powers, 134 Mass. 22.

[6] Flemyng *v.* Hector, 2 M. & W. 172; Hawke *v.* Cole, 62 L. T. Rep. 658; Ash *v.* Guie, 97 Pa. St. 493.

[7] *Post,* § 185.

during the continuance of a state of war, make any contract with a citizen of the United States which involves any communication across the lines of hostilities.[1] Accordingly he cannot appoint an agent in the United States during the continuance of the war.[2] But if he have an agent here at the outbreak of the war, the agency is not terminated or suspended for those purposes not involving a communication across the lines of hostilities, either between the principal and the agent or the agent and third persons.[3]

§ 22. Parties. — Joint Principals.

Two or more persons may be jointly principals in a contract of agency. This has already been illustrated in the case of partnerships and unincorporated clubs.[4] In the case of a partnership each partner represents his copartners and may bind them by the appointment of an agent. But joint-owners of property do not stand in this relationship, and each must assent for himself to the appointment of the agent in order to be bound as a principal.[5] So in unincorporated associations, not being partnerships, one member does not represent the others, nor do a majority represent a minority, except by assent.[6]

§ 23. Parties. — Competency of Agent.

Any person may, as to third persons, act as an agent, unless, perhaps, one who is too young or too imbecile

1 Kershaw *v.* Kelsey, 100 Mass. 561; United States *v.* Grossmayer, 9 Wall. (U. S.) 72.

2 United States *v.* Grossmayer, 9 Wall. 72.

3 Monsseaux *v.* Urquhart, 19 La. An. 482; Ward *v.* Smith, 7 Wall. (U. S.) 447.

4 *Ante*, §§ 19, 20.

5 Keay *v.* Fenwick, L. R. 1 C. P. Div. 745; Perminter *v.* Kelly, 18 Ala. 716.

6 Flemyng *v.* Hector, 2 M. & W. 172; Todd *v.* Emly, 7 M. & W. 427; Devoss *v.* Gray, 22 Oh. St. 159; Newell *v.* Borden, 128 Mass. 31.

to perform at all the act in question.[1] So infants,[2] married women,[3] slaves,[4] and probably lunatics and other incompetents may be the channel of communication between a principal and one with whom he deals. Of course the contract of agency between the principal and the incompetent is subject to the usual rules governing contracts by persons under disability, and the contract of warranty of authority[5] between the agent and the third party would be governed by like considerations.

As between the agent and principal, the agent may be disqualified by the fact that he has an interest in the subject-matter of the agency adverse to that of the principal.[6] As between the principal and a third person the agent may be disqualified by the fact that the agent is secretly acting for both of the parties to the contract to the knowledge of the third person; this would amount to a combination between the agent and the third party to defraud the principal.[7]

§ 24. Parties. — Joint Agents.

The agents entrusted with the authority from the principal may be either several or joint. The only question of difficulty connected with a joint agency is as to the manner in which it must be executed, and that may best be disposed of at this point.

[1] Lyon *v.* Kent, 45 Ala. 656.

[2] Talbot *v.* Bowen, 1 A. K. Marsh. (Ky.) 436; *In re* D'Angibau, L. R. 15 Ch. D. 228.

[3] Hopkins *v.* Mollinieux, 4 Wend. (N. Y.) 465; Butler *v.* Price, 110 Mass. 97.

[4] Lyon *v.* Kent, *supra.*

[5] *Post*, § 183.

[6] Tewksbury *v.* Spruance, 75 Ill. 187; Crump *v.* Ingersoll, 44 Minn. 84; Taussig *v.* Hart, 58 N. Y. 425.

[7] Mayor, etc. of Salford *v.* Lever, L. R. 1891, 1 Q. B. 168; City of Boston *v.* Simmons, 150 Mass. 461.

Where the agency is joint, that is, where two or more persons are authorized jointly to act for the principal, the execution of the agency must generally be joint.[1] But whether the agency is joint or several is a matter of construction to be gathered from the terms of the authority and considerations of custom or necessity.[2] Two cases are clear in which the agency though confided to two or more persons is presumed to be several and not joint, so that one may act for all: the first is the case of a partnership acting as agent,[3] and the second is the case where the agency is a public one or one created by law;[4] in either of these cases one of the joint agents may act for all, and a majority may decide for all.

§ 25. Parties. — Sub-Agents.

Sub-agents may be appointed either, (1) by an agreement between the agent and the sub-agent in which the agent as to the sub-agent is principal, or (2) by an agreement between the agent and the sub-agent in which the agent acts for the principal. In the first case a privity of contract or gratuitous relationship is created between the agent and the sub-agent; in the second case a privity is created between the principal and the sub-agent, provided, of course, the agent was authorized to make such an agreement for the employment of the sub-agent in behalf of his principal.[5] This subject is more fully discussed hereafter, more particularly with reference to the liability of the principal or agent for the conduct of the sub-agent.[6]

[1] Commonwealth *v.* Canal Commissioners, 9 Watts, (Pa.) 466.

[2] Hawley *v.* Keeler, 53 N. Y. 114.

[3] Deakin *v.* Underwood, 37 Minn. 98.

[4] Williams *v.* School District, 21 Pick. (Mass.) 75.

[5] Haluptzok *v.* Great Northern Ry. Co., 55 Minn. 446.

[6] *Post*, §§ 92–95, 147, 160.

§ 26. Form of Contract.—Writing or Seal.

As a general rule the contract of agency may be by parol. The cases in which it must be in writing may be summarized as follows: —

(1) Where by the terms of the contract it is not to be performed within a year. In such cases the contract is required by the Fourth Section of the English Statute of Frauds to be in writing.[1] If the contract may be performed within a year,[2] or if it contemplates a contingency, as death, which would terminate it within a year,[3] it need not be in writing.

(2) In some States the Statute of Frauds provides that, where a contract is required to be in writing and signed by the party to be charged, or his agent thereunto duly authorized, such authority to the agent shall be in writing.[4]

(3) Where the contract between the principal and the third party is required to be under seal the authority of the agent to execute the instrument must itself be under seal.[5] But if the seal is superfluous, it may be disregarded, and a parol authority to execute the instrument will suffice;[6] so also if the instrument be executed in the presence of the principal;[7] so a corporation may by vote of the directors authorize the execution of sealed instru-

[1] Hinckley *v.* Southgate, 11 Vt. 428; Tuttle *v.* Swett, 31 Me. 555.

[2] Roberts *v.* Rockbottom Co., 7 Metc. (Mass.) 46; Russell *v.* Slade, 12 Conn. 455; Moore *v.* Fox, 10 Johns. (N. Y.) 244.

[3] Riddle *v.* Backus, 38 Iowa, 81; Updike *v.* TenBroeck, 32 N. J. L. 105; Jilson *v.* Gilbert, 26 Wis. 637.

[4] See Stimson's Amer. Statute Law, Vol. I. § 5201.

[5] Hanford *v.* McNair, 9 Wend. (N. Y.) 54; Gordon *v.* Bulkeley, 14 Serg. & Rawle, (Penn.) 331; Johnson *v.* Dodge, 17 Ill. 433.

[6] Wagoner *v.* Watts, 44 N. J. L. 126; Worrall *v.* Munn, 5 N. Y. 229; Thomas *v.* Joslin, 30 Minn. 388.

[7] Gardner *v.* Gardner, 5 Cush. (Mass.) 483; Jansen *v.* McCahill, 22 Cal. 563; King *v.* Longnor, 4 Barn. & Adol. 647.

ments, and no other writing or seal is necessary to that end.[1]

§ 27. Legality of Object.

A contract of agency must not contemplate an illegal object. Accordingly a contract of agency for dealing in futures where the object is to bet on the rise or fall of prices,[2] or for lobbying,[3] or selling smuggled goods,[4] or for improperly influencing the action of a third person, as by assuming to advise as a friend when the adviser is secretly the agent of one who is to profit by the advice,[5] or for any other object opposed to law, or public policy, or good morals, is unenforceable.[6]

2. *Gratuitous Agency.*

§ 28. Gratuitous Agency as between Principal and Third Person.

The question of gratuitous agency resolves itself into two parts : (1) as to the liability of a principal to third persons where he acts through a gratuitous agent ; (2) as to the liability of the agent to the principal or to third persons where the agent serves without compensation.

The first phase of the question affords little difficulty. One who acts through another is liable to third persons in the same way as if he had acted without the intervention of an agent, and so far as the third person is concerned it is wholly immaterial whether the agent acts for

[1] Burrill *v.* Nahant Bank, 2 Metc. (Mass.) 163.

[2] Irwin *v.* Williar, 110 U. S. 499.

[3] Trist *v.* Child, 21 Wall. (U. S.) 441.

[4] Armstrong *v.* Toller, 11 Wheat. (U. S.) 258.

[5] Byrd *v.* Hughes, 84 Ill. 174.

[6] Stout *v.* Ennis, 28 Kans. 706 ; Nichols *v.* Mudgett, 32 Vt. 546 ; Keating *v.* Hyde, 23 Mo. App. 555 ; White *v.* Equitable, &c. Union, 76 Ala. 251.

the principal for compensation or gratuitously.[1] The sole inquiry is, had the agent authority to act for the principal? If so, the principal is bound by the agent's act within the apparent scope of the authority. But the considerations as to the competency of the principal apply to a gratuitous agency in the same way as to an agency by contract.[2]

§ 29. Gratuitous Agency as between Principal and Agent.

It is a fundamental dogma of the English law that a consideration is necessary to support a promise. Accordingly a gratuitous promise by an agent to perform an act for the principal is unenforceable. If the agent enters upon the performance of the act, then he may be liable for the negligent manner in which he performs it, either, as is sometimes said, because the consideration then arises from the fact that the principal suffers a detriment in parting with his control over the subject-matter of the agency, or, as is more accurately said, because one who voluntarily meddles with the property rights or *quasi* property rights of another is bound to act as an ordinarily prudent man would act under like circumstances.[3]

The main difference therefore between an agency by contract and a gratuitous agency lies in the fact that the former may be enforced while it remains unacted upon by either party, while the latter can be enforced only when it has been acted upon by the agent, and he has, by his act, involved the interests and rights of the principal. But of this hereafter.[4]

[1] Haluptzok *v.* Great Northern Ry., *supra.*

[2] *Ante,* §§ 14–22.

[3] Thorne *v.* Deas, 4 Johns. (N. Y.) 84; Pollock on Cont. (6th ed.) pp. 170–71; 2 Law Q. Rev. 33.

[4] *Post,* §§ 97, 98.

CHAPTER III.

FORMATION OF THE RELATION BY RATIFICATION.

§ 30. Meaning of the Term.

(1) *Ratification generally.* The assent of the principal to the act of the agent may be given either before the act is performed, or after it is performed. When given before it is performed the assent is in the nature of an appointment of the agent for the performance of the act as explained in the preceding chapter. When given after the act is performed it is in the nature of a ratification of the act, and is intended to clothe the act with the same qualities as if there had been a prior appointment. Two cases of ratification are clearly distinguishable: (1) where the agent had no prior authority for any purpose and the ratification operates as an appointment as agent and as authority to do the act ratified; (2) where the agent had some prior authority, but exceeded it in the act in question, and the ratification operates as an extension of the authority so as to cover the act ratified.

(2) *Definition.* Ratification is the adoption of an act or contract entered into in behalf of the one ratifying by one who had no previous authority to represent the one so ratifying in the doing of the act or the making of the contract.[1]

When such unauthorized act comes to the knowledge of the one in whose behalf it was assumed to be performed,

[1] Negley *v.* Lindsay, 67 Pa. St. 217, 228.

he has an election either to repudiate the act or to accept it. If he elects to accept it, the acceptance or adoption of it constitutes a ratification, and relates back to the time the act was performed in such manner as to involve the principal and the third person in the same legal consequences as would have ensued had the act been authorized in advance. The subject falls into two main heads: (1) Elements of ratification; (2) Legal effects of ratification.

1. *Elements of Ratification.*

§ 31. Analysis of Elements.

The essential elements of ratification are as follows: (1) An act performed by an 'agent' in behalf of an existing 'principal;' (2) The subsequent real assent of the principal to the act so performed in his behalf; (3) The competency of the principal to give a binding assent; (4) In some cases an assent expressed in a particular form; (5) The legality of the act ratified.

§ 32. (I.) Act performed in Behalf of Existing Principal.

Two elements must concur before the basis for ratification can be said to be laid: (1) The principal must be an existing person capable of being ascertained, and (2) The contract must have been made in the name of or in behalf of such existing and ascertainable person.

(1) The principal must be an existing person. If an agent professes to make a contract in behalf of a corporation to be formed, but not yet in existence, the contract is incapable of ratification after the corporation has a legal existence. The corporation may make a new contract upon the same terms as the original one, but this is a different matter from ratification. It is one thing to intend to ratify and to proceed upon the assumption that there is a ratification, and another thing to intend to make

a contract and to proceed upon that assumption.[1] But if after the incorporation the company is found in possession of property or benefits accepted under the terms of the contract, this may be equivalent to proof of a new contract on the terms of the original one.[2] This comes very near the line of ratification, but is distinguishable from it in theory.[3] Perhaps the most logical holding would be to regard the company's liability as resting on an implied contract to pay reasonable value, instead of an express one to pay the agreed price.

(2) The contract must be professedly made in behalf of such principal. No one can sue on a contract except the person who made it, or one who stands in his shoes;[4] or a person who ratified what purported to be a contract made by his agent.[5] If A. professes to be making a contract for B., C. cannot, by an attempted ratification, take advantage of it, nor can C. ratify it so as to become liable on it.[6]

§ 33. (II.) Assent of the Principal.

Ratification, like prior authority by agreement, rests on assent. The assent of the agent is already given by his assuming to act. The assent of the third party is already given by his entering into the contract.[7] The assent of

[1] *In re* Northumberland Avenue Hotel Co., L. R. 33 Ch. D. 16; Stainsby *v.* Frazer's Co., 3 Daly, (N. Y. C. P.) 98.

[2] McArthur *v.* Times Printing Co., 48 Minn. 319.

[3] Howard *v.* Patent Ivory Co., L. R. 38 Ch. D. 156; Paxton Cattle Co. *v.* First National Bank, 21 Neb. 621; Bell's Gap R. R. *v.* Christy, 79 Pa. St. 54; Rockford, &c. R. *v.* Sage, 65 Ill. 328.

[4] Boulton *v.* Jones, 2 H. &. N. 564; Boston Ice Co. *v.* Potter, 123 Mass. 28.

[5] Watson *v.* Swann, 11 C. B. N. S. 756.

[6] Jones *v.* Hope, 3 Times Law Rep. 247; Hawke *v.* Cole, 62 Law Times, 658; Hamlin *v.* Sears, 82 N. Y. 327; Western Pub. Co. *v.* Dist. Tp. of Rock, 84 Ia. 101.

[7] As to whether he can withdraw his assent before ratification, see *post*, § 38.

the principal is therefore all that is required to make the contract binding on him and on the third person. Much the same considerations govern the doctrine of assent in ratification as govern the assent in the acceptance of an offer.[1] These may be summarized as follows: (1) The assent may be express or implied. (2) Silence is not (ordinarily) assent. (3) Assent must be *in toto* and unconditional. (4) Assent must be free from mistake or ignorance as to facts, and from fraud. A further consideration involves the question: (5) Has the third party a right to recede before ratification by the principal?

§ 34. — (1) Assent may be Express or Implied.

Except in cases where a particular form is necessary, the ratification may be either by express words or by conduct. All that the law requires is such a manifestation of the intent of the principal to adopt the act of the agent as would lead the ordinarily prudent man to conclude that the principal has assented. The main difference between the two methods is in the nature of the proof offered to establish the ratification. One other difference has to do with the question whether the principal knew all the material facts when he manifested his assent. If he has expressly adopted the act there may be a presumption that he has either learned all the material facts or has learned all he cares to know of them, and has deliberately assumed the risk as to the others;[2] while if he has impliedly adopted the act, the conduct relied on to establish the assent must have a greater or less probative force according as the principal knows or does not know the facts to which his conduct is sought to be related.[3] While, therefore,

[1] Yet it must not be supposed that ratification is a contract. It is an election to regard a prior acceptance by an unauthorized agent as the assent of the principal. Metcalf *v.* Williams, 144 Mass. 452.

[2] Kelley *v.* Newburyport Horse R., 141 Mass. 496.

[3] Combs *v.* Scott, 12 Allen, (Mass.) 493.

the knowledge of the principal of the material facts connected with the transaction is a material element in ratification,[1] the difficulties of establishing such actual knowledge increase or diminish according as the ratification is by conduct or by words.[2]

(1) *Express Ratification.* Express ratification, like express authority, may ordinarily be in any form, parol or written, and if written, sealed or unsealed.[3] Where, however, a prior authority would require to be in any particular form, a subsequent ratification must be in like form. This general rule is subject to some qualifications to be considered hereafter.[4]

(2) *Ratification by Conduct.* Any conduct by the principal which would lead a reasonable man to conclude that the principal is manifesting an intent to be bound by the agent's contract will be deemed a ratification. This conduct may assume an endless variety of forms. Only a few of these can be here mentioned by way of illustration. By accepting benefits under the contract, a principal will be held to have ratified it. "No rule of law is more firmly established than the rule that if one, with full knowledge of the facts, accepts the avails of an unauthorized treaty made in his behalf by another, he thereby ratifies such treaty, and is bound by its terms and stipulations as fully as he would be had he negotiated it himself."[5] By bringing an action on the contract, a principal will be held to have ratified it, whether the action be against the third person or against the agent for the proceeds of the contract.[6] By promising to pay the agent's

[1] *Post*, § 37.

[2] Hyatt *v.* Clark, 118 N. Y. 563.

[3] *Ante*, § 26.

[4] *Post*, § 40.

[5] Strasser *v.* Conklin, 54 Wis. 102; Hyatt *v.* Clark, 118 N. Y. 563; Pike *v.* Douglass, 28 Ark. 59; Thomas *v.* City N. B., 40 Neb. 501; Wheeler, &c. Co. *v.* Aughey, 144 Pa. St. 398.

[6] Bank of Beloit *v.* Beale, 34 N. Y. 473; Partridge *v.* White, 59 Me.

commissions after full knowledge of the unauthorized contract, the principal ratifies the act.[1] Even an express declaration of repudiation of the contract may be overcome by subsequent conduct, but the proof should be clear and decisive.[2]

§ 35. — (2) Ratification by Silence.

It is a general rule in the law that silence does not give consent,[3] and this is modified only by the consideration that in some special circumstances good faith may require a man to speak or be thereafter estopped by his silence. In the application of these principles to the doctrine of ratification it is necessary to distinguish at the outset between an unauthorized act by one who has no authority to act at all, and a like act by one who has some authority to act but who has exceeded his authority.

(1) *Unauthorized Act by Stranger.* Mere silence by one in whose behalf a stranger has assumed to act would not probably be sufficient evidence of ratification, although, in connection with other circumstances, it might be some evidence.[4] Circumstances may also be present, which, coupled with the silence of the supposed principal, would lead a reasonable man to believe that an agency did in fact exist. In such a case a duty seems to be laid upon the supposed principal to speak in order not to mislead the third party to his injury.[5] The question is after all one as to the *sufficiency* and not the *kind* of evidence, and it

564; Frank *v.* Jenkins, 22 Oh. St. 597; Merrill *v.* Wilson, 66 Mich. 232; Benson *v.* Liggett, 78 Ind. 452.

[1] Gillett *v.* Whiting, 141 N. Y. 71.

[2] City of Findlay *v.* Pertz, 66 Fed. Rep. 427.

[3] Royal Ins. Co. *v.* Beatty, 119 Pa. St. 6.

[4] Ward *v.* Williams, 26 Ill. 447; Philadelphia, &c. R. *v.* Cowell, 28 Pa. St. 329.

[5] Heyn *v.* O'Hagen, 60 Mich. 150; Saveland *v.* Green, 40 Wis. 431.

is clear that silence in one set of circumstances would not have the same evidential force as in another set of circumstances. "It is one thing to say that the law will not imply a ratification from silence, and a very different thing to say that silence is a circumstance from which, with others, a jury may imply it."[1]

(2) *Unauthorized Act by Agent.* Where an agent exceeds his authority, and the principal, after knowledge of the transaction, remains silent, such silence may in itself be sufficient evidence of ratification.[2] In some cases it may amount to conclusive evidence of ratification.[3] The evidential force of the silence is much greater and more cogent where an agency actually exists than where the act is that of a stranger, because the circumstances of the case demand more imperatively that the principal should speak. The time within which he must speak is to be determined by the facts of the case. It must be a reasonable time after he learns of the unauthorized act.[4]

§ 36. — (3) Assent must be in toto and unconditional.

The principal must ratify the whole act or disaffirm the whole. He cannot ratify as to a part and disaffirm as to the rest.[5] A man cannot take the benefits of a contract without bearing its burdens.[6] The principle is fundamental and axiomatic.

[1] Phil. &c. R. *v.* Cowell, *supra.*

[2] Fothergill *v.* Phillips, L. R. 6 Ch. App. 770; Kent *v.* Quicksilver Mining Co., 78 N. Y. 159; Mobile, &c. Ry. *v.* Jay, 65 Ala. 113.

[3] Lee *v.* Fontaine, 10 Ala. 755; Jones *v.* Atkinson, 68 Ala. 167; Alexander *v.* Jones, 64 Iowa, 207.

[4] Mobile, &c. Ry. *v.* Jay, *supra.*

[5] Smith *v.* Hodson, 4 T. R. 211; Brigham *v.* Palmer, 3 Allen, (Mass.) 450; Eberts *v.* Selover, 44 Mich. 519; Mundorff *v.* Wickersham, 63 Pa. St. 87; Billings *v.* Mason, 80 Me. 496.

[6] Bristow *v.* Whitmore, 9 H. L. Cas. 391, 404; Rudasill *v.* Falls, 92 N. C. 222.

§ 37. — (4) Assent must be free from Mistake or Fraud.

In order that the ratification may be binding it is necessary that it should be genuine, that is, it must be the free and intelligent act of the principal. Several circumstances may intervene to prevent the reality of the assent, the chief among these being mistake and fraud.

(1) *Mistake.* The most obvious ground of mistake is that the principal ratified the act believing certain facts to exist when in reality the facts were otherwise. "The general rule is perfectly well settled, that a ratification of the unauthorized act of an agent, in order to be effectual and binding on the principal, must have been made with a full knowledge of all material facts, and that ignorance, mistake, or misapprehension of any of the essential circumstances relating to the particular transaction alleged to have been ratified will absolve the principal from all liability by reason of any supposed adoption or assent to the previously unauthorized act of an agent."[1] While the rule is clear that the principal must know all the material facts before the ratification will become binding, or, rather, that upon discovery of his mistake he may avoid the ratification, the application of the rule calls for some additional consideration. The first is that the principal may choose to ratify knowing that he is ignorant of all the circumstances. In such a case he assumes the risk with knowledge of his ignorance, and is not misled or deceived.[2] The second consideration is that, where the agent was authorized to act, but departed from his instructions, there is a presumption that the principal knows all the facts. This presumption grows out of the doctrine of agency,—that the knowledge of the agent is the knowledge of the principal, since it is the duty of the agent to disclose to his principal all the facts connected with the

[1] Combs *v.* Scott, 12 Allen, (Mass.) 493.

[2] Kelley *v.* Newburyport Horse R., 141 Mass. 496.

agency.[1] This consideration would not prevail where the act was that of a stranger, nor is it admitted as correct in all cases of unauthorized acts by agents.[2]

(2) *Fraud.* If the principal is induced to ratify the contract by the fraud of the third party he can, of course, avoid the ratification.[3]

§ 38. — (5) Has the Third Party a Right to recede before Ratification?

It is a disputed question whether the third party who has entered into a contract with an unauthorized agent has a right to recede from the contract at any time before ratification.

In England it is held that he has not a right to recede on the ground that the contract with the agent binds the third party, though it does not bind the principal, and that a subsequent ratification by the principal relates back to the time when the contract was formed, and places the parties in the same position as if the agent had had prior authority.[4] "It comes to this, that if an offer to purchase is made to a person who professes to be the agent for a principal, but who has no authority to accept it, the person making the offer will be in a worse position as regards withdrawing it than if it had been made to the principal; and the acceptance of the unauthorized agent in the mean time will bind the purchaser to his principal, but will not in any way bind the principal to the purchaser."[5] This view is further supported by some text-writers, and in occasional *dicta* of American judges.[6] While this is

[1] Hyatt *v.* Clark, 118 N. Y. 563. *Post,* § 141.

[2] Combs *v.* Scott, 12 Allen, (Mass.) 493.

[3] Owings *v.* Hull, 9 Pet. (U. S.) 607.

[4] Bolton Partners *v.* Lambert, L. R. 41 Ch. D. 295.

[5] North, J., in *In re* Portuguese, &c. Mines, L. R. 45 Ch. D. 16, 21.

[6] Wharton on Agency, §§ 876–77; Story on Agency, §§ 245–48; Andrews *v.* Ætna Life Ins. Co., 92 N. Y. 596, 604.

the holding of the English courts on this point, they hold that the third person and the unauthorized agent may by mutual assent release the third person from any obligations under the contract at any time before ratification.[1]

In the United States the doctrine generally prevails that the third person may recede from the contract at any time before ratification, on the ground that prior to ratification there is no mutuality, and that if one party is free to be bound or not bound the other must also be free.[2] The decision in Dodge *v.* Hopkins actually goes beyond this point, and holds the unauthorized contract a nullity, and a subsequent ratification also a nullity unless assented to by the third party. But this is obviously too refined for the necessities of business. It is better to treat the contract between the third person and the agent as in the nature of an offer to the principal which the latter may accept or reject by an election operating upon the previous unauthorized acceptance by the agent. It differs from an ordinary offer in contract mainly in this, that it remains open until withdrawn, whereas an ordinary offer lapses by the expiration of time. This avoids the extremes of the English doctrine on the one hand, which treats the unauthorized contract as in effect an irrevocable offer, and of the doctrine of Dodge *v.* Hopkins on the other hand, which treats it as in effect no offer at all. The case is an anomalous one at best and requires anomalous treatment.[3]

§ 39. (III.) Principal must be Competent.

The competency of the principal has already been discussed. The same considerations prevail in respect of the

[1] Walter *v.* James, L. R. 6 Ex. 124.

[2] Dodge *v.* Hopkins, 14 Wis. 630; Atlee *v.* Bartholomew, 69 Wis. 43; Townsend *v.* Coming, 23 Wend. (N. Y.) 435. See also Wilkinson *v.* Heavenrich, 58 Mich. 574; McClintock *v.* South Penn. Oil Co., 146 Pa. St. 144, 161–62.

[3] See 9 Harv. L. Rev. 60; 5 Am. St. Rep. 109.

competency of the principal to ratify an act as to authorize it. Persons under disability cannot conclusively ratify.[1]

The matter presents itself, however, in several aspects: (1) The principal may have been competent when the act was done and competent when it was ratified; (2) he may have been incompetent when it was done and incompetent when it was ratified; (3) he may have been competent when it was done and incompetent when it was ratified; (4) he may have been incompetent when it was done and competent when it was ratified. The first three cases call for no special comment. In the first, the ratification is clearly binding. In the second and third it is as clearly not binding.

The fourth case presents a difficulty. If the incompetent could have appointed an agent, subject only to his right to disaffirm the contract of agency, then clearly he could, on arriving at competency, affirm the agency and thereby ratify the acts of the agent. So, it would seem, he could ratify unauthorized acts of that agent as well as authorized acts. So, too, he could ratify the acts of one who assumed to represent him without any authority. But if the appointment of an agent by the incompetent would be void (as in some States in case of infancy), then clearly the act could not have been authorized when it was performed. How then could it be ratified after it was performed? The conclusion is that the act so done by an agent can not be ratified.[2] But this is dependent upon the answer to the question whether the infant could have appointed the agent.[3]

[1] McCracken *v.* City of San Francisco, 16 Cal. 591, 623–24; Armitage *v.* Widoe, 36 Mich. 124.

[2] Trueblood *v.* Trueblood, 8 Ind. 195; Armitage *v.* Widoe, 36 Mich. 124.

[3] See *ante*, § 15.

§ 40. (IV.) Form of Ratification.

It has already been seen that, with the exception of a few cases, the authority of an agent may be conferred without any formality whatever. The same general rule applies to ratification. Unless the case is one in which the authority, if conferred in the first instance, must have been under seal or in writing, the ratification may be by parol.[1]

(1) *Ratification of Agent's Contract under Seal.* Authority to execute a contract which is required to be under seal, must be conferred by an instrument under seal, and consequently the unauthorized execution of such a contract can only be ratified by an instrument of equal formality.[2] But the constantly growing tendency to do away with the formality of a seal has led to an exception to the above rule, and it seems now to be generally recognized that the execution of a sealed instrument by a partner in the firm name may be ratified by the other partner by parol.[3] The Massachusetts court goes still further and holds that a parol ratification is sufficient, even in cases where the unauthorized execution of the sealed instrument is in the name of an individual.[4] Of course, if the sealed instrument is one upon which no seal is necessary, the seal may be regarded as mere surplusage and the instrument ratified by parol.[5]

(2) *Ratification of Contract required by Statute of Frauds to be in writing.* It has been seen that in some States, the Statute of Frauds provides that where a con-

[1] Goss *v.* Stevens, 32 Minn. 472; Taylor *v.* Conner, 41 Miss. 722.

[2] Heath *v.* Nutter, 50 Me. 378; Spofford *v.* Hobbs, 29 Me. 148; Despatch Line *v.* Bellamy Mfg. Co., 12 N. H. 205.

[3] Peine *v.* Weber, 47 Ill. 41; Holbrook *v.* Chamberlin, 116 Mass. 155.

[4] McIntyre *v.* Park, 11 Gray, (Mass.) 102; Holbrook *v.* Chamberlin, 116 Mass. 155.

[5] Adams *v.* Power, 52 Miss. 828.

tract is required to be in writing and signed by the party to be charged, or his agent thereunto duly authorized, such authority to the agent must also be in writing.[1] Under the rule stated above, it seems clear that when such a contract is executed by the agent without due authorization, his act can only be ratified by an instrument in writing.[2] It is held in one State, however, that a parol ratification is sufficient.[3] If the agent had written authority, but departed from it by signing a contract not authorized by the instrument of agency, a parol ratification of the contract as signed is unavailing.[4]

§ 41. (V.) Legality or Validity of Act ratified.

It is a general rule that the principal may ratify any act which he could have authorized.[5] As he may authorize an act resulting in tort as well as an act resulting in contract, so he may ratify the one as well as the other.[6] The adoption of the benefits of an act made with knowledge of the material facts, carries with it the burdens of the act, whether those burdens arise from contract or from tort.

§ 42. — Exceptions to Rule.

An exception to the general rule is found in the case of notice in behalf of an alleged principal where the notice is one of an existing intent. Such notice cannot be given

[1] *Ante*, § 26.

[2] McDowell *v.* Simpson, 3 Watts, (Pa.) 129. This view finds some support in the case of Ragan *v.* Chenault, 78 Ky. 545, in which it is held that where a statute provides that an agent cannot make a contract of suretyship without written authority, a parol ratification is insufficient.

[3] Hammond *v.* Hannin, 21 Mich. 374.

[4] Kozel *v.* Dearlove, 144 Ill. 23.

[5] McCracken *v.* City of San Francisco, 16 Cal. 591; City of Findlay *v.* Pertz, 66 Fed. Rep. 427.

[6] Dempsey *v.* Chambers, 154 Mass. 330.

by a stranger, or by an agent in excess of authority, and be subsequently ratified so as to avail the principal. The reason is that the party notified has a right to know, not merely the facts on which the notice is based, but the then existing intent of the principal, with reference to such facts so far as they concern the one notified. This he is not informed of authoritatively, and it is immaterial that there is a subsequent authority. Thus, if X. is indorser on a bill which has been dishonored, a notice of dishonor given him by A., who is a stranger to the bill and to the holder, will not avail the holder, and it seems is incapable of ratification by the holder.[1] In this case the holder could have authorized A. to notify X., but cannot ratify the act where it was unauthorized. So a notice to quit by two out of three joint owners will not avail as against a tenant. "The rule of law, that *omnis ratihabitio retrotrahitur*, etc., seems only applicable to cases where the conduct of the parties on whom it is to operate, not being referable to any agreement, cannot in the mean time depend on whether there be a subsequent ratification."[2] Neither can there be a ratification if the rights of strangers have intervened, even though the stranger knows of the unauthorized contract.[3]

§ 43. — Converse of Rule.

The converse of the rule is that an act which could not have been authorized cannot be ratified. It may be that the act if done by the principal or by an authorized agent would have been void; if so, a ratification would be void.[4]

[1] Stewart *v.* Kennett, 2 Camp. 177; Brower *v.* Wooten, 2 Taylor, (N. C.) 70; Chanoine *v.* Fowler, 3 Wend. (N. Y.) 173.

[2] Right *v.* Cuthell, 5 East, 491.

[3] Pollock *v.* Cohen, 32 Oh. St. 514; Taylor *v.* Robinson, 14 Cal. 396.

[4] Armitage *v.* Widoe, 36 Mich. 124; Milford *v.* Water Co., 124 Pa. St. 610.

This generally involves the question of competency of the party, or the form of the act. Or it may be that the act if done by any one would have been illegal; if so, the ratification would be illegal, certainly if the act continues to be illegal when ratified.[1] But there may be two special cases. First, the act may be legal when done but illegal when ratified, or second, the act may be illegal when done but legal when ratified. In either case the ratification is probably inoperative. In the first case, because when the contract became illegal the offer must be regarded as revoked and a subsequent acceptance of it would be too late. In the second case, because, as the ratification relates back to the time of the unauthorized contract, it would bring into existence a contract illegal when made.[2]

§ 44. — Ratification of Forgery.

A special instance in the law of ratification is presented in the case of forgery. If A. forges the name of B. to an instrument can B. ratify the forgery? This is a vexed question on which there is no agreement. It is contended, on the one hand, that so far as the rights and liabilities of B. are concerned there is no more reason why he may not ratify the written contract than why he might not ratify the same contract if it rested in parol.[3] But it is contended, on the other hand, that one who commits a forgery does not assume to act as agent of the person whose name is forged; that the only conceivable motive for ratification is to conceal a crime; that the doctrine of ratification does not apply, and the person attempting to ratify is not bound.[4] While this conflict exists as to ratification, it is

[1] Milford *v.* Water Co., 124 Pa. St. 610.

[2] Milford *v.* Water Co., *supra.*

[3] Greenfield Bank *v.* Crafts, 4 Allen, (Mass.) 447; Hefner *v.* Vandolah, 62 Ill. 483; Howard *v.* Duncan, 3 Lans. (N. Y.) 174.

[4] Henry *v.* Heeb, 114 Ind. 275; Workman *v.* Wright, 33 Oh. St.

generally agreed that the doctrine of estoppel is applicable in cases where the attempted ratification leads innocent third persons to change their legal position, or lose or impair their legal rights.[1] There is also agreement on the proposition that no ratification or estoppel on the part of the principal can deprive the State of the right to prosecute the wrong-doer for forgery.[2]

2. *Legal Effects of Ratification.*

§ 45. Ratification is irrevocable.

Ratification bears many analogies to acceptance of an offer. Among others is the rule that when once the principal has, with knowledge of the facts, free from mistake or fraud, adopted the act of the assumed agent as his own, he cannot afterward withdraw his ratification.[3]

§ 46. Effect as between Principal and Third Party.

Ratification relates back to the time of the contract or act ratified, and the principal and third party are in the same position as if the act has been at that time authorized.[4] The principal becomes immediately liable upon the contract, and liable as well for any fraud committed by the agent in its formation,[5] or any tort connected with its performance.[6] If it is merely an act and not a contract

405; Shisler *v.* Vandike, 92 Pa. St. 447; Owsley *v.* Philips, 78 Ky. 517; Brook *v.* Hook, L. R. 6 Ex. 89; M'Kenzie *v.* British Linen Co., L. R. 6 App. Cas. 82.

[1] M'Kenzie *v.* British Linen Co., *supra;* Casco Bank *v.* Keene, 53 Me. 103; Rudd *v.* Matthews, 79 Ky. 479; Corser *v.* Paul, 41 N. H. 24.

[2] M'Kenzie *v.* British Linen Co., *supra.*

[3] Brock *v.* Jones, 16 Tex. 461; Jones *v.* Atkinson, 68 Ala. 167; Smith *v.* Cologan, 2 T. R. 188 n.

[4] Fleckner *v.* Bank of U. S., 8 Wheat. (U. S.) 338.

[5] Nat. Life Ins. Co. *v.* Minch, 53 N. Y. 144; Lane *v.* Black, 21 W. Va. 617; Fairchild *v.* McMahon, 139 N. Y. 290.

[6] Nims *v.* Mount Hermon Boys' School, 160 Mass. 177.

which is adopted, the principal becomes liable for torts committed within the scope of the act.[1] On the other hand, the question as to whether the third person is bound by a ratification without a new assent on his part depends on the question whether the third person has a right to recede from the contract before ratification. This has already been discussed,[2] with the result that it seems justifiable to say, at least in this country, that the third party is not bound unless he has, by leaving the contract unrevoked, signified to the principal his willingness to be bound. But, of course, such assent on the part of the third person would also relate back to the time of the original contract and create obligations against him as of that date.[3]

§ 47. Effect as between Principal and Strangers.

While as between the parties ratification relates back to the time of the original transaction, it cannot by so doing cut off the intervening rights of strangers to the transaction. Purchasers of the subject-matter of the contract, attaching creditors, and others who acquire rights in the subject-matter of the contract, are protected from the effects of a subsequent ratification.[4]

§ 48. Effect as between Principal and Agent.

Since ratification is equivalent to prior authority it follows that the agent after ratification is, if he has fully informed his principal as to the facts, in the same position as if he had possessed prior authority to do the acts involved in the transaction.[5] He is no longer responsible

[1] Dempsey *v.* Chambers, 154 Mass. 330.

[2] *Ante,* § 38.

[3] State *v.* Torinus, 26 Minn. 1.

[4] *Ante,* § 46; Wood *v.* McCain, 7 Ala. 800; Taylor *v.* Robinson, 14 Cal. 396; McCracken *v.* City of San Francisco, 16 Cal. 591; Cook *v.* Tullis, 18 Wall. (U. S.) 332.

[5] Gelatt *v.* Ridge, 117 Mo. 553.

unless he would have been responsible had he done the acts under express authority.[1] But the agent must, to excuse himself, not only act in good faith, but he must also be sure that he is not mistaken as to the facts communicated. A false statement whether wilful or innocent which induces the principal to ratify, will involve the agent in liability to his principal for loss or damage which accrues because the fact is otherwise than stated.[2] Moreover, the same conduct which might amount to ratification as between the principal and the third party will not always be so construed in favor of the agent in order to relieve him from liability for his own wrongful act.[3]

§ 49. Effect as between Agent and Third Party.

An agent after ratification of his unauthorized act by his principal is in the same relation to the third party as if the acts had been previously authorized. The principal alone is generally liable on a contract which he has ratified,[4] though, if the third party is free to accept or reject the ratification and chooses to reject,[5] the agent would be liable on his warranty of authority.[6] But since prior authority will not relieve an agent from liability for a tort, obviously subsequent ratification will not;[7] although the agent may claim indemnity against the principal if sued for the tort in like case where he could under prior authority.[8]

1 Pickett *v.* Pearsons, 17 Vt. 470; Woodward *v.* Suydam, 11 Ohio, 360; Bray *v.* Gunn, 53 Ga. 144.

2 Bank of Owensboro *v.* Western Bank, 13 Bush, (Ky.) 526.

3 Triggs *v.* Jones, 46 Minn. 277.

4 Story on Agency, § 244.

5 As to which see *ante,* § 38.

6 See *post,* § 183.

7 Josselyn *v.* McAllister, 22 Mich. 300; Richardson *v.* Kimball 28 Me. 463; Wright *v.* Eaton, 7 Wis. 595.

8 *Post,* § 85.

CHAPTER IV.

FORMATION OF THE RELATION BY ESTOPPEL.

§ 50. Agencies not resting on Assent.

The agencies by agreement and ratification rest on assent. The agent is either appointed by the principal to carry out the will of the latter, or the latter adopts the act of the agent as an expression of his own will. The agencies we have now to consider do not rest on assent, but are created by the law on grounds of public policy or convenience irrespective of the consent of the principal.

§ 51. Meaning of Estoppel.

The doctrine of estoppel is based on the idea that when one man induces another to believe in the truth of that which appears to be true, he will not be permitted to deny that it is true if the other has been misled by the representation.[1] The representation may be made by express statement, or by conduct which the reasonable man would construe as equivalent to an express representation. The estoppel may therefore arise from contract, or from acts and conduct,[2] and the acts or conduct may consist in express representations or in implied representations.[3] The essence of estoppel is that a false impression has been created by one man upon the mind of another as to the existence of some fact on the strength of which the latter

[1] Kirk *v.* Hamilton, 102 U. S. 68.

[2] Bigelow on Estoppel, (5th ed.) 453.

[3] *Ibid.*, pp. 556, 570.

is induced to change his legal position. Fraud in the usual sense of that term is not an essential element of estoppel.[1]

§ 52. Application to Law of Agency.

The application of this doctrine to the law of agency is of the first importance. It is involved not only in the question as to the existence of the agency, but also in the question as to its nature and extent.

(1) Estoppel may be relied upon to establish the agency. When one knowingly and without dissent permits another to act for him in a particular transaction, or in a general course of transactions of which the particular transaction is one, he will be estopped from denying the agency of such other as against one who in good faith and in the exercise of reasonable prudence has dealt with such apparent agent relying on such apparent authority.[2] To work this estoppel it is necessary that the party misled should be so misled by the representations or conduct of the alleged principal ; if he is misled by the representations of the agent the principal will not be estopped.[3] But it is not necessary that the representation should be made to the third party directly ; "it is enough if it is made to another and intended or expected to be communicated as the representations of the party making them to the party acting on them, for him to rely and act on."[4]

(2) Estoppel may be relied upon to establish the extent of the agency. While this is to be distinguished from the estoppel to deny the agency the principle on which it is based is fundamentally the same. In the one case the

[1] Brookhaven *v.* Smith, 118 N. Y. 634; Stevens *v.* Ludlum, 46 Minn. 160.

[2] Bigelow on Estoppel, (5th ed.) 565; Martin *v.* Webb, 110 U. S. 7, 15; Travellers' Ins. Co. *v.* Edwards, 122 U. S. 457, 468; James *v.* Russell, 92 N. C. 194; Simon *v.* Brown, 38 Mich. 552.

[3] Rathbun *v.* Snow, 123 N. Y. 343.

[4] Stevens *v.* Ludlum, 46 Minn. 160.

defendant makes two representations both of which are false, namely, that A. is his agent, and that A. as his agent has certain authority. If X. relies, in good faith and in the exercise of ordinary prudence, upon these representations, he may prevent the defendant from denying either of them. In the other case the defendant makes both representations; but one of them, namely, the fact of the agency, is true, while the other, namely, the extent of the agency, is false. He is equally prevented from denying either of them; but he is prevented from denying the one because it is true, while he is prevented from denying the other because he has represented it to be true.[1] This phase of estoppel finds its expression in the general rule of law that one who deals with an agent within the *apparent* scope of his authority is protected.[2] "Where one, without objection, suffers another to do acts which proceed upon the ground of authority from him, or by his conduct adopts and sanctions such acts after they are done, he will be bound, although no previous authority exists, in all respects as if the requisite power had been given in the most formal manner. If he has justified the belief of a third party that the person assuming to be his agent was authorized to do what was done, it is no answer for him to say that no authority had been given, or that it did not reach so far, and that the third party had acted upon a mistaken conclusion. He is estopped to take refuge in such a defence. If a loss is to be borne, the author of the error must bear it."[3]

§ 53. Limits of the Doctrine.

The limits of the doctrine are to be sought in the general law of estoppel. They may be briefly summarized as follows: —

1 Bickford *v.* Menier, 107 N. Y. 490.

2 *Post,* § 102 *et seq.*

3 Bronson's Ex'r *v.* Chappell, 12 Wall. (U. S.) 681; Hill *v.* Wand, 47 Kans. 340.

(1) The representation must be made by the principal, or by one having authority from him to make it.

(2) The representation must be as to a material fact.

(3) The representation must be made with the intent that the other party should act upon it.

(4) The other party must be ignorant of the truth, and his ignorance must not be the result of his own negligence or bad faith.

(5) The other party must actually be induced to act relying on the representation.[1]

Any further discussion of the elements of the doctrine would be foreign to the purpose of this work. Its application will appear in a subsequent chapter.[2]

[1] Bigelow on Estoppel, (5th ed.) p. 570.

[2] *Post*, § 102 *et seq.*

CHAPTER V.

FORMATION OF THE RELATION BY NECESSITY.

§ 54. General Doctrine of Contracts from Necessity.

Aside from contracts which rest upon the agreement of the parties there is a more or less clearly defined class of legal relations in which obligations are enforced by contractual remedies although in fact no contract by agreement existed between the parties. These are called "contracts created by law," or "quasi-contracts."[1] Such is the obligation of an infant to pay for necessaries,[2] of a man to return money received under mistake,[3] of a corporation to return the benefits received under a contract *ultra vires*,[4] or of a man to pay for benefits conferred under statutory authority.[5] The obligation where not a statutory one is created by the courts on grounds of public policy to do justice between the parties.

The principle of quasi-contractual obligation is applied for the purpose of creating an agency where otherwise there would be none. Such agency generally arises from the necessity of the particular situation.

§ 55. Agency of Wife in Purchase of Necessaries.

The typical case is that of the agency of a wife in the purchase of necessaries. It may be that in fact the husband has authorized the wife to pledge his credit, in which case there would be an agency by consent. But in

[1] Keener on Quasi-Contracts, Chap. I.

[2] Trainer *v.* Trumbull, 141 Mass. 527.

[3] Keener, Chap. II.

[4] Central Trans. Co. *v.* Pullman Car Co., 139 U. S. 24.

[5] Steamship Co. *v.* Joliffe, 2 Wall. (U. S.) 450.

many cases the husband not only has not authorized the wife to pledge his credit, but has even forbidden her to do so and has notified third parties of such prohibition. In such case there could clearly be no agency by authority or assent, and yet the husband would be obliged to pay for the necessaries. There may be two theories on which this result is reached, — (1) that the obligation of the husband is to pay for the necessaries without regard to the question of agency,[1] or (2) that there is a compulsory agency created by law under which the wife's act is the husband's act.[2] The first theory finds color in the fact that the husband must pay even if the wife be insane or unconscious, or even if the husband be insane.[3] The second theory is the one, however, which is usually advanced by the courts and may be adopted subject to the qualifications or modifications growing out of the doctrines of status.

§ 56. Agency of Infant Child in Purchase of Necessaries.

Some of the American courts enforce the doctrine that a father is liable for necessaries furnished his infant child where no actual authority is vested in the child to pledge the father's credit. It is probably true that slighter evidence will establish authority in such cases than in cases where the relation does not exist.[4] But in some cases no evidence of such authority exists at all, and hence the agency cannot rest on assent. The English and some of the American courts refuse to enforce any obligation under such circumstances,[5] but some of our

[1] Keener on Quasi-Contracts, pp. 22, 23.

[2] Benjamin *v.* Dockham, 134 Mass. 418; Johnston *v.* Sumner, 3 Hurl. & Nor. 261.

[3] Read *v.* Legard, 6 Ex. 636; Cunningham *v.* Reardon, 98 Mass. 538, cited by Keener on Quasi-Cont. p. 22.

[4] Clark *v.* Clark, 46 Conn. 586; Fowlkes *v.* Baker, 29 Texas, 135. And see Schouler on Domestic Relations, § 241; Jordan *v.* Wright, 45 Ark. 237; Freeman *v.* Robinson, 38 N. J. L. 383.

[5] Mortimore *v.* Wright, 6 M. & W. 482; Shelton *v.* Springett, 11

courts enforce it on the same theory as in the case of the compulsory agency of the wife.[1]

§ 57. Agency of Shipmaster.

A shipmaster has authority in cases of necessity to purchase supplies for the vessel and pledge the credit of the owner.[2] This is analogous to the purchase of necessaries by a wife or child, in that the plaintiff in order to recover must show that the supplies were in fact necessaries. Such authority may, indeed, be thought to be conferred by the contract or assent of the owner aided by custom, but it is closely analogous to the compulsory agencies arising from necessity. So also the shipmaster has authority to sell the cargo or even the vessel itself in case of supreme necessity.[3]

§ 58. Agency of Unpaid Vendor.

An unpaid vendor who is still in possession of the goods may re-sell the same as agent of the vendee and charge the vendee with the difference between the contract price and the amount received on the re-sale. This agency arises "by operation of law," and can be defeated by the vendee only by taking and paying for the goods.[4]

§ 59. Other Illustrations.

The doctrine of agency by necessity has been extended in some modern cases to relations unknown to the common law. The most important instance is that of the employment of medical attendance in railway accidents. Is a

C. B. 452; Kelley *v.* Davis, 49 N. H. 187; Gordon *v.* Potter, 17 Vt. 348; Freeman *v.* Robinson, 38 N. J. L. 383; Carney *v.* Barrett, 4 Oregon, 171.

[1] Gilley *v.* Gilley, 79 Me. 292; Cromwell *v.* Benjamin, 41 Barb. (N. Y.) 558; Watkins *v.* DeArmond, 89 Ind. 553. And see *dictum* in Dennis *v.* Clark, 2 Cush. (Mass.) 347, 352.

[2] McCready *v.* Thorn, 51 N. Y. 454.

[3] Pike *v.* Balch, 38 Me. 302; Gaither *v.* Myrick, 9 Md. 118; Butler *v.* Murray, 30 N. Y. 88.

[4] Dustan *v.* McAndrew, 44 N. Y. 72; Benjamin on Sales, (6th ed.) §§ 782–795, and American note.

railway company liable for services rendered by a physician in the care of injured servants or passengers, where the services are rendered at the request of (say) a conductor? It is held on the one side that it is, on the ground that the emergency creates an agency by necessity in favor of the highest railway official on the scene of the accident or within reach by reasonable means of communication.[1] But this conclusion is denied in other jurisdictions.[2] The grade of the officer may determine the question, but if so, it must be on the ground of assent and not of necessity.[3]

The recent English case of Gwilliam *v.* Twist[4] is an interesting one upon this question. The driver of an omnibus belonging to defendants became intoxicated while on duty and was taken from his seat by a policeman. A man who happened to be standing near, volunteered to drive the omnibus to the defendants' yard, and the driver and conductor acquiesced, the former warning him to drive carefully. The volunteer in negligently turning a corner ran over and injured plaintiff, who brought action for damages against the defendants, owners of the omnibus. The trial court held, with considerable hesitation, that the defendants were liable for the injury, placing its decision upon the ground of agency by necessity; but the Court of Appeal reversed the decision on the ground that the necessity did not sufficiently appear.[5]

[1] Terre Haute, &c. R. *v.* McMurray, 98 Ind. 358; Ib. *v.* Stockwell, 118 Ind. 98; Indianapolis, &c. R. *v.* Morris, 67 Ill. 295.

[2] Sevier *v.* Birmingham, &c. R., 92 Ala. 258; Tucker *v.* St. Louis, &c. Ry. 54 Mo. 177. See Marquette, &c. R. *v.* Taft, 28 Mich. 289, where the court was evenly divided.

[3] Langan *v.* Great W. Ry., 30 L. T. N. S. 173; Swazey *v.* Union Mfg. Co., 42 Conn. 556.

[4] 1895, 1 Q. B. 557; on appeal, 43 W. R. 566.

[5] See also Sloan *v.* Central Iowa Ry. Co., 62 Iowa, 728; Fox *v.* Chicago, &c. Ry. Co., 86 Iowa, 368.

CHAPTER VI.

TERMINATION OF THE RELATION.

§ 60. Ways in which Relation may be terminated.

The relation of principal and agent may be terminated by various methods, and for convenience of treatment, these methods may be classified as follows: (1) by bilateral act; (2) by unilateral act; (3) by operation of law. But to the general rules governing the termination of the agency by these means there is an important exception, (4) where the agency is coupled with an interest or its revocation would involve the agent in liability toward third person.

1. *By Bilateral Act.*

§ 61. By Terms of Original Agreement.

The relation may be limited by the terms of the original agreement, in any one of the following ways: (1) When the contract by its terms is to endure only during a certain period of time, the expiration of that period will dissolve the relation.[1] (2) When the parties manifestly contemplate that the relation shall continue only until the happening of a certain event, the happening of that event likewise operates as a dissolution.[2] (3) When the purpose for which the agency was created, is accomplished, either through the instrumentality of the agent or otherwise, the agent's authority is terminated.[3]

[1] Gundlach *v.* Fischer, 59 Ill. 172.

[2] Danby *v.* Coutts, L. R., 29 Ch. Div. 500.

[3] Moore *v.* Stone, 40 Iowa, 259; Short *v.* Millard, 68 Ill. 292; Ahern *v.* Baker, 34 Minn 98.

In every case, it is a question of the intention of the parties, and such intention, unless expressed by the words of the contract, may be implied from the circumstances of the case.

§ 62. By Subsequent Agreement.

Agency depends for its existence upon the contract by which it was created, and consequently a subsequent agreement between the parties to cancel or rescind their original contract, terminates the relation. The rescinding contract, of course, must have the essential element of consideration, but the abandonment by either party of his rights under the original contract is sufficient.[1]

2. *By Unilateral Act.*

§ 63. Revocation and Renunciation.

Having considered the ways in which the agency may be terminated by the voluntary act of both principal and agent, we have now to treat of its termination by the act of one party alone. This may be effected, (1) by the principal's revocation of his agent's authority ; (2) by the agent's renunciation of his authority. Questions as to remedies for breach of contract by either principal or agent are considered hereafter.[2]

§ 64. Revocation — when possible.

It is clear upon principle, that since the authority of the agent is conferred upon him by the principal, and is to be exercised on his behalf and for his benefit, the agent should not be permitted to continue in the exercise of such authority any longer than the principal desires. The relation is, in a degree, personal and confidential, and the

[1] Anson on Cont. (8th ed.) Pt. V. Ch. i.

[2] *Post*, §§ 79–81.

principal for his own protection should be able to withdraw his confidence at will. It is therefore the general rule of law, that the principal may revoke his agent's authority at any time, and with or without good cause.[1] And this is true even where the principal has expressly or impliedly agreed not to revoke. In such a case, however, the principal, although he has the *power*, has not the *right* to revoke, and the agent has an action against the principal for any damages suffered by him as a result of the revocation.[2]

§ 65. Revocation — what amounts to.

The revocation of the agent's authority may be by the express act of the principal, or it may be implied from the circumstances of the case. In the absence of statute, a sealed or written revocation is unnecessary, even though the authority was originally conferred by a formal instrument.[3] The circumstances from which a revocation will be implied are various. If the principal, after conferring the authority but prior to its execution, disposes of the subject-matter of the agency, or involuntarily loses control over it, a revocation must necessarily be implied.[4] For example, if a principal confers authority upon an agent to sell his house, and before the agent accomplishes his object, the house is destroyed by fire or sold by the principal himself, the agent is clearly deprived of his power, and a revocation of authority is therefore presumed. And so also, if after conferring authority upon an agent

1 Hartley's Appeal, 53 Pa. St. 212; Blackstone *v.* Buttermore, 53 Pa. St. 266; Chambers *v.* Seay, 73 Ala. 372; Hunt *v.* Rousmanier, 8 Wheat. (U. S.) 174.

2 Chambers *v.* Seay, *supra;* Blackstone *v.* Buttermore, *supra;* MacGregor *v.* Gardner, 14 Iowa, 326.

3 Brookshire *v.* Brookshire, 8 Iredell (N. C.) Law, 74.

4 Gilbert *v.* Holmes, 64 Ill. 548.

to perform a specified act, necessarily exclusive, the principal gives the same power to another, the authority of the first agent is thereby revoked.[1] But it is held that the authority of an agent to do a specified act is not necessarily revoked by the subsequent employment of another to attend to all business of the principal.[2] The dissolution of a corporation or partnership, or the severance of the interests of joint principals, revokes the authority of agents.[3]

§ 66. Revocation, Notice of.

A revocation is effectual and binding, only as against those who have notice that it has been made. Consequently, in order to protect himself, the principal must communicate the revocation not only to the agent,[4] but to all persons who, upon the strength of his previous authority, are likely to deal with him.[5] In case the authority is only for the performance of a special act, however, third persons cannot presume that the agency will continue after the performance of that act, and therefore no notice of revocation need be communicated to them.[6] Nor is it necessary to give notice to a sub-agent, deriving his authority from the agent alone.

The method by which the revocation should be communicated varies with each particular case, but the notice must always be sufficient to make the knowledge of the revocation co-extensive with the knowledge of the author-

1 Copeland *v.* Mercantile Ins. Co., 6 Pick. (Mass.) 198.

2 Smith *v.* Lane, 101 Ind. 449.

3 Schlater *v.* Winpenny, 75 Pa. St. 321; Rowe *v.* Rand, 111 Ind. 206.

4 See Robertson *v.* Cloud, 47 Miss. 208.

5 Tier *v.* Lampson, 35 Vt. 179; Fellows *v.* Hartford, &c. Co., 38 Conn. 197; Lamothe *v.* St. Louis, &c. Co., 17 Mo. 204; McNeilly *v.* Continental Life Ins. Co., 66 N. Y. 23.

6 Watts *v.* Kavanagh, 35 Vt. 34.

ity. Thus, to persons who have never dealt with the agent, a general notice through the medium of the public press is sufficient, whether it is seen or not. But to persons who have transacted business with the agent, actual notice must be given, or at least such knowledge of the revocation must be communicated to them as would serve to place a prudent man upon inquiry.[1]

§ 67. Revocation, Effect of, as to Principal and Agent. As was said before, it is a general rule of law that unless the agent's authority is coupled with an interest, the principal has the *power* to revoke at any time, and with or without good cause. It does not always follow, however, that he has the *right* to revoke without incurring liability for breach of contract. Where there is an agreement, express or implied, that the relation shall endure for a definite time, the principal cannot revoke without subjecting himself to liability for the damages resulting to the agent.[2] Of course, this rule does not apply in case the agent has broken an express or implied condition in the original contract. For instance, every contract of agency contains the implied condition that the agent will faithfully, honestly and diligently perform his duty, and if he fails so to do, the principal may revoke his authority without liability.[3] Unless guilty of gross and wilful misconduct, the agent is entitled, upon revocation, to reasonable remuneration for his past services and expenditures.[4]

[1] Claflin *v.* Lenheim, 66 N. Y. 301, 305.

[2] Lewis *v.* Atlas, &c. Ins. Co., 61 Mo. 534; Standard Oil Co. *v.* Gilbert, 84 Ga. 714.

[3] Dieringer *v.* Meyer, 42 Wis. 311.

[4] Sumner *v.* Reicheniker, 9 Kansas, 320.

§ 68. Revocation, Effect of, as to Third Persons.

It has already been seen that the revocation of an agent's authority is effectual as to all persons who have notice that it has been made, the character of the notice depending upon circumstances. If sufficient notice has not been given, and the third person has no knowledge of the revocation, he may presume that the agency still exists, and his subsequent dealings with the agent are binding and enforceable against the principal.[1]

§ 69. Renunciation.

The agent, like the principal, may terminate the relation at will. And so also, his renunciation, if not express, may be implied from the circumstances. Thus, if the agent abandons his work, the principal is justified in regarding his authority as renounced.[2]

The renunciation becomes operative, as between principal and agent, when knowledge of it actually reaches the principal. And the principal, as in the case of his own revocation, must notify third persons in order to protect himself from liability for the subsequent fraudulent dealings of the agent.[3]

If the agency is to endure for an indefinite period, the agent has not only the *power* but the *right* to renounce at any time.[4] But in case there is an express or implied agreement that the agency is to endure for a definite period, a renunciation is a breach of contract and subjects the agent to liability for the damages resulting to the principal. There is an exception to this rule, of course, when the principal, by his own breach, justifies the re-

[1] Fellows *v.* Hartford, &c. Co., 38 Conn. 197; Tier *v.* Lampson, 35 Vt. 179; Lamothe *v.* St. Louis, &c. Co., 17 Mo. 204.

[2] Stoddart *v.* Key, 62 How. Pr. (N. Y.) 137.

[3] Capen *v.* Pac. &c. Ins. Co., 1 Dutcher, (N. J. L.) 67.

[4] Barrows *v.* Cushway, 37 Mich. 481.

nunciation. If an agent renounces the employment he cannot generally recover compensation for services rendered, but some jurisdictions allow a recovery on *quantum meruit*.[1]

3. *By Operation of Law.*

§ 70. Change affecting Subject-Matter.

Contracts may be discharged without the consent of the parties, or irrespective of their consent. Such are the cases where the law creates a discharge on grounds of public policy, convenience, or necessity. Discharge by operation of law is a topic of the general law of contract and need not be specially treated here.[2] So far as contracts of personal service are concerned the subject involves, (1) a change in the law itself, (2) a change affecting the subject-matter or circumstances of the contract, (3) a change affecting the parties to the contract. These changes are generally in the nature of what is termed a subsequent impossibility.

(1) A change in the law itself which renders the continuance of the contract impossible, because illegal, would operate to discharge the contract.[3]

(2) A change affecting the subject-matter or circumstances of the contract may operate to discharge the contract if the contract was made in contemplation of the continued existence of the subject-matter or circumstances as it or they were at the time of the formation of the contract. Thus if the agency be created for the sale of a specific article and the article should perish, without fault, the agency would be terminated.[4] So if the agency

[1] *Post*, § 81.

[2] Anson on Cont. (8th ed.) Pt. V. Ch. iv., v.; Leake on Cont. (3d ed.) 590 *et seq.*

[3] Cordes *v.* Miller, 39 Mich. 581.

[4] Dexter *v.* Norton, 47 N. Y. 62.

contemplated the continued existence of a particular state of things, and, without fault, this condition should cease to exist, the agency would be terminated.[1] But "the parties must have contemplated the continuing of that state of things as the foundation of what was to be done;" otherwise a change in conditions, however seriously it may interrupt the agency, will not discharge the contract.[2] Whether the danger arising from the prevalence of a contagious disease at the place where the service is to be rendered will discharge the contract, is a disputed question.[3]

(3) A change affecting the parties to the contract may be caused by death, insanity, illness, marriage, constraint of law, bankruptcy, and war. These are treated in the succeeding section.

§ 71. Change in Condition of Parties.

(1) *Death.* The death of either party to the contract terminates the agency. It is no longer binding on the survivor nor on the estate of the deceased.[4] The death of the principal revokes the authority of the agent, and any contracts made with him afterwards are a nullity, even though no notice of the revocation of authority is given.[5] The death of one of two joint principals has the like effect.[6] But if the agent's authority be coupled with

[1] Stewart *v.* Stone, 127 N. Y. 500.

[2] Turner *v.* Goldsmith, 1891, 1 Q. B. 544, where the destruction of the principal's manufactory was held not to discharge an agency for the sale of the goods manufactured.

[3] Lakeman *v.* Pollard, 43 Me. 463; Dewey *v.* Union School Dist., 43 Mich. 480.

[4] Lacy *v.* Getman, 119 N. Y. 109.

[5] Farmers', &c. Co. *v.* Wilson, 139 N. Y. 284; Long *v.* Thayer, 150 U. S. 520; *In re* Succession of Lanaux, 46 La. Ann. 1036.

[6] McNaughton *v.* Moore, 1 Haywood, (N. C.) 189; Rowe *v.* Rand, 111 Ind. 206.

an interest the death of the principal does not revoke the authority.[1]

(2) *Insanity.* The after-occurring insanity of the principal or agent, like his death, terminates the agency.[2] And if his insanity has been judicially declared, the decree of the court will be regarded as notice, and the revocation will operate upon all persons, whether or not they have actual knowledge of the insanity. But if the principal has not been formally adjudged insane, persons who, in ignorance of the insanity, deal with the agent, are protected. This, upon the theory that while both principal and third person are innocent and free from blame, the principal, by conferring the original authority, had made the wrong possible, and he must therefore bear the loss.[3] In accordance with the general rule, if the agent's authority is coupled with an interest, the principal's insanity does not terminate the agency.[4]

(3) *Illness.* The illness of the principal would have no effect upon the agency. But the illness of the agent which incapacitated him from performing the duties of the agency would warrant him in renouncing the contract.[5] And it is immaterial that his illness is due to his own fault, since an inquiry as to the cause of the illness is treated as an inquiry into a remote cause.[6] If, however, before renunciation or notice of the termination of the agency, the agent should act for the principal, his acts, would, of course, be binding.

[1] Hunt *v.* Rousmanier, 8 Wheat. (U. S.) 174, 203; Grapel *v.* Hodges, 112 N. Y. 419. *Post,* § 72.

[2] Davis *v.* Lane, 10 N. H. 156; Motley *v.* Head, 43 Vt. 633; Drew *v.* Nunn, L. R. 4 Q. B. D. 661.

[3] *Ante,* § 16.

[4] *Post,* § 72.

[5] Spalding *v.* Rosa, 71 N. Y. 40; Robinson *v.* Davison, L. R. 6 Ex. 269.

[6] Hughes *v.* Wamsutta Mills, 11 Allen, (Mass.) 201 (*semble*).

(4) *Marriage.* The marriage of a principal does not, as a general rule, operate as a termination of the agency. It may, however, revoke an authority the exercise of which would impair rights growing out of the marriage. For instance it is held that a power of attorney to sell land, the home of a single man, is revoked by his marriage.[1] The principal's wife, by the marriage, acquires an interest in the land which can only be divested by her joining in the conveyance, or in the power to convey. Under the common law, a woman was deprived by marriage of all control over her property and the authority of her agent was consequently revoked.[2] But under the modern statutes giving to married women the right to hold and control separate property, this rule, of course, does not apply. The marriage of a woman who is under contract of service does not of itself afford ground for a revocation of the contract by the master.[3] And, as we have seen, married women may act as agents.[4]

(5) *Constraint of Law.* Where the law puts a constraint on one of the parties which renders it impossible for him to continue the relation, the agency is revoked. Thus the arrest and imprisonment of an agent terminates the agency, and it is immaterial that the arrest is due to the fault of the offender.[5] So if a corporation be dissolved by judicial proceedings, the agency is rovoked.[6]

(6) *Bankruptcy.* The mere insolvency of the principal has no effect upon the agency, but if the principal becomes legally bankrupt, and voluntarily or involuntarily surren-

[1] Henderson *v.* Ford, 46 Texas, 627.

[2] Wambole *v.* Foote, 2 Dak. 1.

[3] Edgecombe *v.* Buckhout, 146 N. Y. 332.

[4] *Ante*, § 23.

[5] Hughes *v.* Wamsutta Mills, 11 Allen, (Mass.) 201; Leopold *v.* Salkey, 89 Ill. 412.

[6] People *v.* Globe Ins. Co., 91 N. Y. 174.

ders the control of his property and affairs, the authority of the agent, unless coupled with an interest, is regarded as terminated.[1] It seems, however, that even after bankruptcy, the agent may act for his principal in regard to all matters except those touching the rights and property of which he is divested by the bankruptcy.[2] And it is also held that although the adjudication of the court relates back to the act of bankruptcy, persons who, subsequent to the act of bankruptcy but prior to the adjudication, deal with the agent in good faith, will be protected.[3] The bankruptcy of the agent revokes his authority to deal with the principal's property rights, although he might still perform a purely formal act.[4]

(7) *War*. Although there are several cases to the contrary, it seems to be the law in America, that the existence of war between the country or State of a principal and that of his agent terminates the agency. This is in accord with the general rule that all trading or commercial intercourse between two countries at war is prohibited.[5] The exception is recognized, however, that debts may be paid to the agent of an alien enemy, when such agent resides in the same State with the debtor. But it must be with the mutual assent of principal and agent, and it must not be done with the view of transmitting the funds to the principal during the continuance of the war.[6]

[1] Story on Agency, § 482; Minett *v.* Forrester, 4 Taunt. 541; Parker *v.* Smith, 16 East, 382; *Ex parte* Snowball, L. R. 7 Ch. App. 548.

[2] Dixon *v.* Ewart, Buck, 94; 3 Mer. 322.

[3] *Ex parte* Snowball, L. R. 7 Ch. App. 548; Elliott *v.* Turquand, L. R. 7 App. Cases, 79.

[4] Audenried *v.* Betteley, 8 Allen, (Mass.) 302. As to the agent's right to compensation after bankruptcy, see *post*, § 80.

[5] Kershaw *v.* Kelsey, 100 Mass. 561; United States *v.* Grossmayer 9 Wall. (U. S.) 72. See *ante*, § 22.

[6] Insurance Co. *v.* Davis, 95 U. S. 425; N. Y. Life Ins. Co. *v.* Statham, 93 U. S. 24; Ward *v.* Smith, 7 Wall. (U. S.) 447. See *ante*, § 22.

4. *Irrevocable Agencies.*

§ 72. Doctrine of Irrevocable Agencies.

The general rule is that an authority vested in an agent may be revoked by the principal at any time, and that it is revoked by the death, insanity, etc., of the principal. But to this general rule there are at least two exceptions: (1) in cases where the authority is 'coupled with an interest,' and (2) in cases where the revocation would involve the agent in liability to third persons.

(1) A 'power coupled with an interest' is difficult to define. It is generally said that the agent to come within the doctrine must have an interest in the thing itself which is the subject-matter of the agency as distinguished from an interest in the execution of the power.[1] Thus if an agent be authorized to sell lands and apply the proceeds to a debt due the agent from the principal, the agent is said to have an interest in the execution of the power, but no interest in the subject-matter of the agency, that is, the lands.[2] But if his interest be in the lands, as if he may execute the sale in his own name, then the power is coupled with an interest and is irrevocable.[3] The possession of personal property under a power to sell coupled with an authority to apply the proceeds to the payment of a debt due the agent from the principal, constitutes a power coupled with an interest.[4] But a like power where the agent has not possession and therefore no special property in the articles, is not a power coupled with an interest.[5] An interest in the subject-matter of

[1] Hunt *v.* Rousmanier, 8 Wheat. (U. S.) 174.

[2] Frink *v.* Roe, 70 Cal. 296. But see Gaussen *v.* Morton, 10 B. & C. 731.

[3] Roland *v.* Coleman, 76 Ga. 652.

[4] Knapp *v.* Alvord, 10 Paige's Ch. (N. Y.) 205.

[5] Hunt *v.* Rousmanier, *supra.*

the agency by way of security or indemnity renders the power irrevocable.[1] But an interest by way of compensation in the proceeds of the agency is not such an interest as will render the power irrevocable.[2]

(2) Where the revocation would involve the agent in liability for damages to third persons, the principal may not revoke, nor will the law revoke, the agency. "If the power is in its nature such that the authority cannot be revoked without loss to the agent, the principal may not revoke. This rule has recently been treated as identical with a rule of more limited significance, that 'an authority coupled with an interest is irrevocable.'"[3] Thus if the agent has been entrusted with funds for the payment of the principal's creditor, and has promised the creditor to pay, the principal cannot afterward revoke, because the agent is thereafter liable to the creditor and would suffer loss if his authority to pay could be revoked.[4]

[1] Cases *supra.*

[2] Blackstone *v.* Buttermore, 53 Pa. St. 266; Chambers *v.* Seay, 73 Ala. 372.

[3] Anson on Cont. (7th ed.) p. 358, citing Read *v.* Anderson, L. R. 13 Q. B. D. 779.

[4] Goodwin *v.* Bowden, 54 Me. 424.

PART II.

LEGAL EFFECT OF THE RELATION AS BETWEEN PRINCIPAL AND AGENT.

§ 73. Introduction.

It being assumed that the relation of principal and agent has been formed, we pass to a consideration of the legal consequences of the relation as concerns the principal and agent. The relation when founded on contract imposes mutual obligations. We proceed therefore to inquire: (1) What are the obligations of a principal toward his agent; and (2) What are the obligations of an agent toward his principal?

CHAPTER VII.

OBLIGATIONS OF PRINCIPAL TO AGENT.

§ 74. Source and Nature of Obligations.

The obligations of each party are fixed either by the terms of the contract agreed to by them, or by the terms annexed by law or custom, or by the terms reasonably inferred from the circumstances of the case. The relation being largely a fiduciary one the obligations are correspondingly high, as will appear hereafter.

Turning then to the subject of the obligations of the principal, we may classify them as follows: —

1. The duty to compensate the agent.
2. The duty to reimburse the agent.
3. The duty to indemnify the agent.

§ 75. Compensation.

An express agreement as to compensation will fix definitely the right and amount of recovery for the agent's services. The agreement may further fix the manner of payment or the means of ascertaining when the compensation has been earned, or it may fix a condition upon the happening of which the compensation shall be deemed to be earned. In all such cases the terms fixed by the parties will be conclusive of the reciprocal rights and obligations.[1]

In the absence of an express agreement as to compensation there will arise an implied agreement to pay whatever the services are reasonably worth, under all

[1] Wallace *v.* Floyd, 29 Pa. St. 184; Zerrahn *v.* Ditson, 117 Mass. 553.

circumstances where a reasonable man would infer that the services were not intended to be gratuitous.[1] In these cases the principal question is, was any compensation intended? The answer must be sought in the circumstances of the transaction. If they are such as to lead to a reasonable inference that payment is mutually intended, then payment may be enforced; but if they are such as to lead to a reasonable inference that the services were intended to be gratuitous, then, however valuable they may prove to be, no payment for them can be enforced against the one benefited. In the application of this test some subsidiary considerations may be assumed to be settled. *First,* if the services were rendered on request there is a presumption that compensation was intended,[2] except where the transaction is between near relatives.[3] In the latter case there must be not only the express request but also an express promise, for otherwise the reasonable inference, arising from the relation of the parties, is that the services are intended to be gratuitous.[4] So, also, the presumption arising from the request may be rebutted by the existence of other attendant circumstances, as where the services are competitive, or are rendered on the chance of future employment.[5] *Second,* where there is no express request, the circumstances of the transaction may raise an implied request, or an implied acceptance of an offer, and therewith an implied promise to pay.[6] These cases should be sharply distinguished from those where the services are

[1] McCrary *v.* Ruddick, 33 Iowa, 521.

[2] Weston *v.* Davis, 24 Me. 374; Weeks *v.* Holmes, 12 Cush. (Mass.) 215; Van Arman *v.* Byington, 38 Ill. 442.

[3] Hertzog *v.* Hertzog, 29 Pa. St. 465; Hays *v.* McConnell, 42 Ind. 285; Scully *v.* Scully's Extr., 28 Iowa, 548.

[4] *Ibid.*

[5] Palmer *v.* Haverhill, 98 Mass. 487; Scott *v.* Maier, 56 Mich. 554.

[6] McCrary *v.* Ruddick, 33 Iowa, 521; Shelton *v.* Johnson, 40 Iowa, 84; Garrey *v.* Stadler, 67 Wis. 512.

rendered at the request of an employee of the principal, and the question is whether the employee is an agent by necessity.[1] *Third*, where there is neither an express or implied request, nor an express or implied promise, the services are deemed gratuitous however valuable they may have been.[2]

§ 76. Compensation : Remedies of Agent.

In addition to the general remedies open to all creditors, an agent may have a special remedy in the nature of a lien upon the subject-matter of the agency. Aside from special classes of agents, as factors, bankers and attorneys, the lien is a special or particular one and extends only to the amount claimed for services or expenditures performed or incurred in behalf of the very property upon which the lien exists.[3] This lien extends to property or funds which are the produce or fruit of the agency and which remain in the hands of the agent.[4] The lien, however, is a possessory one and is lost by parting with the possession of the property or funds.[5] In general, the doctrine here follows the doctrine of all common law liens.[6]

General liens, that is, liens for a general balance of account, exist in favor of factors,[7] bankers,[8] and attorneys.[9]

1 See *ante*, § 59.

2 Chadwick *v.* Knox, 31 N. H. 226; Bartholomew *v.* Jackson, 20 Johns. (N. Y.) 28. Cf. Hicks *v.* Burhans, 10 Johns. (N. Y.) 242.

3 McKenzie *v.* Nevius, 22 Me. 138; Muller *v.* Pondir, 55 N. Y. 325.

4 Muller *v.* Pondir, 55 N. Y. 325; Nagle *v.* McFeeters, 97 N. Y. 196; Vinton *v.* Baldwin, 95 Ind. 433.

5 Tucker *v.* Taylor, 53 Ind. 93; Collins *v.* Buck, 63 Me. 459.

6 See Jones on Liens, §§ 1–26.

7 Story on Agency, § 376; Martin *v.* Pope, 6 Ala. 532; McGraft *v.* Rugee, 60 Wis. 406; Matthews *v.* Menedger, 2 McLean, (U. S. C. C.) 145.

8 Jones on Liens, § 241.

9 Bowling Green Savings Bank *v.* Todd, 52 N. Y. 489; Hurlbert *v.* Brigham, 56 Vt. 368.

Other general liens are sometimes created by statute. But the details of this subject are foreign to the purpose of this work.

§ 77. Compensation for Unauthorized Act.

If the service was unauthorized but is subsequently ratified and the benefits accepted by the principal, the agent may, ordinarily, recover for the services in the same way and to the same extent as if the service had been originally authorized.[1] This doctrine must, however, be clearly defined. In the first place the adoption of the act must be intended as a ratification *in toto*, and not merely as an attempt on the part of the principal to avoid further loss, and in the next place it must be remembered that what might establish ratification as between the principal and the third party will not, necessarily, establish it as between the principal and the agent.[2] It is further necessary to distinguish clearly between ratification and a subsequent promise to pay for a gratuitous service; in the latter case there is no consideration for the promise and the agent cannot recover.[3] With these cautions the doctrine may be accepted in broad terms.

§ 78. Compensation: Conditions.

The compensation may be made to depend upon the performance of certain conditions. If so, the performance of the condition is necessary to establish the claim to compensation.[4] If, however, the condition be performed the agent is entitled to his compensation even though the principal refuse to avail himself of the results of the service. This last proposition is illustrated by the cases

[1] Gelatt *v.* Ridge, 117 Mo. 553; Wilson *v.* Dame, 58 N. H. 392; Frixione *v.* Tagliaferro, 10 M. P. C. C. 175.

[2] Triggs *v.* Jones, 46 Minn. 277.

[3] Allen *v.* Bryson, 67 Iowa, 591.

[4] Jones *v.* Adler, 34 Md. 440.

where commissions are promised the agent for the sale of the principal's property, or for the securing of a loan. If the agent finds a purchaser ready, willing and able to purchase on the terms fixed by the principal, he is entitled to his commission although the principal refuse to carry out the sale on those terms.[1] So, if the agent finds one willing to loan to the principal on the terms fixed by the latter, the agent has earned his commission although the principal refuse to accept the loan.[2] In such cases the agent has performed the condition precedent, and the right to compensation is perfected.

§ 79. Compensation: Revocation of Agency by Principal.

Where the principal revokes the agency in breach of the contract the agent is entitled to compensation already earned and to damages for the breach.[3] This proceeds on the theory that the contract is still in existence but that the principal refuses to perform it or allow it to be performed. The agent in such case may sue at once and recover the compensation earned and unpaid plus the probable damages,[4] or he may wait till the expiration of the term of service and recover the compensation plus the actual damages. In the first course his measure of damages is presumptively the total amount of the unearned stipulated compensation; but this may be reduced by affirmative proof by the principal as to the probability of the agent's finding similar employment during the unexpired term.[5] Such proof must be weighty enough how-

[1] Moses *v.* Bierling, 31 N. Y. 462; Love *v.* Miller, 53 Ind. 294.

[2] Vinton *v.* Baldwin, 88 Ind. 104.

[3] Richardson *v.* Eagle Machine Works, 78 Ind. 422; James *v.* Allen County, 44 Oh. St. 226.

[4] Cutter *v.* Gillette, 163 Mass. 95; 39 N. E. Rep. 1010.

[5] Sutherland *v.* Wyer, 67 Me. 64; Hand *v.* Clearfield Coal Co., 143 Pa. St. 408.

ever to convince the jury of the reasonable probability of the agent's securing such employment, the burden being on the principal to establish this.[1] If the second course is pursued the measure of damages is *prima facie* the unearned stipulated compensation, but the principal may show in mitigation of damages what the agent has earned during that time, or what he might have earned had he acted prudently.[2] The right of the principal to diminish the damages by showing what the agent might earn proceeds on the general doctrine of the law that upon a breach of contract it is the duty of the injured party to act prudently and diligently to prevent loss to himself. The application in the case of agency involves the question as to the duty of the agent to seek other employment. He is bound to exercise reasonable care to that end, but he is not bound to accept a different employment,[3] nor in a different locality,[4] nor with an employer against whom reasonable objections would lie.[5]

It is generally held that if the principal revoke the agency before the agent has entered upon the performance of his duties, the right of action accrues at once, and the agent need not wait until the time of performance before bringing his action.[6]

If the revocation of the agency be not a breach of the contract, as where the agency is at the will of the principal,[7] or is revoked because of a breach by the agent

[1] Howard *v.* Daly, 61 N. Y. 362.

[2] Howard *v.* Daly, 61 N. Y. 362; Leatherberry *v.* Odell, 7 Fed. Rep. 641; Horn *v.* Western Land Ass'n, 22 Minn. 233.

[3] Costigan *v.* Mohawk, &c. Rd. Co., 2 Denio, (N. Y.) 609; Wolf *v.* Studebaker, 65 Pa. St. 459.

[4] Costigan *v.* Mohawk, &c. Rd. Co., 2 Denio, (N. Y.) 609; Strauss *v.* Meertief, 64 Ala. 299; Harrington *v.* Gies, 45 Mich. 374.

[5] Strauss *v.* Meertief, 64 Ala. 299.

[6] Dugan *v.* Anderson, 36 Md. 567; Howard *v.* Daly, 61 N. Y. 362.

[7] United States *v.* Jarvis, Daveis, (U. S. C. C.) 274.

himself,[1] no damages can be recovered, but only compensation for services actually rendered. If, however, the agent is guilty of such gross misconduct that the service he has rendered is of no value to his principal, he is not entitled to compensation.[2]

§ 80. Compensation: Revocation of Agency by Law.

The circumstances which will revoke an agency by operation of law have already been pointed out.[3] There may be some incapacity on the part of the principal or some incapacity on the part of the agent. In either case the impossibility in question discharges the contract as to both parties, but does not discharge the liability of the principal for services already rendered. In case of death, insanity, illness, imprisonment, or other incapacity of the agent, he may recover in quasi-contract for benefits already conferred,[4] unless he has expressly stipulated that he shall not be entitled to compensation under such circumstances,[5] or unless he knows at the time he makes the contract that it will be impossible for him to perform it.[6] Even where the illness or imprisonment is caused by the fault of the plaintiff he may still recover, as the illness or imprisonment, and not the wrongful act of the agent, is regarded as the proximate cause of the breach.[7]

Bankruptcy of the principal, however, does not discharge the estate from liability for damages, though it revokes the authority of the agent.[8]

[1] Lawrence *v.* Gullifer, 38 Me. 532; Massey *v.* Taylor, 5 Cold. (Tenn.) 447.

[2] Sumner *v.* Reicheniker, 9 Kans. 320.

[3] *Ante*, §§ 70–71.

[4] Wolfe *v.* Howes, 20 N. Y. 197; Hughes *v.* Wamsutta Mills, 11 Allen, (Mass.) 201; Green *v.* Gilbert, 21 Wis. 401.

[5] Cutter *v.* Powell, 6 T. R. 320.

[6] Jennings *v.* Lyons, 39 Wis. 553.

[7] Hughes *v.* Wamsutta Mills, *supra.*

[8] Vanuxem *v.* Bostwick, 19 W. N. C. (Pa.) 74; s. c. 7 Atl. Rep. 598.

§ 81. Compensation: Renunciation of Agency by Agent.

Where the agent renounces the agency in breach of the contract, it is generally held that he can recover nothing for the services already performed. It is due to his own fault that the contract is not completed, and most of the courts refuse to depart in his behalf from the severe rule of the law, which forbids a man to profit from his own wrong.[1] But a few jurisdictions have been led from considerations of the hardships of the case to permit a recovery in *quantum meruit* for the services actually performed, so far as the value of such services exceeds the damage resulting from the breach.[2] The two classes of cases are irreconcilable, and it is necessary to know what is held in each jurisdiction where the question may arise.

The above applies to the cases of indivisible contracts, or to one partly performed division of a divisible contract.

But how of a divisible contract in which one or more parts have been fully performed? If the agreement is that the agent shall work a year at a given price per month, or at a given commission on actual sales, payable as the work or sales progress, then the agent upon abandoning the contract would be able to maintain an action for the full months he actually served, or the commissions actually earned, subject to a counter-claim for damages for the non-performance of the entire contract. This proceeds upon the theory that in effect there are twelve

[1] Stark *v.* Parker, 2 Pick. (Mass.) 267; Miller *v.* Goddard, 34 Me. 102; Hutchinson *v.* Wetmore, 2 Cal. 310; Ripley *v.* Chipman, 13 Vt. 268; Henson *v.* Hampton, 32 Mo. 408; Martin *v.* Schoenberger, 8 W. & S. (Pa.) 367; Diefenback *v.* Stark, 56 Wis. 462; Timberlake *v.* Thayer, 71 Miss. 279.

[2] Britton *v.* Turner, 6 N. H. 481; McClay *v.* Hedge, 18 Iowa, 66; Downey *v.* Burke, 23 Mo. 228 (but see Henson *v.* Hampton, *supra*); Duncan *v.* Baker, 21 Kans. 99; Parcell *v.* McComber, 11 Neb. 209; Coe *v.* Smith, 4 Ind. 79; Allen *v.* McKibbin, 5 Mich. 449.

contracts in one, and that the breach of (say) the fifth is no bar to an action for the full performance of the first, second, third and fourth. But the fifth, and the succeeding ones, are abandoned, and the defendant is entitled to damages for their breach. The most serious difficulty in these cases is to determine whether a contract is in fact divisible or indivisible.[1] This is really a question of construction depending upon the ascertainment of the intent of the parties. The general tendency seems to be to hold contracts of service entire rather than severable, although payment may be stipulated for by instalments.[2]

If an infant renounce his employment, he may nevertheless recover the value of his services, since an infant may always rightfully avoid such a contract.[3] But remaining in the employment after reaching majority ratifies the contract, and a subsequent breach is within the general rule.[4]

§ 82. Compensation: Agent acting for both Parties.

Where an agent acts for both parties, his right to compensation from either depends upon the knowledge or want of knowledge by the principal that his agent was acting for the other party. If therefore A. acts as agent for both X. and Y. in a transaction between the two, A. may recover from both if each knew that A. was acting for the other also;[5] but A. cannot recover from either

[1] On this see Anson on Cont. (7th ed.) pp. 300–304; Norrington *v.* Wright, 115 U. S. 188; Cahen *v.* Platt, 69 N. Y. 348; Gerli *v.* Poidebard Silk Mfg. Co., (N. J.) 31 Atl. Rep. 401.

[2] Diefenback *v.* Stark, 56 Wis. 462; Wilson *v.* Board of Education, 63 Mo. 137; Davis *v.* Maxwell, 12 Metc. (Mass.) 286.

[3] Judkins *v.* Walker, 17 Me. 38; Moses *v.* Stevens, 2 Pick. (Mass.) 332; Wheatly *v.* Miscal, 5 Ind. 142; Lufkin *v.* Mayall, 25 N. H. 82.

[4] Forsyth *v.* Hastings, 27 Vt. 646.

[5] Bell *v.* McConnell, 37 Oh. St. 396; Alexander *v.* University, 57 Ind. 466; Adams Mining Co. *v.* Senter, 26 Mich. 73.

if neither knew of the double agency;[1] and if the agent has been paid in ignorance of this fact the money may be recovered back by the principal.[2] But how if X. knew A. was also acting for Y., but Y. did not know A. was acting for X.? Clearly A. cannot recover from Y. Can he recover from X.?

If, however, the province of the agent is merely to bring the parties together, and not to advise as to the terms of their contract, he may recover from both parties if he act as the agent of both, since there is nothing inconsistent with a double agency in such a case.[3] And if, in accordance with the rules of a stock exchange, a broker who has orders from one customer to purchase and from another to sell a certain stock, procures another member of the exchange to act for one of the parties, the transaction will be upheld.[4] If two agents agree that they will share the commissions received on an exchange of their principals' property, the agreement is illegal as it contemplates a fraud on the principals.[5]

§ 83. Compensation: Illegal Services.

Where the services of the agent have been rendered in an unlawful undertaking he can recover no compensation. This applies to lobbying contracts,[6] contracts for improperly influencing executive officers,[7] marriage brokerage contracts,[8] contracts of brokers for dealing in betting

[1] Scribner *v.* Collar, 40 Mich. 375; Rice *v.* Wood, 113 Mass. 133; Lynch *v.* Fallon, 11 R. I. 311; McDonald *v.* Maltz, 94 Mich. 172.

[2] Cannell *v.* Smith, 142 Pa. St. 25.

[3] Montross *v.* Eddy, 94 Mich. 100.

[4] Terry *v.* Birmingham N. Bk., 99 Ala. 566.

[5] Levy *v.* Spencer, 18 Colo. 532.

[6] Trist *v.* Child, 21 Wall. (U. S.) 441.

[7] Tool Co. *v.* Norris, 2 Wall. (U. S.) 45. Cf. Lyon *v.* Mitchell, 36 N. Y. 235.

[8] Duval *v.* Wellman, 124 N. Y. 156.

'futures,' [1] and the like.[2] Where a statute or ordinance provides that any person acting as real estate broker without a license shall be subject to a penalty, a broker acting without a license cannot recover his commissions.[3] Where the statute forbids an attorney to be present at the taking of depositions upon interrogatories unless both sides are represented, he cannot recover compensation for such services in violation of the statute.[4] At common law an agreement of an attorney to carry on a suit and look to the proceeds of the suit alone for his compensation is champertous and void.[5] But this rule has been much modified in the modern law, and such agreements are now generally upheld in the United States.[6]

§ 84. Reimbursement.

An agent is entitled to be reimbursed for all sums which he has paid out, or become individually and solely liable for, in the due course of the agency and for the principal's benefit.[7] The expenses or outlays must have been reasonably necessary in due course, and not unreasonable in amount, or occasioned by the default or negligence of the agent himself.[8] Thus an attorney who, under implied authority, has indemnified an officer for making a levy, may recover from the client the loss suffered in consequence of such indemnity.[9]

[1] Irwin *v.* Williar, 110 U. S. 499.

[2] Bixby *v.* Moor, 51 N. H. 402.

[3] Buckley *v.* Humason, 50 Minn. 195.

[4] Comfort *v.* Graham, 87 Iowa, 295.

[5] Ackert *v.* Barker, 131 Mass. 436; Blaisdell *v.* Ahern, 144 Mass. 393.

[6] Reece *v.* Kyle, 49 Ohio St. 475; Stanton *v.* Embrey, 93 U. S. 548; Fowler *v.* Callan, 102 N. Y. 395.

[7] Maitland *v.* Martin, 86 Penn. St. 120; Ruffner *v.* Hewitt, 7 W. Va. 585; Warren *v.* Hewitt, 45 Ga. 501.

[8] Godman *v.* Meixsel, 65 Ind. 32.

[9] Clark *v.* Randall, 9 Wis. 135.

§ 85. Indemnity.

The agent is entitled to indemnity against the consequences of all acts performed in the execution of his authority which are not illegal.[1] Even as to the performance of illegal acts he may claim indemnity if he did not know they were illegal and if they were not in fact contrary to good morals or general public policy.[2] Thus an auctioneer who sells for his principal goods belonging to a third person is entitled to indemnity in case he is obliged to respond to the true owner for conversion.[3] So an innkeeper who detains a person under arrest at the solicitation of an officer may recover indemnity if he is obliged to pay damages to the involuntary guest for false imprisonment.[4]

If the transaction is illegal, and known to the agent to be so, or if though not known to the agent to be illegal, it is a prohibited act, or against general public policy, the agent is not entitled to indemnity. Thus the English courts held prior to the Gaming Act of 1892,[5] that an agent who has paid money for his principal or incurred liabilities on wagers could recover since wagers were unenforceable or void, and not illegal.[6] Since the Gaming Act which renders wagers illegal, the holding has been otherwise.[7] In this country wagering contracts are generally illegal, and not merely void, and disbursements and liabilities of the agent are, if he knows the transaction

[1] D'Arcy *v.* Lyle, 5 Binney, (Pa.) 441; Saveland *v.* Green, 36 Wis. 612.

[2] Bibb *v.* Allen, 149 U. S. 481, 498; Moore *v.* Appleton, 26 Ala. 633; 34 Ala. 147.

[3] Adamson *v.* Jarvis, 4 Bing. 66; Castle *v.* Noyes, 14 N. Y. 329.

[4] Fletcher *v.* Harcot, Hutton, 55.

[5] 55 Vict. c. 9.

[6] Thacker *v.* Hardy, L. R. 4 Q. B. D. 685; Read *v.* Anderson, L. R. 13 Q. B. D. 779.

[7] Tatam *v.* Reeve, 1893, 1 Q. B. 44.

is a wager, at his own risk since he becomes *particeps criminis.*[1] If the transaction is one which the agent ought to know is illegal, he cannot recover indemnity although in fact he believed it to be legal.[2]

§ 86. Non-Assignability of Obligations or Rights.

The rule of law is strict that no one can assign his obligations.[3] Accordingly the principal cannot assign to a third person the obligations which by his contract he undertakes toward his agent. On the other hand the general rule is that rights or benefits under a contract may be assigned.[4] Yet an exception occurs in the case of agency. A principal cannot assign his rights to the services of the agent, since the agent is not bound to assume a fiduciary relation toward the assignee or consent to be governed by the latter.[5] It follows that a principal can assign neither his rights nor his obligations under the contract of agency.

[1] Harvey *v.* Merrill, 150 Mass. 1.

[2] Coventry *v.* Barton, 17 Johns. (N. Y.) 142.

[3] *Post,* § 94.

[4] Anson on Cont. (8th ed.) Pt. III. Ch. ii.

[5] *Ibid.*; Hayes *v.* Willio, 4 Daly, (N. Y. C. P.) 259.

CHAPTER VIII.

OBLIGATIONS OF AGENT TO PRINCIPAL.

1. *Agents by Contract.*

§ 87. Statement of Obligations.

The obligations of the agent to the principal are in the main as follows: —

1. The duty to obey the instructions of the principal.
2. The duty to exercise the skill, judgment and care necessary to the prudent discharge of the agency.
3. The duty to act with the highest good faith in the management of the principal's interests.
4. The duty to account fully for all the proceeds and profits of the agency.
5. The duty to act in person, except where authorized by his principal or by custom to act through sub-agents.

§ 88. (I) Obedience.

Agency is a means of expressing the will of the principal. The agent contracts that he will serve as the means to that end, and the measure of his obedience is his conformity to the dominant will. So long as the agent correctly carries out the will of his principal he is protected, but if he fails to be directed by it, and loss ensues, he becomes liable for the deviation.[1] It is no answer even that he used reasonable care and diligence in the course he pursued; he pursues it at his own risk since it is

[1] Adams *v.* Robinson, 65 Ala. 586; Frothingham *v.* Everton, 12 N. H. 239; cases cited below.

contrary to his instructions. Thus where the principal directed the agent to return a draft at once if it was not paid, but the agent held the draft in order to give the drawee an opportunity to communicate with the drawer, and loss ensued, the agent was held liable for the loss.[1] So where an agent is directed by his principal to send a claim for collection to A., but sends it to B., and loss ensues, the agent is liable, and it is no defence that he acted prudently in sending it to B., since he had no right of choice whatever under his instructions.[2] So where a landlord gave his agent a license for the lessee to assign the lease, but directed the agent not to deliver it until the lessee paid the arrears of rent, and the agent on receipt of a check delivered the license, and the check was dishonored, the agent was held liable for the loss.[3] So if the agent parts with the principal's goods contrary to instructions, he becomes liable for conversion.[4] Generally however he is liable simply for a breach of the contract.

§ 89. (II) Prudence.

An agent is bound to bring to the performance of his service, and to exercise in such performance, a reasonable degree of skill, care and diligence. The measure of such skill, care and diligence is governed by the nature of the undertaking, and by the circumstances of the case, but generally speaking, it may be said to be such a degree as is ordinarily observed by prudent men engaged in similar undertakings, and under similar circumstances.[5] Thus, an agent to purchase a farm must possess and exercise

[1] Whitney *v.* Merchants' Union Exp. Co., 104 Mass. 152.

[2] Butts *v.* Phelps, 79 Mo. 302.

[3] Pape *v.* Westacott, 1894, 1 Q. B. 272.

[4] Laverty *v.* Snethen, 68 N. Y. 522.

[5] Leighton *v.* Sargent, 27 N. H. 460; Wright *v.* Central R. Co., 16 Ga. 38; Heinemann *v.* Heard, 50 N. Y. 27, 35; Whitney *v.* Martine, 88 N. Y. 535.

only that knowledge and skill which is common to all prudent dealers in land; while an agent to select and purchase a valuable and intricate machine is bound to display the skill and caution of an expert machinist. Likewise, even in the same profession or business, the skill and prudence required may depend upon circumstances. For example, a country physician cannot be expected to exercise the same skill in surgery as a physician in a large manufacturing community.[1]

In general, the same rules apply to a breach of the contract resulting from the agent's negligence, as to a breach resulting from the agent's disobedience of instructions. An agent is presumed by law to warrant that he possesses and will exercise such a degree of skill as is reasonably demanded by the nature and circumstances of his undertaking; and for a breach of this implied warranty he will of course be liable in damages. But he does not undertake an absolute liability.[2] If the principal has knowledge or notice of the agent's deficiency in skill, the presumption of a warranty is negatived.[3]

§ 90. (III) Good Faith.

The relation existing between a principal and his agent is a fiduciary one, and consequently the most absolute good faith is essential. The principal relies upon the fidelity and integrity of the agent, and it is the duty of the agent, in return, to be loyal to the trust imposed in him, and to execute it with the single purpose of advancing his principal's interests.[4]

Upon the general principle just stated the courts will not permit an agent to take any position, or to acquire any

[1] Small *v.* Howard, 128 Mass. 131.

[2] Page *v.* Wells, 37 Mich. 415.

[3] Felt *v.* School Dis., 24 Vt. 297.

[4] Michoud *v.* Girod, 4 How. (U. S.) 503.

rights or interests that are antagonistic to those of the principal. He should not attempt to act for both parties to the same transaction without their consent,[1] or in any way to use his authority for his own benefit.[2] Thus, an agent with instructions to lease or purchase property for his principal, cannot, except with his principal's consent, lease or purchase it from himself.[3] Nor will one authorized to sell or let property, be permitted to become the purchaser or lessee.[4] In either case the principal may repudiate the transaction. And this is true, even though the motive of the agent is perfectly honest, and his action beneficial to the principal. The law sees only the evil and dangerous tendency of such transactions, and upon grounds of public policy refuses to enforce them in any case.[5]

An agent cannot, through a failure to perform his duty, acquire interests in conflict with those of his principal. For example, an agent instructed to pay the taxes on his principal's property, and neglecting so to do, cannot acquire a valid title to the land by purchase upon tax sale, but will be regarded as a trustee for his principal.[6]

[1] Raisin *v.* Clark, 41 Md. 158; Walker *v.* Osgood, 98 Mass. 348; N. Y., &c. Ins. Co. *v.* Ins. Co., 20 Barb. (N. Y.) 468; Hinckley *v.* Arey, 27 Me. 362; Meyer *v.* Hanchett, 39 Wis. 419. *Cf.* Rupp *v.* Sampson, 16 Gray, (Mass.) 398; Orton *v.* Scofield, 61 Wis. 382; Nolte *v.* Hulbert, 37 Oh. St. 445.

[2] Bunker *v.* Miles, 30 Me. 431.

[3] Conkey *v.* Bond, 36 N. Y. 427; Taussig *v.* Hart, 58 N. Y. 425; Tewksbury *v.* Spruance, 75 Ill. 187; Boswell *v.* Cunningham, 32 Fla. 277; Davis *v.* Hamlin, 108 Ill. 39; Greenfield Sav. Bk. *v.* Simons, 133 Mass. 415.

[4] Kerfoot *v.* Hyman, 52 Ill. 512; Eldridge *v.* Walker, 60 Ill. 230; Martin *v.* Moulton, 8 N. H. 504; People *v.* Township Bd., 11 Mich. 222.

[5] Michoud *v.* Girod, 4 How. (U. S.) 503; People *v.* Township Bd., 11 Mich. 222; Taussig *v.* Hart, 58 N. Y. 425.

[6] Barton *v.* Moss, 32 Ill. 50; Krutz *v.* Fisher, 8 Kans. 90; Fisher *v.* Krutz, 9 Kans. 501; Geisinger *v.* Beyl, 80 Wis. 443.

And an agent whose duty it is to compromise a claim against his principal, may not purchase the claim at a discount, and then enforce it in full against his principal.[1] An attorney engaged to advise on a title cannot purchase an outstanding adverse title and set it up against his client; he will hold the adverse title in trust for the latter.[2]

Upon the same doctrine one who deals with an agent knowing that the latter is not in that transaction showing good faith toward his principal, deals at his peril as a party to the agent's bad faith or fraud.[3] Good faith requires the agent to give notice to the principal of all facts coming to his knowledge which may affect the principal's interests.[4]

§ 91. (IV.) Accounting.

It is a duty necessarily incident to the relation of principal and agent, that the agent should account to his principal for all money and property received by him or coming into his hands by virtue of the agency.[5] And this includes all profits which have accrued to the agent as a result of his transactions,[6] whether such transactions were within or without the scope of his authority.[7]

(1) *Keeping of Accounts.* If the nature of the undertaking requires, it is the duty of an agent to keep reasonably full, regular and accurate accounts of his business, including both receipts and disbursements, and to preserve all vouchers and other evidential papers which may be of

[1] Noyes *v.* Landon, 59 Vt. 569.

[2] Eoff *v.* Irvine, 108 Mo. 378.

[3] Hegenmyer *v.* Marks, 37 Minn. 6.

[4] *Ibid.;* Devall *v.* Burbridge, 4 Watts & Serg. (Pa.) 305.

[5] Jett *v.* Hempstead, 25 Ark. 462; Baldwin *v.* Potter, 46 Vt. 402.

[6] Gardner *v.* Ogden, 22 N. Y. 327; Dutton *v.* Willner, 52 N. Y. 312; Lafferty *v.* Jelley, 22 Ind. 471.

[7] Watson *v.* Union Iron, &c. Co., 15 Brad. (Ill.) 509.

value to his principal.[1] If, by reason of the agent's carelessness, the money or property of his principal becomes so commingled with that of the agent that they cannot be separated, the whole mass must upon well known doctrines be surrendered to the principal.[2] And if such commingled mass of funds or property is lost, the misfortune must be borne by the agent alone.[3]

(2) *Rendering of Accounts.* In the absence of an express or implied agreement or of circumstances pointing to the contrary, it may be said that it is the duty of an agent to render to his principal an account of his transactions upon demand, or within a reasonable time.[4] And as a rule, no action can be maintained against an agent for money received by him, until after he has failed to comply with a demand of payment.[5]

(3) *Set-off.* Although the right of set-off or counterclaim ordinarily exists in favor of an agent, he will not be permitted to enforce it in cases where such enforcement would be in direct violation of the agent's duty. For example, where a principal directed his agent to collect certain rents and to apply them first to the payment of certain demands due to third persons, and then to the payment of a mortgage held by the agent; but the agent collected the rents and applied them all to the payment of his own claim, it was held, in an action by the principal for the money, that the agent could not set off his own demand, on the ground that it would be a breach of his trust so to do.[6]

[1] Haas *v.* Damon, 9 Iowa, 589.

[2] Hart *v.* Ten Eyck, 2 Johns. Ch. (N. Y.) 62; Williams *v.* Williams, 55 Wis. 300.

[3] Bartlett *v.* Hamilton, 46 Me. 435.

[4] Leake *v.* Sutherland, 25 Ark. 219.

[5] Heddens *v.* Younglove, 46 Ind. 212.

[6] Tagg *v.* Bowman, 108 Pa. St. 273.

(4) *Following Trust Funds.* If an agent has come into the possession of property or funds which are impressed with a trust in favor of his principal, the principal may follow such property or funds, or the proceeds of such property, so long as they can be identified, or until they reach the hands of a *bona fide* purchaser for value.[1] And if they become so commingled with the property or funds of the agent that identification is impossible, the entire mass will be subject to a charge in favor of the principal to the amount of the trust fund.[2]

(5) *Principal's Title, Agent not to deny.* It has already been seen that it is the duty of an agent to be loyal to his trust. Akin to that rule is one to the effect that an agent may not deny his principal's title.[3] When, by virtue of his fiduciary relation to the principal, an agent comes into the possession of the principal's money or property, and is subsequently called upon by the principal to account for it, he will not be allowed, as a general rule, to dispute the title of the principal in such money or property. He may show in defence, however, that he has been divested of the property by one holding a paramount title,[4] or that the principal's title has either been terminated or transferred to the person under whom he claims.[5] Likewise, an agent cannot, in defence of an action by his principal to recover money in his hands, set up the illegal-

[1] Roca *v.* Byrne, 145 N. Y. 182; Peak *v.* Ellicott, 30 Kans. 156; Van Alen *v.* Am. Nat. Bk. 52 N. Y. 1; Nat. Bk. *v.* Ins. Co., 104 U. S. 54; McLeod *v.* Evans, 66 Wis. 401; Knatchbull *v.* Hallett, L. R. 13 Ch. Div. 696.

[2] Peak *v.* Ellicott, 30 Kans. 156; Knatchbull *v.* Hallett, L. R. 13 Ch. Div. 696.

[3] Collins *v.* Tillou, 26 Conn. 368.

[4] Bliven *v.* Hudson River Rd. Co., 36 N. Y. 403, 406; Western Trans. Co. *v.* Barber, 56 N. Y. 544, 552.

[5] Marvin *v.* Ellwood, 11 Paige's Ch. (N. Y.) 365.

ity of the transaction under which he received it or of the purpose to which it was to be devoted.[1]

§ 92. (V.) Appointment of Sub-Agents.

A sub-agent is one appointed to do some act or exercise some authority in place of the agent. The doctrine upon this point is commonly said to be embodied in the maxim, *delegatus non potest delegare,* — a delegate cannot delegate. The maxim is a correct statement of the law so far as the obligation of the agent is concerned, but is subject to qualification in so far as the performance of the obligation is concerned. There are therefore two questions involved in the problem as to the right of an agent to appoint a sub-agent. The first and simplest is whether the agent may use a sub-agent as a means of carrying out the purposes for which the agency is created, remaining himself solely liable to the principal for the manner in which the agency is executed. The second and more difficult is whether the agent may delegate to a sub-agent not only the power to act for the principal but also the obligations resting primarily on the agent, so that in case of disobedience or negligence the sub-agent shall be liable to the principal and the agent be absolved. The first question has to do with the delegation of duties. The second has to do with the assignability of obligations. A third question, often confused with the second, but in reality quite distinct, has to do with the power of the agent to make a contract of employment in behalf of his principal.

§ 93. Same: (1) Delegation of Duties.

One who contracts to do a particular thing is generally responsible to the other contracting party only for results and not for methods. Accordingly the instrumentalities

[1] Kiewert *v.* Rindskopf, 46 Wis. 481; Snell *v.* Pells, 113 Ill. 145.

by which the promisor carries out his promise are left to his own discretion.[1] But it may be that the promisee has contracted, expressly or impliedly, not only that a thing shall be done but also that it shall be done in a particular way or by means of particular instrumentalities. This is peculiarly true in contracts of personal service, for the principal or master generally intends to stipulate for the personal skill, judgment, discretion and character of his agent. Accordingly an agent cannot generally delegate to any one else the performance of duties involving these qualities. The doctrine is broader than the field of agency,[2] but it finds its peculiar application in that field. While the rule is as stated it is to be qualified by two considerations : (1) custom or necessity may import into the contract of agency a stipulation that the agent may delegate the performance of his duties to another; (2) the rule does not extend to merely mechanical, ministerial or executive acts not involving skill or discretion.

(1) It is generally true that an agent employed to buy or sell property for his principal cannot delegate the duty of buying or selling to a sub-agent, because the principal contracts for the judgment and discretion of the agent in this behalf.[3] But this rule bends before a usage by which agents are authorized in particular cases to sell through sub-agents.[4] A bank entrusted with the collection of commercial paper payable at a distance has, by necessity, the authority to employ a sub-agent at the place of payment to make the collection ; whether it has authority to

[1] Rochester Lantern Co. *v.* Stiles, &c. Co., 135 N. Y. 209 ; British Waggon Co. *v.* Lea, L. R. 5 Q. B. D. 149.

[2] Robson *v.* Drummond, 2 Barn. & Adol. 303. A physician or artist is not an 'agent,' yet neither could delegate his duties.

[3] Wright *v.* Boynton, 37 N. H. 9 ; Hunt *v.* Douglass, 22 Vt. 128.

[4] Laussatt *v.* Lippincott, 6 Serg. & Rawle, (Pa.) 386 ; Harralson *v.* Stein, 50 Ala. 347.

make the sub-agent the agent of the principal, is another question.[1]

(2) While an agent cannot generally delegate a duty involving discretion, he may delegate one which is merely mechanical, ministerial or executive in its nature. Thus if he is vested with discretion to make commercial paper he cannot delegate the exercise of this discretion to a sub-agent, but he may, after having exercised his own discretion, direct a sub-agent to perform the mechanical act of writing and signing the paper.[2] So in the execution of other contracts, as an insurance policy,[3] or a bill of lading.[4] And in general a merely mechanical or ministerial act may be performed by a sub-agent under the direction of the agent.[5]

§ 94. Same: (2) Transfer of Obligation.

It is a strict rule of law that a party cannot release himself from his contractual obligations by his own act. Subject to certain exceptions he may assign his rights under a contract, but he can never assign his obligations without the consent of the other party, for B. cannot compel A. to look to C. where A. has by contract the right to look to B.[6] Accordingly it may be laid down that an agent cannot transfer or assign to a sub-agent the obligation which he has undertaken toward the principal, so as to create a privity of contract between the sub-agent and the principal and exonerate himself from further liability. Such

[1] *Post*, § 95.

[2] Commercial Bank *v.* Norton, 1 Hill, (N. Y.) 501.

[3] Grady *v.* American Cent. Ins. Co., 60 Mo. 116.

[4] Newell *v.* Smith, 49 Vt. 255.

[5] Williams *v.* Woods, 16 Md. 220; Sayre *v.* Nichols, 7 Cal. 535; Renwick *v.* Bancroft, 56 Iowa, 527; Eggleston *v.* Boardman, 37 Mich. 14.

[6] Arkansas, &c. Co. *v.* Belden, &c. Co. 127 U. S. 379; La Rue *v.* Groezinger, 84 Cal. 281; Rochester Lantern Co. *v.* Stiles, &c. Co. 135 N. Y. 209.

assignment of obligation is effective only when the principal consents to substitute the sub-agent in place of the agent.

§ 95. Same: (3) Sub-Agency by Authorized Contract.

When an agent makes a contract within the scope of his authority he is discharging his obligation to his principal and is creating an obligation between the principal and the third party. Among other contracts which an agent may be authorized to make is the contract of employment or the hiring of servants and agents. The authority to make such contracts of employment in behalf of the principal may be express or implied. Many cases of implied authority to engage additional agents have been confused in the books with cases of the appointment of sub-agents.

The problem is well illustrated in cases where A. deposits in his home bank for collection commercial paper payable at a distance. In such a case A. knows that the home bank must send it to a correspondent bank at the place where it is payable. The problem is whether A., under these circumstances, simply authorizes the home bank to make use of a sub-agent in the collection of the paper,[1] or whether he authorizes the home bank to employ an additional agent in his behalf. If the first, then the home bank is liable for the manner in which the sub-agent performs the duty and the sub-agent is liable to the home bank; if the second, then the correspondent bank is liable to the principal and the home bank is exonerated if it has used due care in the selection of the additional agent. The courts differ widely in the view taken of this situation. One class of cases holds that A. contracts for the skill and judgment of the home bank in the collection of the paper, leaving the bank free to employ such instrumental-

[1] *Ante*, § 93.

ities as it sees fit, but assuming himself no responsibility for the conduct of the sub-agents.[1] Another class of cases holds that A. under such circumstances contemplates the appointment of a sub-agent, and impliedly authorizes the home bank to make such an appointment in his behalf; that the obligation of the home bank is to use due care in making such appointment; and that there arise two contracts, (1) the contract of the first bank with A. to use due care in selecting a sub-agent, and (2) the contract of the second bank with A. to use due care in the collection of the paper.[2] On the first view there is no privity of contract between A. and the correspondent bank, while on the second there is such privity. The same question arises in the case of the appointment of a notary by the bank;[3] and in other like cases.[4]

It will be observed that the question in these cases is not as to the power of the home bank to appoint a sub-agent, but as to the power of the home bank to create a contract between the principal and a third party. It is not the delegation of power but the possession of power that is involved. And it is believed that this is the question in every case where it is sought to establish a privity of contract between the principal and a so-called

[1] Exchange N. B. *v.* Third N. B., 112 U. S. 276; Simpson *v.* Waldby, 63 Mich. 439; Power *v.* First N. B., 6 Mont. 251; Allen *v.* Merchants' Bank, 22 Wend. (N. Y.) 215.

[2] Guelich *v.* National State Bank, 56 Iowa, 434; Dorchester Bk. *v.* New England Bk., 1 Cush. (Mass.) 177; Merchants' N. B. *v.* Goodman, 109 Pa. St. 422; Daly *v.* Bank, 56 Mo. 94.

[3] Ayrault *v.* Pacific Bank, 47 N. Y. 570; Bank *v.* Butler, 41 Oh. St. 519.

[4] Dun *v.* City N. B., 58 Fed. Rep. 174, where it was held that one who seeks through a commercial agency information as to the standing of a person residing in a distant city, contemplates the employment of a sub-agent at the place where the third person lives and becomes the principal of such sub-agent, to whom, and not to the commercial agency, he must look for damages for negligence or fraud.

sub-agent.[1] The appointment of the sub-agent may involve the liabilities of the principal to third parties. In such cases it is only a question as to whether the agent had authority, express or implied, to appoint such sub-agent, and it is immaterial whether the sub-agent serve for compensation or gratuitously.[2] The power to appoint a sub-agent may arise from necessity,[3] or from custom.[4]

Unless there be some authority express or implied for so doing, the agent cannot bind the principal by a contract with a sub-agent.[5]

§ 96. Del Credere Agents.

A *del credere* agent is one who, in consideration of an additional compensation, undertakes to guarantee the payment to the principal of the debts arising and becoming due through his agency. His powers and duties are, in general, of the same nature and extent, as those of an ordinary agent, or factor. The authorities do not agree, however, whether the legal effect of his special undertaking is to make him a mere surety for the vendee, or primarily liable for the proceeds of the sale.[6] In England, it has been held that he is merely a surety; that is to say, that he guarantees the solvency of the vendee, and in case of default, undertakes, himself, to pay;[7] but later cases clearly modify this.[8] In the United States, on

[1] Barnard *v.* Coffin, 141 Mass. 37; Bradstreet *v.* Everson, 72 Pa. St. 124; Cummins *v.* Heald, 24 Kans. 600.

[2] Haluptzok *v.* Great Northern Ry. Co., 55 Minn. 446.

[3] *Ante,* § 93; Gwilliam *v.* Twist, 1895, 1 Q. B. 557; 43 W. R. 566.

[4] Arff *v.* Star Fire Ins. Co., 125 N. Y. 57; Carpenter *v.* German Am. Ins. Co., 135 N. Y. 298.

[5] Fairchild *v.* King, 102 Cal. 320.

[6] Lewis *v.* Brehme, 33 Md. 412.

[7] Morris *v.* Cleasby, 4 M. & S. 566; Hornby *v.* Lacy, 6 M. & S. 166.

[8] Couturier *v.* Hastie, 8 Ex. 40; Wickham *v.* Wickham, 2 Kay & Johns. 478.

the other hand, it is generally held, that the *del credere* agent is primarily liable for the proceeds of the goods sold, as for goods sold to him.[1] The question becomes of importance, under the provisions of the Statute of Frauds. If the *del credere* agent be regarded as a mere surety, his contract is to answer for the debt of another, and must therefore be in writing. But if he is himself absolutely liable in the first instance, his undertaking is an original one, and not within the provisions of the Statute.[2]

It is sometimes difficult to determine whether a transaction amounts to a sale between A. and B. or the creation of a *del credere* agency. It is stated broadly that "the law implies a mere consignment of goods for sale upon a *del credere* commission, and not a sale thereof, where the contract provides that the consignee shall receive them, and return periodically to the consignor the proceeds of the sales, at prices charged by the latter, the consignee guarantying payment thereof."[3]

2. *Gratuitous Agents.*

§ 97. Obligations of Gratuitous Agents.

The agent may undertake to perform a service for the principal gratuitously. In such case the promise, being without consideration, is unenforceable, and the agent is not liable for refusing or neglecting to perform.[4] But if the agent enter upon the performance of the undertaking he is bound to exercise that degree of care and skill which

[1] Lewis *v.* Brehme, 33 Md. 412; Sherwood *v.* Stone, 14 N. Y. 267; Swan *v.* Nesmith, 7 Pick. (Mass.) 220; Wolff *v.* Koppel, 5 Hill, (N. Y.) 458.

[2] Sherwood *v.* Stone, *supra;* Swan *v.* Nesmith, *supra.*

[3] National Cordage Co. *v.* Sims, (Neb.) 62 N. W. Rep. 514; *ante,* § 6.

[4] Thorne *v.* Deas, 4 Johns. (N. Y.) 84, where the subject is exhaustively discussed.

is proportioned to the risk to the interests involved.[1] The simplicity of the rule as stated is marred by the frequent use in the authorities of the terms "ordinary" and "gross" negligence. It is often said that a gratuitous agent or mandatory is liable only for "gross" negligence.[2] Aside from the objection to the use of these fluid terms in the law of negligence, the rule as thus stated seems contrary to sound public policy; and the objections increase when to the exception is added an exception to the effect that where the undertaking involves skill the mandatory is bound to possess the skill to do what he undertakes.[3] And it is further said that a gratuitous agent is liable for wilful or malicious wrongs to third persons committed in the course of his agency.[4] Liability for negligence depends upon circumstances, for negligence is the want of care according to the circumstances. Hence the gratuitous agent or mandatory must use the care which the ordinarily prudent man would use in like case, and that is a question of fact. Such is the conclusion of the United States Supreme Court: "The general doctrine, as stated by the text writers and in judicial decisions, is that gratuitous bailees of another's property are not responsible for its loss unless guilty of gross negligence in its keeping. But gross negligence in such cases is nothing more than a failure to bestow the care which the property in its situation demands; the omission of the reasonable care required is the negligence which creates

[1] Spencer *v.* Towles, 18 Mich. 9; Williams *v.* Higgins, 30 Md. 404; Passano *v.* Acosta, 4 La. 26.

[2] Shiells *v.* Blackburne, 1 H. Bl. 158; Beardslee *v.* Richardson, 11 Wend. (N. Y.) 25; Lampley *v.* Scott, 24 Miss. 528; Eddy *v.* Livingston, 35 Mo. 487.

[3] Durnford *v.* Patterson, 7 Martin, (La.) 460; Gill *v.* Middleton, 105 Mass. 477; Wilson *v.* Brett, 11 Mees. & Wels. 113; McNevins *v.* Lowe, 40 Ill. 209.

[4] Hammond *v.* Hussey, 51 N. H. 40.

the liability; and whether this existed is a question of fact for the jury to determine, or by the court where a jury is waived."[1] And in a recent case in New York where a banker made a gratuitous loan for A., it was held that the banker was bound "to exercise the skill and knowledge of a banker engaged in loaning money for himself and for his customers, because of the peculiar character and scope of his agency, because of his promise of careful attention, and because the contract (*sic*) was made in reliance upon his business character and skill."[2]

§ 98. Gratuitous Bank Directors.

The question of gratuitous agency arises frequently in the case of directors of corporations who serve without compensation, and the discussion has revolved particularly around the question as to the liability of bank directors for losses occasioned through their alleged negligence. What amount of care is a bank director, serving without compensation, required to exercise in the management of the affairs of the bank? Several answers have been given to this question. A very common answer is that he is liable only for fraud or gross negligence amounting to fraud.[3] Another answer is that he is liable for the want of that care and prudence "that men prompted by self-interest generally exercise in their own affairs."[4] A third answer is that he is liable for negligence (without an epithet) and that negligence consists in the want of care according to the circumstances; that the circumstances do not warrant a director in being judged by the standard of the man who is conducting his own business,

[1] Mr. Justice Field in Preston *v.* Prather, 137 U. S. 604, 608–9.

[2] Isham *v.* Post, 141 N. Y. 100.

[3] Swentzel *v.* Penn Bank, 147 Pa. St. 140; Bank *v.* Bossieux, 4 Hughes, (U. S. C. C.) 387, 398, 3 Fed. R. 817.

[4] Hun *v.* Cary, 82 N. Y. 65.

but by the standard of the ordinarily prudent bank director as that is fixed by experience and usage.[1] The last answer seems the most reasonable, and even in the cases in which "gross" negligence is made the measure of liability, the reasoning results in the adoption of this standard.[2] The question sometimes turns on whether the duty of the directors is to the stockholders or to the depositors, it being urged that as to the former they are agents, while as to the latter they are trustees;[3] but in either case the care required is the care proportioned to the risk, that is, the care that an ordinarily prudent business man would give under similar circumstances.

[1] Briggs *v.* Spaulding, 141 U. S. 132 (*semble*); Delano *v.* Case, 121 Ill. 247; Williams *v.* McKay, 40 N. J. Eq. 189.

[2] See Swentzel *v.* Penn Bank, *supra*, where the court says that the care to be exercised is "ordinary care." "Not, however, the ordinary care which a man takes of his own business, but the ordinary care of a bank director in the business of a bank. Negligence is the want of care according to the circumstances, and the circumstances are everything in considering this question. The ordinary care of a business man in his own affairs means one thing; the ordinary care of a gratuitous mandatory is quite another matter. The one implies an oversight and knowledge of every detail of his business; the other suggests such care only as a man can give in a short space of time to the business of other persons, from whom he receives no compensation." Yet after this excellent statement the court holds "the rule to be that directors, who are gratuitous mandatories, are only liable for fraud, or for such gross negligence as amounts to fraud!"

[3] Hun *v.* Cary, 82 N. Y. 65; Williams *v.* McKay, 40 N. J. Eq. 189.

PART III.

LEGAL EFFECT OF THE RELATION AS BETWEEN THE PRINCIPAL AND THIRD PARTIES.

§ 99. Introduction.

We have now considered, (1) the manner in which the relation of principal and agent may be formed, and (2) the legal effect of the formation of the relation as between the principal and agent. We have now to consider, (3) the legal effect of the execution of the agency as between the principal and third persons with whom the agent may deal. The main object of agency is to bring the principal into contractual relations with third persons. In executing the agency the agent may disclose his principal or he may not; he may make admissions or declarations affecting the principal's interests; he may receive notice of facts affecting the principal's interests; or he may be guilty of fraud or other torts affecting such interests. Accordingly we have now to consider each of these five possible cases, and to determine the legal consequences of each. We have, in addition, to consider the liabilities of the third person to the principal.

CHAPTER IX.

CONTRACT OF AGENT IN BEHALF OF A DISCLOSED PRINCIPAL.

1. *In Agencies generally.*

§ 100. General Considerations.

The normal case of agency is that in which the agent acts for a disclosed principal, in whose name, and in whose behalf he enters into contracts with third persons. In so doing the agent may (1) act within the actual scope of his authority, or (2) act outside of the actual, but within the apparent scope of his authority, or (3) act outside of the apparent scope of his authority. The legal effect of the contract will vary in accordance with the variance in these three particulars.

§ 101. Contracts actually authorized.

It is obvious that if the principal has actually authorized the contract specifically or generally, that he will be bound by it in the same manner as if he had made it in person. The agent in such a case is merely an instrumentality which correctly manifests the will of the prinpal. This is the object of the agency and the object is attained. Every consideration that leads to the enforcement of contracts made in person calls equally for the enforcement of the contract made under these circumstances. It is immaterial by what means the agent derives his authority so long as it is sufficient. It may spring from the consent of the principal or from the necessities of the situation.[1]

§ 102. Contracts apparently authorized.

It may happen, however, that the principal has authorized his agent to make a contract or to make contracts, but has placed certain restrictions or limitations upon the agent as to the terms of the transaction. These restrictions the agent may disregard. In such a case the will of the principal is not correctly manifested. Is he nevertheless bound by the contract?

The solution of this problem depends upon a consideration much more vital than the interests or rights of the principal. It depends upon a consideration of the rights of the public generally, and of those persons specially who may deal with the agent. If agency is to be admitted as a means of transacting business, it is essential that the business world should be able to deal with agents, in a reasonable and prudent manner, without assuming the risk that the agent may turn out in the end to have exceeded his actual authority. This consideration leads to the conclusion that where a principal has vested his agent with apparent authority to make a certain contract, and the agent, acting within the scope of such apparent authority, does make a contract with a person who reasonably believes the agent to possess the authority which he seems to possess, the principal is bound by such contract, even though the agent's authority was in fact limited in such a way that the contract was wholly unauthorized.[2] The sole inquiry in such a case is whether the third person, acting with average prudence and good faith, was justified in believing that the agent possessed the necessary authority. If so, the principal must bear

[1] See Chapters II. and V.

[2] Butler *v.* Maples, 9 Wall. (U.S.) 766; Johnson *v.* Hurley, 115 Mo. 513.

the risk, because he has held out the agent as possessing the authority which he seems to possess, and is not in a position to maintain that third parties should know that what appears to be true is not true.[1]

§ 103. Apparent Scope of Authority. — Meaning.

The principal is bound by contracts made by his agent within the apparent scope of the agent's authority. But what is the meaning of "apparent scope of authority," and how is such authority ascertained and measured?

The apparent scope of an agent's authority is such authority as a reasonably prudent man, in like circumstances with X. and with like means of knowledge and information, would naturally infer the agent to possess. Perhaps there is no express decision that this is the test; but this is clearly the rationale of the doctrine. The cases are numerous and decisive to the point, that the third person may prudently conclude that the principal intends the agent to exercise those powers which ordinarily and properly belong to the character in which the principal holds the agent out to the world. "When a general agent transacts the business intrusted to him, within the usual and ordinary scope of such business, he acts within the extent of his authority; and the principal is bound, provided the party dealing with the agent acts in good faith, and is not guilty of negligence which proximately contributes to the loss."[2] If the third party knows the limitation, he does not in good faith rely upon the apparent authority, and cannot hold the principal.[3] If he may not prudently infer that the agent possesses

[1] *Ante*, §§ 51, 52.

[2] Wheeler *v.* McGuire, 86 Ala. 398; Butler *v.* Maples, 9 Wall. (U. S.) 766; Munn *v.* Commission Co., 15 Johns. (N. Y.) 44; Hatch *v.* Taylor, 10 N. H. 538.

[3] Peabody *v.* Hoard, 46 Ill. 242.

the powers exercised, he is negligent, and it is his own negligence and not the conduct of the principal that is the proximate cause of his loss.[1]

In order to establish the apparent authority of the agent, therefore, it is necessary to show: (1) that the principal held out the agent under circumstances from which a reasonably prudent man might infer such authority; (2) that, acting prudently, and in good faith, X. believed the agent to possess such authority.

It is sometimes said that where the facts are undisputed the question of authority is one of law for the court;[2] but, in accordance with the general principles applicable to similar questions, it would seem that this question is for the court when the facts are undisputed, and but one inference can reasonably be drawn from the facts, but that if the facts are in dispute, or if reasonable men might differ as to the inferences to be drawn from the facts, the doubt should be resolved by the jury.[3] If the authority be contained in a writing upon which X. relied, or ought to have relied, its interpretation is for the court in accordance with the general rules governing written instruments.[4]

§ 104. Same. — General and Special Agents.

It is often said that the rules as above stated apply to a general agency, but not to a special agency. "The distinction is well settled between a general and a special agent. As to the former, the principal is responsible for the acts of the agent, when acting within the general

[1] Hazeltine *v.* Miller, 44 Me. 177; Gulick *v.* Grover, 33 N. J. L. 463.

[2] Gulick *v.* Grover, *supra.*

[3] Huntley *v.* Mathias, 90 N. C. 101; Franklin Bank Note Co. *v.* Mackey, 83 Hun, (N. Y.) 511.

[4] Savings Fund Soc. *v.* Savings Bank, 36 Pa. St. 498.

scope of his authority, and the public cannot be supposed connusant of any private instructions from the principal to the agent; but where the agency is a special and temporary one, there the principal is not bound if the agent exceeds his employment."[1] "The acts of the former bind the principal, whether in accordance to his instructions or not; those of the latter do not, unless strictly within his authority."[2] "A special agent cannot bind his principal in a matter beyond or outside of the power conferred, and the party dealing with a special agent is bound to know the extent of his authority."[3] And many other cases use language to the same effect.

It is believed, however, that this distinction is misleading. The difference between a 'general' agency and a 'special' agency is not an absolute but a relative one. It is a difference in degree and not in kind. In the case of a general delegation of powers the authority is necessarily broad, and a third person may reasonably infer that the agent possesses the powers usually conferred upon such agents under such circumstances, and will not be bound to search for secret limitations.[4] In the case of a special delegation of powers the authority conferred is usually narrow and is limited to the accomplishment of the special purpose. Third persons may not reasonably infer that the powers are greater than those expressly and openly granted. They are therefore put upon inquiry to ascertain the exact scope of the authority, and do not act as prudent men unless they make such inquiry. But if they make such inquiry, with all prudence and good faith, and fail to discover some secret limitation upon the agent's authority, do they still act at their peril in dealing with

[1] Munn *v.* Commission Co., 15 Johns. (N. Y.) 44.

[2] Rossiter *v.* Rossiter, 8 Wend. (N. Y.) 494.

[3] Blackwell *v.* Ketcham, 53 Ind. 184.

[4] Butler *v.* Maples, *supra;* Bentley *v.* Doggett, 51 Wis. 224.

him? It is believed not. It is believed that precisely the same rules now apply to the special agency as to the general agency, namely, that one who deals in good faith and with due prudence may rely upon that appearance of authority with which the principal has clothed the agent. "No man is at liberty to send another into the market, to buy or sell for him, as his agent, with secret instructions as to the manner in which he shall execute his agency, which are not to be communicated to those with whom he is to deal; and then, when his agent has deviated from those instructions, to say that he was a special agent — that the instructions were limitations upon his authority — and that those with whom he dealt, in the matter of his agency, acted at their peril, because they were bound to inquire, where inquiry would have been fruitless, and to ascertain that, of which they were not to have knowledge."[1] This doctrine places special agencies upon the same footing as general agencies; each is to be measured by the appearance of authority upon which reasonably prudent men may rely. "The rule is, that if a special agent exercise the power exhibited to the public the principal will be bound, even if the agent has received private instructions which limit his special authority."[2]

§ 105. Same. — Public Agents.

"Different rules prevail in respect to the acts and declarations of public agents from those which ordinarily govern in the case of mere private agents. Principals, in the latter category, are in many cases bound by the acts and declarations of their agents, even where the act or declaration was done or made without any authority, if it appear that the act was done or declaration was made by

1 Hatch *v.* Taylor, 10 N. H. 538.

2 Howell *v.* Graff, 25 Neb. 130; Byrne *v.* Massasoit Packing Co., 137 Mass. 313.

the agent in the course of his regular employment; but the government or public authority is not bound in such a case, unless it manifestly appears that the agent was acting within the scope of his authority, or that he had been held out as having authority to do the act, or was employed in his capacity as a public agent to do the act or make the declaration for the government. . . . Although a private agent, acting in violation of specific instructions, yet within the scope of his general authority, may bind his principal, the rule as to the effect of the like act of a public agent is otherwise, for the reason that it is better that an individual should occasionally suffer from the mistakes of public officers or agents, than to adopt a rule which, through improper combinations or collusion, might be turned to the detriment and injury of the public."[1]

§ 106. Same. — Elements of Authority.

Several elements combine to make up what is termed the apparent scope of the agent's authority, or that appearance of authority upon which the public may rely. These are (1) the powers actually conferred; (2) the powers necessarily or reasonably incidental to those actually conferred; (3) the powers annexed by custom or usage to those actually conferred; (4) the powers which the principal has by his conduct led third persons reasonably to believe that his agent possesses.[2]

(1) *Powers actually conferred.* — The principal is, of course, bound by what he expressly authorizes. On the other hand, he is bound by no more than he actually authorizes in cases where the third party knows the exact

[1] Whiteside *v.* United States, 93 U. S. 247, 256–57, *citing* Story on Agency, § 307 *a*; Lee *v.* Munroe, 7 Cranch, (U. S.) 366; Mayor *v.* Eschbach, 18 Md. 276, 282. As to liability of public agent for his own acts, see *post*, § 203.

[2] Huntley *v.* Mathias, 90 N. C. 101.

terms of the authority, as where it is contained in a power of attorney. "It is as fundamental as it is elementary in the law of agency that a formal instrument conferring authority will be construed strictly, and can be held to include only those powers which are expressly given, and those which are necessary and essential to carry into effect those which are expressed."[1] Thus it has been held that a power of attorney to an agent to sell all lands owned by the donor of the power in a certain county would not be construed to cover lands purchased by the donor subsequent to the execution of the power.[2] But this has been criticised as too strict a construction.[3] Where the instrument is capable of two interpretations, and the agent and third party deal in the light of one of them in good faith, the principal is bound even though he intended it to mean otherwise.[4]

(2) *Powers incidental to those conferred.* — The express authority of the agent includes all means reasonably necessary to the accomplishment of the object of the agency. What means are thus reasonably necessary, seems to be a mixed question of law and fact. "Sometimes the powers are determined by mere inference of law; in other cases by matter of fact; in others by inference of fact; and in others still, to determine them becomes a question of mixed law and fact."[5] The nature and extent of such incidental powers are varied and beyond the province of this work to enumerate in detail. A few illustrations must suffice. An agent employed to travel and sell goods has the implied

[1] Harris *v.* Johnston, 54 Minn. 177; Penfold *v.* Warner, 96 Mich. 179.

[2] Penfold *v.* Warner, *supra;* Weare *v.* Williams, 85 Iowa, 253.

[3] 35 Am. St. Rep. 593, *citing* Fay *v.* Winchester, 4 Met. (Mass.) 513; Bigelow *v.* Livingston, 28 Minn. 57.

[4] Ireland *v.* Livingston, L. R. 5 H. L. 395; Minnesota, &c. Co. *v.* Montague, 65 Iowa, 67.

[5] Huntley *v.* Mathias, 90 N. C. 101.

power to hire a horse for such purpose.[1] And the principal is liable for the horse hire even though he has furnished the agent with money to pay for it, and has forbidden the agent to hire it on credit.[2] But the manager of a hotel has no implied authority to hire horses for the use of guests and render the principal liable for their safe-keeping and return.[3] An agent authorized to sell goods has implied power to warrant the goods in such manner as is usual in such sales.[4] And the weight of authority is now in favor of the proposition that an agent authorized to sell and convey real property may, unless specially restricted, sell and convey with general warranty.[5] An agent authorized to sell goods has implied power to receive payment for the goods provided he has possession of them, and is authorized to deliver; but if he has not possession there is no implied authority to receive payment.[6] An agent has implied power to borrow money only where the transaction of the business confided to him absolutely requires the exercise of the power in order to carry it on; it will not be implied merely because its exercise would be convenient or advantageous.[7] Some agents have, however, a customary power to borrow money, as cashiers of banks[8] and masters of ship.[9]

[1] Huntley *v.* Mathias, 90 N. C. 101.

[2] Bentley *v.* Doggett, 51 Wis. 224.

[3] Brockway *v.* Mullin, 46 N. J. L. 448. See also Wallis Tobacco Co. *v.* Jackson, 99 Ala. 460.

[4] Benj. on Sales (Bennett's ed. 1892) § 624, and notes pp. 629–30; cases cited *post,* § 107.

[5] Le Roy *v.* Beard, 8 How.(U. S.) 451; Schultz *v.* Griffin, 121 N.Y. 294.

[6] Higgins *v.* Moore, 34 N. Y. 417; Butler *v.* Dorman, 68 Mo. 298.

[7] Bickford *v.* Menier, 107 N. Y. 490; Consolidated Nat. Bk. *v.* Pacific, &c. Co., 95 Cal. 1; Heath *v.* Paul, 81 Wis. 532; Bryant *v.* Bank, 1893, App. Cas. 170.

[8] Crain *v.* First N. B., 114 Ill. 516; Barnes *v.* Ontario Bk., 19 N. Y. 152.

[9] The power of masters of ships to borrow money rests strictly on

(3) *Powers annexed by custom.* Custom or usage may aid materially in determining the authority of an agent. Where a principal creates an agency which is generally governed by established usages, it is presumed that he intends such usages to govern the agency so created.[1] It is upon this consideration that the courts reach the conclusion that a bank cashier has power to borrow money;[2] or a factor to sell on credit;[3] or an attorney to control the procedure of an action at law.[4] The general rules as to the validity of usages govern. The usage must be reasonable, nor contrary to positive law, well-established, and publicly known;[5] or if it be not general it must be known to the principal.[6] Even when a usage fulfils all necessary conditions it will not prevail as against positive instructions known to the parties.[7] The doctrine as to custom is well illustrated in the case of stock-brokers who buy and sell stock on margins, or otherwise, in behalf of customers. The customer is bound by the customs of the market in which he deals, and if the custom permits the broker to repledge the stock for his own debt, the principal will be bound by the custom.[8] The doctrine finds a further illustration in the much mooted question as to the power of an agent to warrant goods sold for his principal.[9]

imperative necessity, which, it seems, must be shown to exist in order to charge the principal. McCready *v.* Thorn, 51 N. Y. 454; Stearns *v.* Doe, 12 Gray, (Mass.) 482. Cf. Arey *v.* Hall, 81 Me. 17. *Post*, § 116.

1 Hibbard *v.* Peek, 75 Wis. 619; Adams *v.* Ins. Co., 95 Pa. St., 348.

2 Crain *v.* First N. B., 114 Ill. 516.

3 Pinkham *v.* Crocker, 77 Me. 563; Daylight Burner Co. *v.* Odlin, 51 N. H. 56.

4 Moulton *v.* Bowker, 115 Mass. 36.

5 United States *v.* Buchanan, 8 How. (U. S.) 83; Jackson *v.* Bank, 92 Tenn. 154.

6 Walls *v.* Bailey, 49 N. Y. 464.

7 Day *v.* Holmes, 103 Mass. 306.

8 Skiff *v.* Stoddard, 63 Conn. 198.

9 *Post*, § 107.

In some cases the court will take judicial notice of the existence of the custom,[1] but generally it is a matter of proof. If sought to be established by proof, it must be shown to be so prevailing that parties may be presumed to contract with reference to it.[2]

(4) *Powers inferred from conduct of principal.* The conduct of the principal may be such as to lead to a reasonable inference that the agent has certain powers, and if so the principal will be estopped to deny the existence of such powers. "If a man, whatever his real meaning may be, so conducts himself that a reasonable man would take his conduct to mean a certain representation of facts, and that it was a true representation, and that the latter was intended to act upon it in a particular way, and he, with such belief, does act in that way to his damage, the first is estopped from denying that the facts were as represented."[3] The doctrine is the general doctrine of estoppel and calls for no special consideration in this place.[4]

§ 107. Apparent Scope of Authority. — Illustrations.

(1) *Agent authorized to sell.* An agent authorized to sell possesses impliedly or by custom the following authority: (*a*) to receive payment if the agent has possession of the goods but not otherwise;[5] (*b*) to fix the terms of the sale so far as reasonably within the customs of such agencies and sales;[6] (*c*) to warrant the quality of the goods sold if such goods are customarily sold with such a

[1] Ahern *v.* Goodspeed, 72 N. Y. 108; Talmage *v.* Bierhause, 103 Ind. 270.

[2] Herring *v.* Skaggs, 62 Ala. 180, s. c. 73 Ala. 446.

[3] Carr *v.* Ry. Co., L. R. 10 C. P. 307, 317; Austrian *v.* Springer, 94 Mich. 343.

[4] See *ante*, §§ 51, 52; Johnson *v.* Hurley, 115 Mo. 513.

[5] Higgins *v.* Moore, 34 N. Y. 417; Butler *v.* Dorman, 68 Mo. 298; Law *v.* Stokes, 32 N. J. L. 249. Cf. next case cited.

[6] Putnam *v.* French, 53 Vt. 402; Daylight Burner Co. *v.* Odlin, 51 N. H. 56.

warranty by agents of like kind,[1] but not if the article be not usually sold with a warranty,[2] or with a warranty like the one in question,[3] or if the agent be one not usually authorized to warrant.[4] He has no implied authority to sell at auction;[5] to exchange the goods by way of barter with a third person;[6] to sell on credit[7] unless clearly justified by custom, as in the case of factors; to pledge or mortgage the goods;[8] or, after a sale is once made, to rescind the contract or modify its terms.[9] These rules apply, in the main, to agents authorized to sell realty as well as to those authorized to sell personalty.[10]

(2) *Agent authorized to purchase.* An authority to purchase is construed somewhat more strictly than an authority to sell. Except where "it is the custom of the trade to buy on credit," "the law does not raise any presumption that such agent may bind his principal by a purchase on credit, but the contrary."[11] This, of course, where the agent is supplied with funds; if he be not supplied with funds, the direction to buy will imply the authority to buy on credit.[12] He can buy neither more, nor

1 Ahern *v.* Goodspeed, 72 N. Y. 108; Pickert *v.* Marston, 68 Wis. 465.

2 Smith *v.* Tracy, 36 N. Y. 79; Argersinger *v.* Macnaughton, 114 N. Y. 535; Herring *v.* Skaggs, 62 Ala. 180, *s. c.* 73 Ala. 446.

3 Wait *v.* Borne, 123 N. Y. 592; Upton *v.* Suffolk County Mills, 11 Cush. (Mass.) 586; Palmer *v.* Hatch, 46 Mo. 585.

4 Cooley *v.* Perrine, 41 N. J. L. 322, *s. c.* 42 N. J. L. 623; Dodd *v.* Farlow, 11 Allen, (Mass.) 426.

5 Towle *v.* Leavitt, 23 N. H. 360.

6 Taylor *v.* Starkey, 59 N. H. 142.

7 Payne *v.* Potter, 9 Iowa, 549.

8 Wheeler, &c. Co. *v.* Givan, 65 Mo. 89.

9 Smith *v.* Rice, 1 Bailey, (S. C.) 648.

10 Le Roy *v.* Beard, 8 How. (U. S.) 451; Schultz *v.* Griffin, 121 N. Y. 294.

11 Komorowski *v.* Krumdick, 56 Wis. 23; Wheeler *v.* McGuire, 86 Ala. 398; Berry *v.* Barnes, 23 Ark. 411.

12 Sprague *v.* Gillett, 9 Met. (Mass.) 91.

less, nor any different kind of goods, than his instructions specify,[1] nor than third persons may reasonably infer that he has authority to contract for.[2] He may be presumed to have such powers as are reasonably incidental to the transaction, as, to fix the terms, and, if authorized to purchase on credit, to make the necessary representations as to the solvency of the principal.[3]

(3) *Agent authorized to manage a business.* Where an entire business is placed under the management of an agent the authority of the agent may be presumed to be commensurate with the necessities of his situation. He is to conduct the business as it is, buying and selling, hiring workmen or agents, and otherwise acting as a prudent man would in the conduct of a like enterprise. For all contracts made within these limits the principal is liable; but not for contracts outside of these limits. Thus the manager of a hotel may bind his principal for the necessary supplies of the house,[4] but not for those that are not shown to be necessary.[5] A manager of a shop has authority to buy the goods necessary to keep it in running order.[6] But there is no implied authority to make negotiable paper;[7] nor to borrow money except where the power is absolutely indispensable;[8] nor to sell the entire business;[9] nor to pledge or mortgage it.[10]

1 Olyphant *v.* McNair, 41 Barb. (N. Y.) 446.

2 Butler *v.* Maples, 9 Wall. (U. S.) 766.

3 *Ibid.* Watteau *v.* Fenwick, 1893, 1 Q. B. 346; Hubbard *v.* Tenbrook, 124 Pa. St. 291.

4 Beecher *v.* Venn, 35 Mich. 466.

5 Wallis Tobacco Co. *v.* Jackson, 99 Ala. 460. Cf. Cummings *v.* Sargent, 9 Met. (Mass.) 172.

6 Watteau *v.* Fenwick, *supra;* Hubbard *v.* Tenbrook, *supra;* Banner Tobacco Co. *v.* Jenison, 48 Mich. 459.

7 McCullough *v.* Moss, 5 Denio, (N. Y.) 567; New York Iron Mine *v.* First N. Bank, 39 Mich. 644.

8 Bickford *v.* Menier, 107 N. Y. 490.

9 Vescelius *v.* Martin, 11 Colo. 391.

10 Despatch Line *v.* Mfg. Co., 12 N. H. 205.

§ 108. Contracts unauthorized.

If the agent has neither actual nor apparent authority for his act the principal is not bound, for (1) he never authorized the contract, and (2) he never led a reasonably prudent man to believe that he authorized it. The third party must therefore look to the agent alone for redress.[1] If an agent be appointed by words *in præsenti,* but it is agreed that the agency shall not begin until the happening of some condition, the principal is not liable for contracts entered into by the agent in the interim unless the third party has been misled by the exhibition by the agent of an unconditional power, or by other conduct equivalent to a "holding out" on the part of the principal.[2] A third person has no right to rely upon the representations of the agent as to his authority.[3]

§ 109. Contracts voidable.

A principal is not bound by contracts made within the scope of the authority where they are brought about by fraud or collusion between the agent and the third party. Thus if the third party promise the agent a commission or reward for bringing about a contract between the one promising and the principal of the agent, the contract so induced will be voidable at the election of the principal. "Any agreement or understanding between one principal and the agent of another, by which such agent is to receive a commission or reward if he will use his influence with his principal to induce a contract, or enter into a contract for his principal, is pernicious and corrupt, and cannot be enforced at law. . . . Such agreements are a fraud upon the principal, which entitle him to avoid a

[1] Jackson *v.* Bank, 92 Tenn. 154; Rice *v.* Peninsular Club, 52 Mich. 87.

[2] Rathbun *v.* Snow, 123 N. Y. 343.

[3] *Ibid.*

contract made through such agency."[1] But the principal may elect to take the benefit of the contract notwithstanding the fraud, and in such case the third party will be bound. And this is so even if the principal be a public corporation, as a city, since the contract is neither *malum in se* nor *malum prohibitum*, but one which the city might have made.[2] And after such election it may sue the third party for fraud, and the agent for money had received to its use.[3]

2. *In Particular Agencies.*

§ 110. Introductory.

Little has been said heretofore as to the scope of particular agencies bearing distinctive names, nor will the purpose of this work admit of any extended discussion of the subject. It will be useful, however, to call attention at this point to the fact that some agents have by custom a wider apparent authority than others, and that for the most part these are agents who are regularly engaged in transacting a special kind of business for the public generally. They are not, like common carriers and innkeepers, obliged to serve everybody who applies, and yet it is largely the custom to do so; and because of this, and the settled nature of their business, they are governed by well understood mercantile customs, in the light of which the principal on the one hand and the third person on the other are always presumed to deal. Another class of agents are those who serve but one principal, but from the nature of the principal's business are representing him in dealings with the public generally. These also, not because of their own business, as in the first class, but because of their principal's business, are governed by well understood mercantile customs. The first class is illus-

[1] City of Findlay *v.* Pertz, 66 Fed. Rep. 427.

[2] *Ibid.* [3] *Ibid.* *Post*, § 175.

trated by the agencies of factors, brokers, auctioneers, and attorneys at law. The second class is illustrated by the agencies of cashiers of banks and shipmasters.

§ 111. Factors.

(1) *Definition.* A factor is an agent whose regular business it is to receive consignments of goods and sell them for a commission. He may sell for the ordinary commission for the services of such an agent, or he may sell for an increased commission and guarantee his principal in the collection of the price. In the first case, he is called simply a factor or commission merchant; in the second, he is called a *del credere* factor or commission merchant, and is said to sell on a *del credere* commission.[1] If he accompanies a vessel and represents shippers at the ports where the vessel may touch, he is termed a supercargo.

(2) *Scope of Authority.* As between the principal and the factor, the latter is bound to obey his instructions, and is liable like any other agent for any damages suffered from his failure to do so. He can depart from such instructions only when justified by an emergency in the nature of reasonable necessity,[2] or where he acts to protect himself from loss on his own advances or disbursements.[3] But as between the principal and third persons, the former is bound by the contracts made by the factor within the apparent scope of his authority. And this is very large. Custom has annexed to the agency powers so extended that buyers of the goods are generally protected when they buy in the usual manner and in the course of commercial dealings, and these customs have been supplemented by

[1] *Ante*, § 96.

[2] Greenleaf *v.* Moody, 13 Allen, (Mass.) 363.

[3] Davis *v.* Kobe, 36 Minn. 214; Weed *v.* Adams, 37 Conn. 378. Cf. Sims *v.* Miller, 37 S. C. 402.

legislation looking to the same end.[1] Accordingly the factor has power to sell the goods and confer an indefeasible title as against the principal; to warrant them so far as warranties are usual in the sale of similar goods;[2] to receive payment in a sale for cash, or negotiable paper in a sale on credit;[3] to sell on credit so far as it is usual in similar cases to do so;[4] and even to pledge the goods when necessary to secure the payment of charges against them or a draft drawn against the prospective proceeds by the principal.[5] He has no authority to barter the goods in exchange for others;[6] or to receive anything for them except lawful currency; or to compromise or arbitrate or subsequently extend the time of payment of the amount due on the sale.[7] The factor may sell in his own name, and it follows that the customary powers partake largely of the powers of an owner. The limitation is that the agent must *sell*, not pledge, or barter; but even this limitation has been removed by statute in many jurisdictions.[8]

(3) *Rights and Liabilities of Principal.* For all contracts made by the factor within the scope of the authority, as above explained, the principal is liable, and under the Factors Acts he is bound even where the factor pledges or barters the goods for his own benefit.[9] And this is true whether the principal be disclosed or not. In like man-

[1] *Post*, § 171.

[2] Randall *v.* Kehlor, 60 Me. 37: Argersinger *v.* Macnaughton, 114 N. Y. 535.

[3] Pinkham *v.* Crocker, 77 Me. 563; Daylight Burner Co. *v.* Odlin, 51 N. H. 56; Goodenow *v.* Tyler, 7 Mass. 36.

[4] Goodenow *v.* Tyler, *supra.*

[5] Boyce *v.* Bank, 22 Fed. Rep. 53.

[6] Wheeler, &c. Co. *v.* Givan, 65 Mo. 89.

[7] Carnochan *v.* Gould, 1 Bailey, (S. Car.) 179; Howard *v.* Chapman, 4 C. & P. 508.

[8] *Post*, § 171.

[9] *Ibid.*

ner the principal may avail himself of the benefits of the contract, whether disclosed or not.[1] The subject of foreign principals dealing through domestic factors is discussed hereafter.[2]

§ 112. Brokers.

(1) *Definition.* A broker is an agent whose business it is to make a bargain for another, or bring persons together to bargain, and receive a commission on the transaction as compensation. He differs from a factor in that he does not usually have possession of the property which is the subject matter of the transaction, and in that he deals in the name of his principal. The field of brokerage is much larger than that of factorage. The factor buys and sells goods. The merchandise broker also does that: but there are in addition note and exchange brokers who buy and sell negotiable paper and foreign exchange; stock brokers who buy and sell stocks, bonds and other securities; real estate brokers who buy and sell, rent and mortgage real estate; insurance brokers who negotiate insurance usually for the one insured; and other classes of brokers named for the particular character of business transacted.

(2) *Scope of Authority.* The scope of a broker's authority is much narrower than that of a factor. A merchandise broker is engaged, for instance, in selling goods for his principal, but it is doubtful whether he has any authority to warrant them,[3] although of course a warranty in the nature of a condition would, if false, avoid the contract;[4] and a 'commercial traveler' who represents but one principal is to be distinguished from a broker.[5] He may give

[1] *Post,* § 129. [2] *Post,* § 187.

[3] Dodd *v.* Farlow, 11 Allen, (Mass.) 426.

[4] Forcheimer *v.* Stewart, 65 Iowa, 593.

[5] As in Pickert *v.* Marston, 68 Wis. 465.

credit, but only if usage warrants.[1] But he has no authority to sell in his own name or to agree to barter or pledge, nor has he any authority to receive payment since he has not possession of the goods.[2] As to other brokers than those engaged in buying and selling goods, their powers are fixed almost wholly by custom, and the principal is bound by all contracts within the limits of the custom.[3]

(3) *Liability of Principal.* A principal is liable for the contract of his broker within the scope of the authority, and also for his frauds,[4] but not beyond the scope of the agency.[5]

§ 113. Auctioneers.

(1) *Definition.* An auctioneer is an agent whose business it is to sell property publicly to the highest bidder and receive a commission on the proceeds of the sale. He may receive compensation otherwise, or may work gratuitously, but his habit is, and therefore an element of his business is, to receive commissions. He represents the seller in making the terms of the sale, but may and usually does represent the buyer also in reducing the terms to writing, to satisfy the statute of frauds.[6] Until the fall of the hammer he is the agent of the seller; after that he is the agent of both parties.

(2) *Scope of Authority.* As to his principal an auctioneer must obey instructions like any other agent. As to third persons authority is to be gathered from the

[1] White *v.* Fuller, 67 Barb. (N. Y.) 267.

[2] Higgins *v.* Moore, 34 N. Y. 417; Crosby *v.* Hill, 39 Ohio St. 100.

[3] Skiff *v.* Stoddard, 63 Conn. 198; Markham *v.* Jaudon, 41 N. Y. 235, 256.

[4] Samo *v.* Ins. Co., 26 U. C. C. P. 405, aff'd 2 Can. Sup. C. 411.

[5] Clark *v.* Cumming, 77 Ga. 64.

[6] Walker *v.* Herring, 21 Gratt. (Va.) 678; Johnson *v.* Buck, 35 N. J. L. 338.

customs usually followed in auction sales. These are: to sell for cash, and not on credit or for other goods or for negotiable paper;[1] to receive the price in cash at the time of the sale, or such a deposit of cash as is prescribed by the terms of the sale; and, if it be not paid, to bring an action in his own name for its recovery;[2] to follow the terms of the sale, when these are known, and no others, so that if the terms prescribe for an interest-bearing note, with surety, cash cannot be received instead.[3] Ordinarily he has no implied authority to warrant the quality of the goods sold.[4] If he exceeds the authority actually conferred, and that implied from the nature of the agency, the principal is not bound.[5] But if he keeps within the authority, the principal is liable for refusing to complete the contract.[6]

§ 114. Attorneys at Law.

(1) *Definition.* An attorney at law is an agent whose business it is, as a duly qualified officer of a court, to represent his principal in the conduct of litigation or other legal proceedings. A distinction exists in England between barristers, who represent the client at the bar, that is, when actually before the court, and solicitors, who represent the client generally throughout a legal proceeding.[7] In the United States, however, the distinctions between barristers, or advocates, or counsel, and solicitors,

[1] Broughton *v.* Silloway, 114 Mass. 71.

[2] Thompson *v.* Kelly, 101 Mass. 291; Johnson *v.* Buck, *supra.*

[3] Morgan *v.* East, 126 Ind. 42.

[4] Blood *v.* French, 9 Gray, (Mass.) 197; Payne *v.* Leconfield, 51 L. J. Q. B. 642.

[5] Bush *v.* Cole, 28 N. Y. 261.

[6] Cockcroft *v.* Muller, 71 N. Y. 367.

[7] See Sweet's Law Dictionary, 19 Am. Law Rev. 677. For the history of the rise of attorneys at law as a special class, see 1 Pollock and Maitland's Hist. of Eng. Law, 190-196.

or attorneys, or proctors, has practically dissappeared. The term attorney at law now includes the notion formerly conveyed by these separate terms. The courts generally have the power to prescribe the qualifications of those who appear before them to represent litigants, and it has even been doubted whether the legislature could, without constitutional sanction, deprive the courts of this power.[1]

(2) *Scope of Authority.* The attorney is appointed to conduct the affairs of his client in court, and has therefore a very wide discretion in their management. All the usual and customary steps in a proceeding may be taken under this implied or customary authority and will bind the client. "An attorney at law has authority, by virtue of his employment as such, to do in behalf of his client all acts, in or out of court, necessary or incidental to the prosecution and management of the suit, and which affect the remedy only, and not the cause of action."[2] It has been generally held in the United States that this limitation of the authority to the control over remedies precludes the power to compromise the claim, either before or after judgment.[3] In England the holding is otherwise, and in some of the United States.[4] But it is held that he may submit the claim to arbitration.[5] He may agree that property shall be sold pending an appeal as to the validity of a lien, for which a decree of sale has already been entered, and the money paid into court to abide the decision on the appeal.[6] He may direct a levy as a

[1] Matter of Goodell, 39 Wis. 232.

[2] Moulton *v.* Bowker, 115 Mass. 36; Clark *v.* Randall, 9 Wis. 135.

[3] Whipple *v.* Whitman, 13 R. I. 512; Maddux *v.* Bevan, 39 Md. 485; Watt *v.* Brookover, 35 W. Va. 323; Preston *v.* Hill, 50 Cal. 43.

[4] Prestwich *v.* Poley, 18 C. B. N. S. 806; Bonney *v.* Morrill, 57 Me. 368.

[5] Brooks *v.* New Durham, 55 N. H. 559; Sargeant *v.* Clark, 108 Pa. St. 588. Cf. McPherson *v.* Cox, 86 N. Y. 472.

[6] Halliday *v.* Stuart, 151 U. S. 229.

proper remedy for the collection of a claim, and if the levy be wrongful the principal is liable.[1] In general he may control the management of the proceeding, but he "may not compromise the rights of his client outside of his conduct of the action, or accept less than the full satisfaction sought, or release his client's right, or subject him to a new cause of action."[2]

§ 115. Bank Cashiers.

(1) *Definition.* "The cashier is the executive officer, through whom the whole financial operations of the bank are conducted. He receives and pays out its moneys, collects and pays its debts, and receives and transfers its commercial securities. Tellers and other subordinate officers may be appointed, but they are under his direction, and are, as it were, the arms by which designated portions of his various functions are discharged."[3] A bank cashier is the chief executive agent of the bank; the directors are the deliberative managing agents. "It is not wholly unapt to liken the board of directors to a bench of judges, and the cashier to the clerk of the court."[4]

(2) *Scope of Authority.* Custom has fixed with considerable precision the authority of a bank cashier, and this authority he may be presumed to possess without special delegation from the directors, and even as against a special restriction unknown to a third person dealing with the bank. The question whether he does or does not possess authority to do any particular act is ordinarily one for the court and not for the jury.[5] By the powers inherent in his office a cashier has authority to draw

1 Howell *v.* Caryl, 50 Mo. App. 440.

2 Lewis *v.* Duane, 141 N. Y. 302, 314.

3 Merchants' Bank *v.* State Bank, 10 Wall. (U. S.) 604, 650.

4 1 Morse on Banking, sec. 152.

5 Merchants' Bank *v.* State Bank, *supra.*

checks or drafts upon the funds of the bank deposited with other banking or trust companies;[1] to indorse and transfer for collection, discount, or sale the negotiable paper or securities owned by the bank;[2] to buy and sell bills of exchange;[3] to borrow money;[4] to collect the moneys due the bank;[5] and to certify checks drawn by depositors against funds in the bank.[6] He has no power to bind the bank to accept a draft to be drawn in the future,[7] or to bind the bank on a certification of his own check,[8] or as accommodation indorser of his own note or bill.[9]

§ 116. Shipmasters.

(1) *Definition.* A shipmaster is an agent who has entrusted to him the management and government of the ship upon a voyage. He is the first or head officer upon a merchantman, and as such is responsible for the safety of the ship and cargo, and is vested in consequence with very extensive powers.[10]

(2) *Scope of Authority.* As regards the navigation of the vessel the master has absolute control and authority. As regards discipline his authority is extensive, but its wilful abuse will not render the owner liable to a seaman,

[1] Mechanics' Bank *v.* Bank of Columbia, 5 Wheat. (U. S.) 326.

[2] Wild *v.* Bank, 3 Mason, (U. S. C. C.) 505.

[3] *Ibid.*

[4] Barnes *v.* Ontario Bank, 19 N. Y. 152; Crain *v.* Bank, 114 Ill. 516.

[5] Concord *v.* Bank, 16 N. H. 26.

[6] Merchants' Bank *v.* State Bank, *supra;* Cooke *v.* State Bank, 52 N. Y. 96. A verbal certification was held good in Espy *v.* Bank, 18 Wall. (U. S.) 604. Denying a cashier's inherent power to certify checks, see Mussey *v.* Eagle Bank, 9 Met. (Mass.) 306.

[7] Flannagan *v.* California N. Bank, 56 Fed. Rep. 959.

[8] Claflin *v.* Farmers', &c. Bk., 25 N. Y. 293.

[9] West St. Louis Sav. Bk. *v.* Shawnee County Bk., 95 U. S. 557.

[10] Hubbell *v.* Denison, 20 Wend. (N. Y.) 181; Martin *v.* Farnsworth, 1 Jones & Spencer (N. Y. City Superior Court), 246.

though it might to a passenger.[1] And such discipline is justified at all only on the high seas and not in port.[2] As regards authority to make contracts, the nature and extent of such authority is determined by the customs of the seas and the necessities of the situation. He has authority to make "contracts relative to the usual employment of the ship; to give a warranty in such contracts; to enter into contracts for repairs and necessaries to the ship;" to sell a perishable cargo to preserve it from destruction, or a wrecked ship and cargo where it is impossible or highly imprudent to attempt to carry them to their destination; to hypothecate the ship, freight, and cargo in case of extreme necessity; to borrow money in case of extreme necessity.[3] The further discussion of a shipmaster's powers belongs to a treatise on shipping and admiralty law.

[1] Gabrielson *v.* Waydell, 135 N. Y. 1.

[2] Padmore *v.* Piltz, 44 Fed. Rep. 104.

[3] Evans on Agency, (2d ed.) pp. 146–152, Ewell's ed. pp. 176–182; Story on Agency, §§ 116–123; McCready *v.* Thorn, 51 N. Y. 454.

CHAPTER X.

CONTRACT OF AGENT IN BEHALF OF AN UNDISCLOSED PRINCIPAL.

§ 117. Introductory.

It sometimes happens that an agent makes a contract in his own name and ostensibly for his own benefit, but in reality for the benefit of an undisclosed principal. In such a case there are two relations established,— (1) the relation of the agent to the third person under the contract made in the agent's name, and (2) the relation of the principal to the third person under the contract made for the principal's benefit. The first relation will be discussed in a subsequent chapter.[1] We are now concerned with the liabilities and rights of the undisclosed principal.

In order to make clear the outlines of a difficult branch of the law we will discuss: (1) the doctrine of the privity of contract in the English law and its general application to the subject of the undisclosed principal; (2) the rules applicable to the liability of an undisclosed principal; (3) the rules applicable to the rights of an undisclosed principal.

1. *The Doctrine of Privity of Contract.*

§ 118. General Statement of the Doctrine.

A fundamental notion of the common law is that a contract creates strictly personal obligations between the contracting parties. "A person has a right to select and determine with whom he will contract, and cannot have

[1] *Post,* § 196 *et seq.*

another person thrust upon him without his consent."[1] It was this notion that lay at the basis of the common law rules as to the non-assignability of contracts;[2] it has even yet yielded only to the extent of allowing an assignee to enforce rights owing to his assignor where the assignor has fully performed his obligations, and it can make no difference to the defendant to whom he pays money or delivers goods, or where the assignee can fairly be deputized to discharge the assignor's duties, the latter remaining liable for any breach.[3] It is still a question of much difficulty as to how far executors or administrators succeed to the rights and obligations of their decedents under operation of law.[4] The doctrine is very comprehensive that "you have a right to the benefit you contemplate from the character, credit, and substance of the party with whom you contract."[5]

Even if B. makes a promise to C., upon a consideration moving from the latter, expressly for the benefit of D., D. cannot in England maintain an action upon the promise.[6] In the United States, however, such actions are generally allowed, at least where at the time of the promise there is a duty or obligation owing from C. to D. which C. seeks to discharge or provide for by his contract with B. This has

1 Boston Ice Co. *v.* Potter, 123 Mass. 28; Boulton *v.* Jones, 2 H. & N. 564.

2 Pollock on Cont. (6th ed.) 204, 701; Ames, 3 Harv. L. Rev. 338–9.

3 Arkansas &c. Co. *v.* Belden Co., 127 U. S. 379; Rochester Lantern Co. *v.* Stiles, &c. Co., 135 N. Y. 209; La Rue *v.* Groezinger, 84 Cal. 281; Robson *v.* Drummond, 2 B. & Ad. 303; British Waggon Co. *v.* Lea, L. R. 5 Q. B. D. 149.

4 Dickinson *v.* Calahan's Adm'rs, 19 Pa. St. 227; Lacy *v.* Getman, 119 N. Y. 109; Drummond *v.* Crane, 159 Mass. 577.

5 Humble *v.* Hunter, 12 Q. B. 310, 317; Boston Ice Co. *v.* Potter, *supra;* Arkansas, &c. Co. *v.* Belden Co., *supra.*

6 Tweddle *v.* Atkinson, 1 B. & S. 393. *Accord.* Exchange Bank *v.* Rice, 107 Mass. 37; Borden *v.* Boardman, 157 Mass. 410; Linneman *v.* Moross, 98 Mich. 178.

been put upon the doctrine of agency and subsequent ratification;[1] upon the doctrine of a kind of common law 'trust' enforceable as for money or other thing had and received to the benefit of C;[2] upon the doctrine "that the law, operating upon the act of the parties, creates the duty, establishes the privity, and implies the promise and obligation on which the action is founded;"[3] and upon a doctrine of convenience, namely, that "it accords the remedy to the party who in most instances is chiefly interested to enforce the promise, and avoids multiplicity of actions."[4] The doctrine as applied in the United States is confessedly an anomaly, but serves to illustrate the fact that anomalous doctrines are sometimes admitted into the law where they aid to work out substantial justice, and that the strict common law rule as to privity of contract has important exceptions.

§ 119. Application to Agency generally.

The general doctrines of agency do not run counter to the fundamental dogma, as to privity of contract. Where the principal is disclosed the third party deals with him, and not with the agent, and relies upon his character, credit, and substance, and not upon that of the agent. The agency is merely a means through which the minds of the principal and the third party meet in mutual agreement. When once the contract is formed the agent drops out. The difficulties arising from unauthorized contracts subsequently ratified have already been discussed.[5] The difficulties arising in the enforcement of rights against the

[1] See opinion of Johnson, C. J., and Denio, J., in Lawrence *v.* Fox, 20 N. Y. 268.

[2] See Vrooman *v.* Turner, 69 N. Y. 280; Jefferson *v.* Asch, 53 Minn. 446.

[3] McDowell *v.* Laev, 35 Wis. 171.

[4] Lehow *v.* Simonton, 3 Colo. 346; Wood *v.* Moriarty, 15 R. I. 518.

[5] *Ante*, § 38.

agent upon an unauthorized contract not subsequently ratified will be discussed hereafter.[1] We have now to consider the difficulties attending the enforcement of rights against an undisclosed principal, and the greater difficulties attending the enforcement of rights by an undisclosed principal.

§ 120. Application to Contracts for Undisclosed Principal.

A more serious difficulty presents itself in the doctrines peculiar to undisclosed principals. In the case of a contract made by an agent in his own name, as principal, the third party obviously relies upon the character, credit, and substance of the agent alone, and intends to incur obligations to the agent and to no one else. So far at least as X. is concerned it is a contract between A. and X., and P. is never for a moment in X.'s contemplation. The strict application of the common law rule would lead to the conclusion, therefore, that P. could neither sue nor be sued upon the contract.

Yet just the opposite conclusion prevails. The case escapes the common law doctrine and establishes the sweeping rule that an undisclosed principal may both sue and be sued upon a contract made in his behalf or to his secret use by his agent. The rule is probably the outcome of a kind of common law equity, powerfully aided and extended by the fiction of the identity of principal and agent and the doctrine of reciprocity or mutuality of contractual obligations. The rule has two distinct parts: (1) that the undisclosed principal may be sued; (2) that the undisclosed principal may sue. The first is probably based upon the notion that it is inequitable to allow the principal to take the benefits of a contract made by his agent and compel the third person to look only to the agent for compensation. The second is based upon the

[1] *Post*, § 183.

notion that contract obligations require mutuality, and that, since the principal may sue he must also be liable to be sued. The fiction of identity is employed to establish a real or true assent on the part of the principal in place of an assent or promise constructed by the law, such as is created in all that class of obligations known as quasi-contracts.

§ 121. Suits against Undisclosed Principal.

The action against an undisclosed principal rests logically upon the ground that the principal's estate has had the benefit of the contract and ought to bear the burden. This doctrine is as old as the Year Books in which we read that an action of debt was maintained against an abbot on the count that the plaintiff had lent money and sold a horse to a monk, "which money and horse came to the profit of the house, etc."[1] It is illustrated in many modern cases, where, clearly, the decision need not go further than the doctrine that where the principal's estate is unjustly enriched at the expense of the third party's, the latter may maintain assumpsit for the value of the benefit conferred.[2] Such an action does not logically rest upon a true contractual obligation arising from the assent of the parties, but upon a quasi-contractual obligation created by the law on grounds of justice and fair dealing. But for the aid of the fiction of identity of principal and agent the courts might have been driven into so treating it, and limiting the recovery to the measure of benefits conferred. In that case the doctrine would never have been extended to include the second half of the rule which gives the undisclosed principal an action against the third party.

[1] Y. B. 34 & 35 Edw. I. pp. 566-9 (1307).

[2] Wilson *v.* Hart, 7 Taunt. 295; Kayton *v.* Barnett, 116 N. Y. 625; Henderson *v.* Mayhew, 2 Gill, (Md.) 393.

This is illustrated in the case of Kayton *v.* Barnett.[1] X. having declined to sell to P., the latter procured A. to purchase. X. expressly stated that he would not sell to P., and A. thereupon assured X. that he was not buying for P. but for himself. X. was nevertheless allowed to maintain an action against P. for the price. The court through Follett, Ch. J., said: "Notwithstanding the assertion of the plaintiffs that they would not sell to the defendants, they, through the circumvention of Bishop and the defendants, did sell the property to the defendants, who have had the benefit of it, and have never paid the remainder of the purchase price pursuant to their agreement. Bishop was the defendants' agent. Bishop's mind was, in this transaction, the defendants' mind, and so the minds of the parties met, and the defendants having, through their own and their agent's deception, acquired the plaintiffs' property by purchase, cannot successfully assert that they are not liable for the remainder of the purchase-price because they, through their agent, succeeded in inducing the defendants to do that which they did not intend to do, and, perhaps, would not have done had the defendants not dealt disingenuously."

Here is a curious mixture of the equitable notion that the defendant ought to reimburse the plaintiff for the benefits received, and the notion that the defendant had in verity promised to do so because his agent had promised, and the agent's mind is the principal's mind and so the minds of the parties have met.

But the doctrine once established that the contract obligation rests upon assent, and it will speedily be extended beyond the cases where benefits have been conferred, and the third party will be given an action upon a bilateral executory contract.[2] And actions will be given

[1] 116 N. Y. 625.

[2] Episcopal Church *v.* Wiley, 2 Hill Ch. (S. C.) 584, *s. c.* 1 Riley Ch. (S. C.) 156.

in cases where the principal is guilty of no inequitable conduct, as where, for instance, he has given his agent funds with which to purchase, and the agent has purchased in his own name on credit, under circumstances where, had the agency been known, it would be reasonable to infer that he had authority to purchase on credit.[1]

§ 122. Suits by Undisclosed Principal.

Having reached the conclusion, by aid of the fiction of identity, that the minds of the parties have met, it is easy to invoke the doctrine of reciprocity or mutuality of contract and hold that the undisclosed principal may also sue the third party, although, in fact, the third party never undertook and never intended to undertake an obligation in favor of the principal.[2] "The contract of the agent is the contract of the principal, and he may sue or be sued thereon, though not named therein; and notwithstanding the rule of law that an agreement reduced to writing may not be contradicted or varied by parol, it is well settled that the principal may show that the agent who made the contract in his own name was acting for him."[3] And so it follows that a contract made between A. and B., each believing the other to be acting in his own behalf, may be shown to be a contract between P. and X., the two undisclosed principals.[4]

Earlier cases which held that only the promisee in the

[1] See remarks of Wallace, J., in Fradley *v.* Hyland 37 Fed. Rep. 49, 52–3, and the conclusion, "But it is probably too late to consider the questions thus suggested upon principle." See also Watteau *v.* Fenwick, 1893, 1 Q. B. 346; Hubbard *v.* Tenbrook, 124 Pa. St. 291.

[2] Taintor *v.* Prendergast, 3 Hill, (N. Y.) 72; Eastern R. Co. *v.* Benedict, 5 Gray, (Mass.) 561.

[3] Ford *v.* Williams, 21 How. (U. S.) 287; Burton *v.* Goodspeed, 69 Ill. 237.

[4] Darrow *v.* Horne Produce Co, 57 Fed. Rep. 463.

written instrument could sue upon it,[1] must be regarded as overruled or overwhelmed by later decisions which proceed on the theory that the nominal promisee (the agent) and the real promisee (the principal) are identical.

§ 123. Parol Evidence Rule.

It is now settled law that the admission of parol evidence to show that a written contract made in the name of the agent was in fact made in behalf of an undisclosed, or, if disclosed, unnamed principal, does not violate the rule against the admission of parol evidence to vary the terms of a written contract.[2] "Whatever the original merits of the rule that a party not mentioned in a simple contract in writing may be charged as principal upon oral evidence, even where the writing gives no indication of an intent to bind any other person than the signor, we cannot reopen it, for it is as well settled as any part of the law of agency."[3] This rule must be viewed in connection with two others: (1) that parol evidence is not admissible to introduce into a sealed instrument or a negotiable instrument a party not named or described in the instrument;[4] (2) that parol evidence is not admissible to discharge the agent from liability on a contract made in his name, for "to allow evidence to be given that the party who appears on the face of the instrument to be personally a contracting party, is not such, would be to allow parol evidence to contradict the written agreement, which cannot be done."[5]

[1] United States *v.* Parmele, 1 Paine, (U. S. C. C.) 252. Cf. Huntington *v.* Knox, 7 Cush. (Mass.) 371.

[2] Ford *v.* Williams, 21 How. (U. S.) 287; Huntington *v.* Knox, 7 Cush. (Mass.) 371; Darrow *v.* Horne Produce Co., 57 Fed. Rep. 463.

[3] Byington *v.* Simpson, 134 Mass. 169.

[4] *Post*, §§ 127-8, 134-5.

[5] Higgins *v.* Senior, 8 M. & W. 834.

2. *Liability of an Undisclosed Principal.*

§ 124. General Rule.

Subject to the exceptions hereafter enumerated, an undisclosed principal is liable to a third person with whom his agent has dealt within the scope of the agency in the same way and to the same extent as a disclosed principal, although the third person gave exclusive credit to the agent supposing him to be the principal.[1] This does not rest upon the doctrine of "holding out the agent," since obviously the third party has not been misled in that respect. It rests upon the anomalous doctrines already explained, and has been compared to the liability of a dormant partner.[2] "Once it is established that the defendant was the real principal, the ordinary doctrine as to principal and agent applies — that the principal is liable for all the acts of the agent which are within the authority usually confided to an agent of that character, notwithstanding limitations, as between the principal and the agent, put upon that authority. It is said that it is only so where there has been a holding out of authority — which cannot be said of a case where the person supplying the goods knew nothing of the existence of a principal. But I do not think so. Otherwise, in every case of undisclosed principal, or at least in every case where the fact of there being a principal was undisclosed, the secret limitation of authority would prevail and defeat the action of the person dealing with the agent and then discovering that he was an agent and had a principal."[3]

To this general rule there are, however, certain well

[1] Kayton *v.* Barnett, 116 N. Y. 625; Hubbard *v.* Tenbrook, 124 Pa. St. 291; Watteau *v.* Fenwick, 1893, 1 Q. B. 346; and other cases cited below.

[2] Watteau *v.* Fenwick, *supra.*

[3] *Ibid.*, per Wills, J. See criticism in 9 Law Q. Rev. 111.

defined exceptions or qualifications which must now be noticed.

§ 125. First Exception. — State of Accounts.

The right of the third person to proceed against the undisclosed principal is subject to the state of accounts between the principal and agent. The exact nature and extent of this exception is, however, involved in some uncertainty.

(1) *Origin of the doctrine.* The leading case on this subject is Thomson *v.* Davenport [1] where the *dictum* was pronounced that, "if a person sells goods (supposing at the time of the contract he is dealing with a principal), but afterwards discovers that the person with whom he has been dealing is not the principal in the transaction, but agent for a third person, though he may in the meantime have debited the agent with it, he may afterward recover the amount from the real principal; subject, however, to this qualification, that the state of the account between the principal and the agent is not altered to the prejudice of the principal." This *dictum* was said to be too broad in Heald *v.* Kenworthy,[2] and the doctrine was there declared to be that, "if the conduct of the seller [the third person] would make it unjust for him to call upon the buyer for the money; as for example, where the principal is induced by the conduct of the seller to pay his agent the money on the faith that the agent and seller have come to a settlement on the matter, or if any representation to that effect is made by the seller, either by words or conduct, the seller cannot afterwards throw off the mask and sue the principal." In a later English case [3] a distinction was drawn between the case where the exist-

[1] 9 Barn. & Cress. 78, 86; 2 Smith's Leading Cases.

[2] 10 Ex. 739.

[3] Armstrong *v.* Stokes, L. R. 7 Q. B. 598.

ence of a principal is wholly undisclosed, and the agent contracts as principal, and the case where the existence of a principal is disclosed, but the principal is unnamed and unknown; the doctrine of Thomson *v.* Davenport being held applicable to the first state of facts, and the doctrine of Heald *v.* Kenworthy to the second. But in Irvine *v.* Watson,[1] this distinction is said to be "difficult to understand," and the doctrine of Heald *v.* Kenworthy is expressly approved. The controversy therefore is as to whether settlement in good faith by the principal with the agent will discharge the principal, or whether the settlement must have been in reliance upon such conduct on the part of the third person as will work an estoppel against the latter.

(2) *English doctrine.* The English doctrine now is that the principal is discharged from liability to the third person only where the third person has by his conduct led the principal to believe that there has been a settlement between the third person and the agent, or that, with knowledge of the principal's liability, the third person elects to give credit exclusively to the agent.[2]

(3) *American doctrine.* The doctrine in the United States seems to have followed the *dictum* in Thompson *v.* Davenport. The principal is said to be discharged where he has in good faith paid the agent or made such a change in the state of the account between the agent and himself that he would suffer loss if he should be compelled to pay the seller.[3]

[1] L. R. 5 Q. B. Div. 414.

[2] Irvine *v.* Watson, *supra;* Davison *v.* Donaldson, L. R. 9 Q. B. Div. 623; Pollock on Cont. (6th ed.) 99.

[3] Fradley *v.* Hyland, 37 Fed. Rep. 49; Thomas *v.* Atkinson, 38 Ind. 248; Laing *v.* Butler, 37 Hun, (N. Y.) 144; Knapp *v.* Simon, 96 N. Y. 284; Story on Agency, § 449; 23 Am. L. Rev. 565.

§ 126. Second Exception. — Election to hold Agent.

Where the third party, after discovering the principal, unequivocally elects to regard the agent as the sole responsible contracting party, he cannot afterwards proceed against the principal.[1] What constitutes a final or unequivocal election is a question of fact, though the conduct may be so decisive as to establish an election in point of law, or so indecisive as to render unwarranted a finding that there was an election. Bringing an action against the agent has an evidential force, but does not necessarily constitute an election.[2] It is generally held that an unsatisfied judgment is not conclusive proof of an election;[3] though the ruling is otherwise in England.[4]

It has been held that where at the time the contract is made the third party knows the principal, but accepts a written instrument in the name of the agent, he makes an election to look to the agent alone, and parol evidence is inadmissible to charge the principal.[5] But this is doubtful.[6]

§ 127. Third Exception. — Contract under Seal.

Where the contract between the agent and third party is under seal (the seal not being merely superfluous), the principal is not liable. It is a strict rule of the common law that only the parties named or described in a sealed instrument can sue or be sued upon it.[7] This rule applies

[1] Kingsley *v.* Davis, 104 Mass. 178; Kendall *v.* Hamilton, L. R. 4 App. Cas. 504.

[2] Cobb *v.* Knapp, 71 N. Y. 348; Curtis *v.* Williamson, L. R. 10 Q. B. 57.

[3] Beymer *v.* Bonsall, 79 Pa. St. 298; Maple *v.* R. Co., 40 Ohio St. 313.

[4] Pollock on Cont. (6th ed.) 100, *citing* Priestly *v.* Fernie, 3 H. & C. 977.

[5] Chandler *v.* Coe, 54 N. H. 561.

[6] Merrill *v.* Kenyon, 48 Conn. 314.

[7] *Post*, § 188; Briggs *v.* Partridge, 64 N. Y. 357; Borcherling *v.* Katz, 37 N. J. Eq. 150.

equally to a principal who is disclosed in the negotiations, but unnamed in the formal contract.

§ 128. Fourth Exception.— Negotiable Instrument.

Only the party whose name appears as the obligor on a negotiable instrument can be sued upon it. Parol evidence is therefore inadmissible to charge an undisclosed or unnamed principal upon such an instrument.[1] But if there be an ambiguity on the face of the paper as to whether the principal or agent is intended to be bound, parol evidence is admissible to remove the ambiguity. This will be fully discussed in a succeeding chapter.[2]

3. *Rights of an Undisclosed Principal.*

§ 129. General Rule.

Subject to the exceptions and qualifications hereafter enumerated, an undisclosed principal may bring an action in his own name upon contracts made by his agent in his behalf, although the third party supposed that he was dealing with the agent as principal.[3] This rule is said to be the necessary corollary of the one which gives the third person a right of action against the undisclosed principal, since mutuality of remedial rights is clearly just. It follows that two undisclosed principals may contract through their respective agents, and that the contract will give to each (subject to the enumerated exceptions) the same rights and liabilities as if they had been disclosed principals or had contracted in person.[4] This right of the principal is superior to the right of the agent, and when the prin-

[1] *Post,* § 189; Sparks *v.* Dispatch Transfer Co., 104 Mo. 531; Brown *v.* Parker, 7 Allen, (Mass.) 337.

[2] *Post,* §§ 186–195.

[3] Huntington *v.* Knox, 7 Cush. (Mass.) 371; Taintor *v.* Prendergast, 3 Hill, (N. Y.) 72; Barham *v.* Bell, 112 N. Car. 131.

[4] Darrow *v.* Horne Produce Co., 57 Fed. Rep. 463.

cipal has once given notice of his intention to exercise it, the third party will settle with the agent at his peril.[1] If the contract be in writing (not under seal or negotiable), it does not violate the rule against varying the terms of written instruments by parol to admit parol evidence for the purpose of showing the real principal.[2] But it would vary the instrument to admit parol evidence to discharge the agent.[3]

§ 130. First Exception. — State of Accounts.

The right of the principal to sue the third party is subject to the equities and the state of the accounts existing between the agent and the third party at the time the right is asserted. In other words the principal cannot assert his rights without leaving to the third party exactly the same rights as if the agent had been in fact the principal.[4] The cases applying this doctrine have been mainly those where the agent sold goods in his own name, and under these circumstances the distinction is made between the case where the agent has possession of the goods, and where he has not. In the former case the right of set-off which might be asserted against the agent may be asserted against the undisclosed principal; in the latter case it may not.[5] But the doctrine is equally applicable to contracts other than those for the sale of goods.[6]

It seems to be immaterial whether the agent is authorized to contract in his own name or not; if the principal seeks to enforce the contract he must take it subject to all

[1] Pitts *v.* Mower, 18 Me. 361; Huntington *v.* Knox, *supra.*

[2] Darrow *v.* Horne Produce Co., *supra.*

[3] *Post*, § 197.

[4] Montagu *v.* Forwood, 1893, L. R. 2 Q. B. 350; Gardner *v.* Allen, 6 Ala. 187; Peel *v.* Shepherd, 58 Ga. 365; Taintor *v.* Prendergast, 3 Hill, (N. Y.) 72.

[5] Bernshouse *v.* Abbott, 45 N. J. L. 531.

[6] Montagu *v.* Forwood, *supra.*

defences that might have been set up against the agent.[1] But the third person must have believed that the agent was contracting as principal. If he knew he was contracting as agent, though he did not know whose agent, he cannot set off claims or equities.[2] It is even held that if the agent is one who commonly contracts for undisclosed principals, though also for himself, the third person can not assume that the agent is contracting for himself, and would not be entitled to claim a set-off as against an undisclosed principal.[3]

§ 131. Second Exception. — Estoppel.

Where the principal has, by representing the agent to be the principal, or by standing by and allowing innocent third persons to deal with the agent as principal, induced such innocent third persons to change their legal relations in such a way as to make it inequitable for the principal to claim the rights of an undisclosed principal, he will be estopped from maintaining an action in his own name.[4] Perhaps this exception is only an extension of the previous one. In that the principal is estopped to press his rights to the extent that the third person would be injured; in this it is assumed that he cannot press his rights at all without injury to the third person. There seems to be no considered authority on this point.

§ 132. Third Exception.—Exclusive Credit to Agent.

Where the third person has clearly expressed his inten-

1 *Ex parte* Dixon, L. R. 4 Ch. Div. 133; Stevens *v.* Biller, L. R. 25 Ch. Div. 31.

2 Ilsey *v.* Merriam, 7 Cush. (Mass.) 242; Evans *v.* Waln, 71 Pa. St. 69.

3 Miller *v.* Lea, 35 Md. 396; Evans *v.* Waln, 71 Pa. St. 69; Cooke *v.* Eshelby, L. R. 12 App. Cas. 271. See criticism of this doctrine in 3 Law Q. Rev. 358.

4 Ferrand *v.* Bischoffsheim, 4 C. B. N. S. 710, 716; Pollock on Cont. (6th ed.) 98.

tion to deal with the agent as principal, or where he has dealt with the agent on terms of trust and confidence, or the nature of the contract is fiduciary, the undisclosed principal cannot claim the benefits of the contract. "Every man has a right to elect what parties he will deal with. . . . And as a man's right to refuse to enter into a contract is absolute, he is not obliged to submit the validity of his reasons to a court or jury."[1] The intention to deal only with the agent may be found in the recitals of the written contract,[2] or the negotiations attending an oral one.[3] In the first case the question would be one of construction for the court; in the latter, of fact for the jury. The intention may be further inferred from the nature of the contract, as where it is fiduciary, or for personal skill or service.[4] But in the latter case it would seem that if the agent has personally discharged the trust or performed the service, his undisclosed principal may recover the compensation.[5]

§ 133. Fourth Exception. — Varying Written Instrument. Where in a written instrument the agent has represented himself in express terms or recitals as the real and only principal, the undisclosed principal cannot maintain an action in his own name, since parol evidence would be inadmissible to vary the express terms and recitals of the written instrument.[6] This is the result of a rule of evi-

1 Winchester *v.* Howard, 97 Mass. 303; Humble *v.* Hunter, 12 Q. B. 310.

2 Humble *v.* Hunter, *supra.*

3 Winchester *v.* Howard, *supra.*

4 Pollock on Cont. (6th ed.) p. 97; Eggleston *v.* Boardman, 37 Mich. 14.

5 Warder *v.* White, 14 Ill. App. 50, *citing,* Grojan *v.* Wade, 2 Starkie, 391.

6 Humble *v.* Hunter, 12 Q. B. 310; Schmaltz *v.* Avery, 16 Q. B. 655; Darrow *v.* Horne Produce Co., 57 Fed. Rep. 463.

dence merely. If the representation were one relied upon by the third party as establishing the personality or credit of the person with whom he was dealing, it would be equally effective whether in writing or parol, under the doctrines of the preceding section.

§ 134. Fifth Exception.* — Sealed Instruments.

Where the contract is under seal the principal cannot bring an action upon it in his own name, owing to the technical rule, that only the parties named or described in a deed can sue or be sued upon it. He must proceed in the name of the agent.[1]

§ 135. Sixth Exception. — Negotiable Instrument.

Only the party named as payee in a negotiable instrument can sue upon it.[2] This is due to the technical rule of the law merchant which confines the rights and liabilities upon negotiable instruments to the parties named or described therein. But if there be any ambiguity on the face of the instrument as to who is intended to be the payee, parol evidence is admissible to remove the ambiguity. And, unlike the case of the maker, drawer, or acceptor, the addition of a descriptive term like "agent," "treasurer," "cashier," etc., is now generally held to create such an ambiguity.[3] The same reason does not exist for forbidding a person not named as payee to sue

* The fifth and sixth exceptions apply as well to the case of a disclosed principal, who is not named or described in the formal instrument.

[1] Violett *v.* Powell, 10 B. Mon. (Ky.) 347; see *post,* § 188.

[2] Grist *v.* Backhouse, 4 Dev. & Battle, (N. C.) 362; Moore *v.* Penn, 5 Ala. 135; United States Bk. *v.* Lyman, 1 Blatchf. (U. S. C. C.) 297; *s. c.* 2 Fed. Cas. 709.

[3] Baldwin *v.* Bank, 1 Wall. (U. S.) 234; Commercial Bank *v.* French, 21 Pick. (Mass.) 486; Nave *v.* First Nat. Bk., 87 Ind. 204.

as for forbidding a person not named as payor to be sued, namely, that certainty is required as to the obligors on negotiable instruments in order that they may circulate freely. Accordingly the technical rule forbidding an unnamed payee to sue has dwindled to narrow limits.

CHAPTER XI.

ADMISSIONS AND DECLARATIONS OF THE AGENT.

§ 136. Object in proving Admissions of Agent.

The admissions or declarations of an agent may be sought to be offered in evidence against the principal for any one of three purposes: (1) To establish the fact of the agency; (2) to establish the nature or extent of the authority; (3) to establish the existence or non-existence of some fact (other than the two named above) which is material to the issue in controversy between the parties. The competency of the admission or declaration will depend in the first instance upon the purpose for which it is offered, and secondarily upon the relation of the admission or declaration to the transaction in question and the general scope of the agency.

§ 137. When always inadmissible.

The admissions or declarations of an agent cannot be given in evidence against the principal, either (1) to establish the fact of the agency, or (2) to establish the nature or extent of the authority.[1] The reason is obvious. The declaration of the agent that he is agent, or that he has certain delegated powers, is merely an attempt to clothe himself with authority, and has no tendency to prove that he possesses in fact the authority which he claims. He is holding himself out as agent, whereas the requirement is that the principal should hold him out as agent in order to work an estoppel against the principal. It is therefore error to

[1] Hatch *v.* Squires, 11 Mich. 185; Mitchum *v.* Dunlap, 98 Mo. 418; Butler *v.* C., B. & Q. Ry. Co., 87 Iowa, 206.

admit evidence of what the agent has said as to his own powers in an action to hold the principal, and the error is not cured by a charge to the jury that the agency cannot be proved by the agent's own declarations, and it is even doubtful whether the withdrawing of such evidence from the consideration of the jury would cure the error.[1] Since his express declarations are incompetent to prove his authority, *a fortiori* his conduct is incompetent. It is therefore improper to charge a jury that they may find the fact of the agency or of the authority if the conduct of the agent was such as to lead the third party to believe that he was authorized.[2] It is the conduct of the principal and not of the agent from which authority must be inferred.

This is far from saying, however, that an agent is an incompetent witness to prove the fact of the agency or authority. Where parol evidence as to the existence of the agency or extent of the authority is admissible at all, the agent is as competent a witness as any other person to testify under oath to facts within his knowledge touching the agency. Even the old rule of evidence which excluded the testimony of a party in interest made an exception in favor of the evidence of an agent produced to prove the fact of the agency.[3] And this applies equally where a husband is the agent of his wife or a wife of her husband.[4] But if the authority be conferred in writing, parol evidence of any kind is generally inadmissible,[5] unless it be where the question of authority is only incidentally involved.[6]

[1] Comegys *v.* American Lumber Co., 8 Wash. 661.

[2] Leu *v.* Mayer, 52 Kans. 419.

[3] 1 Greenleaf on Ev. § 416; Gould *v.* Norfolk Lead Co., 9 Cush. (Mass.) 338; Thayer *v.* Meeker, 86 Ill. 470.

[4] O'Conner *v.* Insurance Co., 31 Wis. 160; Roberts *v.* N. W. Nat. Ins. Co., (Wis.) 62 N. W. Rep. 1048.

[5] Neal *v.* Patten, 40 Ga. 363.

[6] Columbia Bridge Co. *v.* Geisse, 38 N. J. L. 39.

§ 138. When admissible. — General Rule.

In order that the admission or declaration of an agent may be binding on his principal, the following elements must concur: (1) the fact of the agency must be established; (2) the admission or declaration must be in regard to some matter within the scope of the agent's authority; (3) the admission or declaration must (*a*) constitute a part of the '*res gestæ*' of a transaction in which the agent was acting for his principal, and (*b*) serve to characterize that transaction.

The first two elements do not call for special discussion. They involve considerations already familiar to the reader. There must be an agency and the agent must be acting within the scope of his authority in order that any act of his may be binding on his principal. This is as true of his statements as of his conduct. If the admissions or declarations have reference to acts which the agent had no authority to perform, or to any matter foreign to the agency, they stand on the same level as statements of strangers and are clearly inadmissible.[1]

§ 139. When admissible. — Res Gestæ.

It is said that the declaration of an agent to be competent evidence against his principal must meet two requirements: (*a*) it must constitute a part of the *res gestæ* of a transaction in which the agent was acting for his principal; (*b*) it must be one which naturally accompanies the transaction and illustrates or unfolds its character or quality.[2]

(*a*) The first requirement is briefly stated in the familiar

[1] 1 Greenleaf on Ev. § 113; Fogg *v.* Pew, 10 Gray, (Mass.) 409; Lamm *v.* Port Deposit, &c. Assn., 49 Md. 233.

[2] White *v.* Miller, 71 N. Y. 118, 134; Butler *v.* Manhattan Ry. Co., 143 N. Y. 417, 422.

rule that the declaration must constitute a part of the *res gestæ*. This merely means that what an agent says or does in the conduct of a transaction for his principal is treated as if it had been said or done by the principal, under the application of the fiction of identity. The term *res gestæ* is simply a convenient symbol for conveying this idea. It really adds nothing, and, because of its literal vagueness and its somewhat different use in other branches of the law, has led to some darkening of counsel. If the phrase "of the *res gestæ*" were omitted from the first sentence in this section, the idea conveyed would be precisely the same.

The first inquiry is, therefore, whether the declaration was made as part of a transaction in which the agent was acting for the principal. If made before or after the transaction, it is incompetent as against the principal. This is stated very clearly in the leading case of White *v.* Miller:[1]

"The general rule is, that what one person says, out of court, is not admissible to charge or bind another. The exception is in cases of agency; and in cases of agency, the declarations of the agent are not competent to charge the principal upon proof merely that the relation of principal and agent existed when the declarations were made. It must further appear that the agent, at the time the declarations were made, was engaged in executing the authority conferred upon him, and that the declarations related to, and were connected with the business then depending, so that they constituted a part of *res gestæ*."[2]

In the application of this rule the courts have not been entirely harmonious in deciding when the declaration is a part of the transaction. Clearly a subsequent narration by

[1] 71 N. Y. 118, 135.

[2] See also Fairlie *v.* Hastings, 10 Ves. 123.

the agent is not.[1] Clearly a contemporaneous statement by way of inducement or representation is.[2] In contract cases there seems to be little difficulty in deciding whether the declaration falls within the first or the second of these classes, for the moment of the formation or completion of the contract marks the termination of the transaction.[3] But in cases of tort the moment when the transaction ends so that subsequent statements become narrative is more difficult to determine, and the courts have shifted the line in accordance with the peculiar circumstances of each case and their interpretation of the rule. The general test is that the declaration should be in such close connection with the main act constituting the tort as to be clearly spontaneous and undesigned, leaving no opportunity for the playing of a part. If strictly contemporaneous the declaration is clearly admissible.[4] If unquestionably subsequent both as to time and causal relation the declaration is clearly inadmissible.[5]

If in point of time subsequent, but in point of causal relation to the main act substantially contemporaneous, the declaration will be admitted by some courts and rejected by others. One class of cases holds that if the

[1] Stiles *v.* Western R., 8 Met. (Mass.) 44; Phelps *v.* James, 86 Iowa, 398; Empire Mill Co. *v.* Lovell, 77 Iowa, 100; White *v.* Miller, *supra.*

[2] Baring *v.* Clark, 19 Pick. (Mass.) 220; Dick *v.* Cooper, 24 Pa. St. 217; Burnside *v.* Grand Trunk Ry., 47 N. H. 554.

[3] Declarations in the course of a transaction amounting to warranties or to fraud may be distinguished. In such cases the warranty or the fraud is the main fact to be established. See, for example, Nelson *v.* Cowing, 6 Hill, (N. Y.) 336; Jeffrey *v.* Bigelow, 13 Wend. (N. Y.) 518; Smalley *v.* Morris, 157 Pa. St. 349. Declarations which are authorized are also to be distinguished, as where two persons converse by telephone through the agency of a telephone operator. Oskamp *v.* Gadsden, 35 Neb. 7.

[4] As in Elledge *v.* National City, &c. Ry., 100 Calif. 282.

[5] As in Williamson *v.* Cambridge R., 144 Mass. 148.

declaration is clearly the result of the main act alone, and not of that plus possible reflection on the part of the agent or servant, it is admissible; another class rejects this doctrine as too refined for practical application, and holds to the rule requiring a proximity in time, which might properly be described as instantaneously successive. This difference of judicial opinion is well illustrated in Vicksburg, &c. Railroad Co. *v.* O'Brien,[1] the Supreme Court of the United States standing five to four against the admission of the declaration of a locomotive engineer made from ten to twenty minutes after an accident. The minority dissented on the ground that the modern cases have relaxed the stringency of the rule requiring 'perfect coincidence' of time. Perhaps the weight of American authority favors such relaxation, guarded by the qualification that the peculiar facts of each case must determine whether the declaration is undesigned and spontaneous.[2]

(*b*) The second requirement is that the declaration should be one which illustrates or unfolds the character or quality of the main act. "While proximity in point of time with the act causing the injury is in every case of this kind essential to make what was said by a third person [agent], competent evidence against another [principal] as part of the *res gestæ*, that alone is insufficient, unless what was said may be considered part of the principal fact, and so a part of the act itself. But as in this case the . . . [remark] was not one naturally accompanying the act, or calculated to unfold its character or quality, it was not admissible as *res gestæ*. . . . *Res gestæ* in a case like this implies substantial coincidence in time, but if declarations of third persons are not in their nature a part of the fact,

[1] 119 U. S. 99.

[2] Alabama, &c. R. *v.* Hawk, 72 Ala. 112; Ohio, &c. Ry. *v.* Stein, 133 Ind. 243; Harriman *v.* Stowe, 57 Mo. 93; Hermes *v.* Chicago, &c. Ry., 80 Wis. 590.

they are not admissible in evidence, however closely related in point of time."[1]

§ 140. Limitation of the Rule. — Adverse Interest.

A qualification of the above rule exists in cases where the agent is known to be acting for himself, or to have an adverse interest. Where, for example, the president of a company pledges the stock of the company for a personal loan, his representations as to its genuineness do not bind the company. The pledgee should know in such a case that the agent's personal interest may lead him to betray his principal. "It is an old doctrine, from which there has never been any departure, that an agent cannot bind his principal, even in matters touching his agency, where he is known to be acting for himself, or to have an adverse interest."[2]

[1] Butler *v.* Manhattan Ry. Co., 143 N. Y. 417, 423; Barker *v.* St. Louis, &c. R., (Mo.), 28 S. W. Rep. 866.

[2] Manhattan Life Ins. Co. *v.* Forty-second Street, &c. R., 139 N. Y. 146.

CHAPTER XII.

NOTICE TO AGENT.

§ 141. General Statement of the Rule.

It is a general statement of the law that notice to the agent is notice to the principal. In other words, the principal is chargeable with all the knowledge that his agent has in a transaction in which the agent is acting for the principal.[1] If this were not so a purchaser could always free himself from the possible equities arising from the acquisition of knowledge of adverse rights in or to the property purchased, by purchasing through an agent. It is against the policy of the law to place one who deals through an agent in a better position than one who deals in person.

But the rule has a wider sweep than this. One who deals through an agent may be placed in a worse position than one who deals in person. By the application of the fiction of identity all the knowledge present in the mind of the agent, whenever or however acquired, may be treated as the knowledge of the principal. In other words, if P. employs A., and it happens that A. possesses information affecting the transaction, P. will be charged with this knowledge ; whereas, if P. employs B., who happens not to possess such information, P. will not be charged with notice.

The subject of notice has, therefore, two branches: (1) Where the notice is acquired by the agent in the course

[1] Hyatt *v.* Clark, 118 N. Y. 563.

of the transaction in respect of which it is invoked; (2) where the notice is acquired by the agent outside of the transaction in respect of which it is invoked, either (*a*) while he is agent, or (*b*) before the agency begins.

§ 142. Notice Acquired during the Transaction.

All the authorities agree that notice acquired by the agent in the course of the transaction which it affects, is notice to the principal. "The rule that notice to the agent is constructive notice to the principal, is based on the presumption that the agent has communicated to the principal the facts connected with the subject-matter of his agency which came to his notice. . . . Where others than the principal and agent are concerned, the presumption that the agent has discharged his duty to his principal in communicating facts of which he has notice, is as conclusive as the presumption that the principal remembers the facts brought home to him personally."[1]

It therefore follows that as to notice acquired by the agent in the course of the transaction in respect of which the notice is invoked, the principal is bound as fully as if he acquired the notice in person, and whether the agent remembered the fact at the final conclusion of the transaction or not.

§ 143. Notice acquired outside of Transaction but in General Scope of Agency.

A distinction must be drawn between an agent, like an attorney, who acts for his principal in totally different transactions, perhaps separated by a considerable period of time, and an agent, like a bank cashier or a general manager, who is engaged in a continuous series of transactions, all incidents of the conduct of a general business.

As to the first, it is believed that the rule as to notice

[1] Bierce *v.* Red Bluff Hotel Co., 31 Cal. 160, 166.

is the same as in the case where the notice is acquired before the agency begins.

As to the second, the rule as established by many of the courts is the same as in the case of notice acquired in the particular transaction. "The general rule is well established that notice to an agent of a bank, or other corporation, intrusted with the management of its business, or of a particular branch of its business, is notice to the corporation, in transactions conducted by such agent, acting for the corporation, within the scope of his authority, whether the knowledge of such agent was acquired in the course of the particular dealing, or on some prior occasion."[1] "Where the agency is continuous, and concerned with a business made up of a long series of transactions of a like nature, of the same general character, it will be held that knowledge acquired as agent in that business in any one or more of the transactions, making up from time to time the whole business of the principal, is notice to the agent and to the principal, which will affect the latter in any other of those transactions in which that agent is engaged, in which that knowledge is material."[2]

§ 144. Notice acquired before Agency begins.

There are two views as to the effect of notice acquired by the agent before the agency begins. It is believed that notice acquired by the agent in a prior disconnected agency for the same principal is to be treated as notice acquired before the agency begins.

(1) The first view is that the principal is never to be charged with notice of any fact learned by the agent before the agency begins. This rests upon the notion that the identity of the principal and agent exists only during the time the agency exists. "The true reason of

[1] Cragie *v.* Hadley, 99 N. Y. 131, 134.

[2] Holden *v.* New York and Erie Bank, 72 N. Y. 286, 292.

the limitation is a technical one, that it is only during the agency that the agent represents, and stands in the shoes of his principal. Notice to him then is notice to his principal. Notice to him twenty-four hours before the relation commenced is no more notice than twenty-four hours after it had ceased would be."[1]

(2) The second view is that notice acquired by an agent before the agency begins is notice to the principal, *provided* that the fact is present in the mind of the agent at the time of the transaction as to which the notice is invoked, and *provided* that the agent is at liberty to disclose it.[2] The qualifications to the rule are important. It must be shown that the agent remembered the fact in question — had it present in his mind — at the time he was acting for the principal; in the absence of such proof the knowledge will not be imputed to the principal.[3] Some cases hold that "if the agent acquires his information so recently as to make it incredible that he should have forgotten it, his principal will be bound."[4] It must also appear that he was at liberty to disclose it, that is, that he would not be violating his duty to another principal in so doing.[5] And it appears that the burden is upon the one alleging the notice to establish these facts.[6]

§ 145. General Qualifications.

There are two general qualifications which must be considered in connection with the general rule of notice.

[1] Houseman *v.* Girard, &c. Ass'n, 81 Pa. St. 256, 262; McCormick *v.* Joseph, 83 Ala. 401; Satterfield *v.* Malone, 35 Fed. Rep. (Penn. Circuit) 445.

[2] The Distilled Spirits, 11 Wall. (U. S.) 356; Fairfield Savings Bank *v.* Chase, 72 Me. 226; Lebanon Savings Bank *v.* Hollenbeck, 29 Minn. 322; Dresser *v.* Norwood, 17 C. B. N. S. 466.

[3] Constant *v.* University of Rochester, 111 N. Y. 604.

[4] Brothers *v.* Bank, 84 Wis. 381, 395.

[5] Constant *v.* University, *supra*.

[6] *Ibid.*

(1) The fact constituting the notice must have a material bearing upon the subject-matter within the scope of the agency. It is not enough that it has a material bearing upon the subject-matter outside the scope of the agency. An agent may be given only a very limited and special power over the subject-matter, and the fact in question may have no bearing upon the exercise of that power. In that case the knowledge of the agent would not be imputed to the principal. "The knowledge or notice must come to an agent who has authority to deal in reference to those matters which the knowledge or notice affects. The facts of which the agent had notice must be within the scope of the agency, so that it becomes his duty to act upon them or communicate them to his principal. As it is the rule that whether the principal is bound by contracts entered into by the agent depends upon the nature and extent of the agency, so does the effect upon the principal of notice to the agent depend upon the same conditions."[1]

(2) It can never be reasonably inferred that an agent will communicate his knowledge to his principal where it is clearly against his own interest to do so.[2] Accordingly a principal is not bound by notice acquired by his agent in a transaction where the agent is acting adversely to his principal,[3] or has colluded with third persons to defraud his principal.[4] This is analogous to the case where an agent commits a wilful tort for his own purposes, and not as a means of performing the business intrusted to him.[5]

[1] Trentor *v.* Pothen, 46 Minn. 298.

[2] Innerarity *v.* Merchants' Nat. Bk., 139 Mass. 332.

[3] Frenkel *v.* Hudson, 82 Ala. 158.

[4] Western Mortg. & Invest. Co. *v.* Ganzer, 63 Fed. Rep. 647; Hudson *v.* Randolph, 66 Fed. Rep. 216.

[5] Allen *v.* South Boston R., 150 Mass. 200. Cf. Bank *v.* American Dock & Trust Co., 143 N. Y. 559.

§ 146. Application of Rule to Corporations.

The general rule that notice to an agent acting within the scope of his authority and in regard to the subject-matter of the agency, is notice to the principal, applies to corporations as well as to individual principals.[1] Indeed, it is probably in reference to corporations that the rule is most frequently invoked, for as is said in one case: "A corporation cannot see or know anything except by the eyes or intelligence of its officers."[2] Generally speaking, however, its application to both individuals and corporations is governed by the same limitations, and it is therefore only necessary to note, in this section, that subject to a few exceptions, notice to either a stockholder[3] or a single director[4] of a corporation is not regarded as notice to the corporation. "If the note is discounted by a bank, the mere fact that one of the directors knew the fraud or illegality will not prevent the bank from recovering; but if the director who has such knowledge acts for the bank, in discounting the note, his act is the act of the bank, and the bank is affected with his knowledge."[5] But if "the officer who has such knowledge has also such connection with or interest in the subject-matter of the transaction as to raise the presumption that he would not communicate the fact in controversy, there is no imputation of notice to the corporation."[6]

[1] Story on Agency, § 140 *a*.

[2] Factors &c. Co. *v.* Maine Dry Dock, &c. Co., 31 La. Ann. 149.

[3] Housatonic Bk. *v.* Martin, 1 Metc. (Mass.) 294; Union Canal Co. *v.* Loyd, 4 W. & S. (Penn.) 393.

[4] Fairfield Sav. Bk. *v.* Chase, 72 Me. 226; Farrel Foundry Co. *v.* Dart, 26 Conn. 376.

[5] Bank *v.* Cushman, 121 Mass. 490.

[6] Hatch *v.* Ferguson, 66 Fed. Rep. 668; Innerarity *v.* Bank, 139 Mass. 332.

§ 147. Notice to Sub-Agent.

Does notice to a sub-agent stand upon the same footing as notice to an agent? The question was fully discussed in the leading case of Hoover *v.* Wise,[1] and the decision reached by a divided court was that if the agent has power to appoint a sub-agent notice given to the sub-agent is notice to the principal, but if the agent has not power to appoint a sub-agent then notice to the sub-agent is not notice to the principal. The dissent in this case was, perhaps, rather on the ground that the agent had authority to appoint the sub-agent than that the rule of law enunciated by the majority was incorrect. The case is a typical one. A principal employs an agent to make a collection or to transact some other business which may require the assistance of an attorney at law. The agent employs an attorney, and the notice with which the principal is sought to be charged is given to or acquired by the attorney. Hoover *v.* Wise holds that this is not notice to the principal since the attorney is the agent of the agent and not of the principal. As Mr. Justice Miller points out in a dissenting opinion, "the effect of the decision is, that a non-resident creditor, by sending his claim to a lawyer through some indirect agency, may secure all the advantages of priority and preference which the attorney can obtain of the debtor, well knowing his insolvency, without any responsibility under the Bankrupt Law." The view taken in this case by the majority has not generally prevailed. It may be said to be the general rule that, where the business confided to the agent reasonably contemplates that the assistance of an attorney at law may be required, the agent has authority to appoint an attorney, and notice to the attorney will be notice to the principal.[2]

[1] 91 U. S. 308.

[2] Bates *v.* American Mortgage Co., 37 S. C. 88; Davis *v.* Waterman, 10 Vt. 526; Ryan *v.* Tudor, 31 Kans. 366.

So if, by custom, as in the case of insurance agencies, it is usual to appoint sub-agents, notice to such a sub-agent will be notice to the principal.[1]

[1] Arff *v.* Star Fire Ins. Co., 125 N. Y. 57; Carpenter *v.* German Am. Ins. Co., 135 N. Y. 298.

CHAPTER XIII.

LIABILITY OF PRINCIPAL FOR TORTS OF AGENT.

1. *Liability for Torts generally.*

§ 148. Non-Contractual Obligations by Agency.

In addition to the contractual obligations which may be created against one by the act of his agent, there are various non-contractual obligations which may be created in the same manner under the doctrines of representation. This is particularly true where the representative is a servant intrusted with the management of mechanical instrumentalities or of affairs involving the general social relations. In such cases it is held that one who appoints another to represent him in the conduct of matters where the rights of others are or may be involved, is answerable for every wrong committed by the representative in the course of the service, or within its apparent scope, certainly if committed for the master's benefit,[1] and in some cases if committed for the benefit of the representative himself. And it is immaterial whether the master authorized or directed the act; the first inquiry is whether it was within the scope of the service, and a secondary inquiry may be whether it was for the master's benefit. "This rule is obviously founded on the great principle of social duty, that every man in the management of his own affairs, whether by himself or by his agents or servants, shall so conduct them as not to injure another; and if he does not, and another thereby sustains damage, he shall answer for

[1] Pollock on Torts, (4th ed.) p. 67 *et seq.*

it;"[1] that is, he shall answer for it under circumstances where the injury, if committed in person, would constitute a breach of legal duty.

The rule is applicable to the relation of principal and agent as well as to the relation of master and servant, so far as torts may be committed by a representative whose chief office is to bring his principal into contractual relations.[2] But from the nature of the case the ways in which an agent may, as agent, commit torts are more limited than the ways in which a servant may commit them. The wrongs involving fraud or malice, as deceit, malicious prosecution, slander of title, libel and slander, are the ones which most commonly occur in connection with this relation.

§ 149. When Principal Liable for Tort of Agent.

The tort of an agent may be either: (1) a tort commanded or ratified by the principal; (2) a tort not commanded or ratified, but which is within the course of the employment and for the master's benefit; (3) a tort not commanded or ratified, but which is apparently within the course of the employment and for the agent's benefit; (4) a tort not commanded or ratified and which is not within the course of the employment.

(1) It is universally conceded that the principal is liable for all torts which he commands or ratifies.[3] Obviously this should be so, for if he chooses to accomplish a wrong by the instrumentality of an agent, or if he chooses to 'profit' by one accomplished by the instrumentality of an agent, he should be liable in the same way as if he had acted in person.

1 Farwell *v.* Boston, &c. R., 4 Met. (Mass.) 49.

2 Barwick *v.* English Joint Stock Bank, L. R. 2 Ex. 259.

3 Dempsey *v.* Chambers, 154 Mass. 330; Pollock on Torts, (4th ed.) p. 69.

(2) It is almost universally conceded that the principal is liable for all torts committed by an agent in the course of the employment and for the principal's benefit, although the principal neither commanded nor ratified the tort.[1] This rests on the principle already enunciated that where one chooses to manage his affairs through an agent he is bound to see that the affairs are managed with due regard to the safety of others.[2] Given the three elements, (*a*) an agent, (*b*) acting in the course of his employment (*c*) for the principal's benefit, and a sufficient basis is laid for the obligation of the principal to indemnify the public generally against the misconduct of the agent while so acting. The scope of this rule and the deviations from it will be considered in connection with the subject of the agent's frauds.

(3) It is a disputed question whether the principal is liable for the torts committed by an agent in the course, or apparent course, of the employment but for the agent's benefit. It will be observed that the elements here are, (*a*) an agent (*b*) acting in the course of the employment (*c*) for his own benefit. The dispute arises as to whether the 'great principle of social duty' is to be extended to cover responsibility for the fidelity of the agent in the use he makes of the instrumentalities intrusted to him by the principal. A typical case is that of a railway servant who, while primarily about his master's business, blows his whistle or lets off steam or uses some other instrumentality intrusted to him, not for any real or supposed benefit to his master, but for some end or pleasure of his own. Whether the master is liable for this misuse of the instrumentalities for the servant's benefit, is the disputed point.[3]

[1] Barwick *v.* English Joint Stock Bank, L. R. 2 Ex. 259.

[2] Pollock on Torts, (4th ed.) p. 71.

[3] That the master is liable: Bittle *v.* Camden, &c. R. Co., 55 N. J. L. 615; Cobb *v.* Columbia, &c. R., 37 S. Car. 194. That the master is not liable: Stephenson *v.* Southern Pacific Co., 93 Cal. 558.

The typical case in contractual agency arises under fraud and will be considered under that head.

(4) It is universally conceded that the principal is not liable for torts committed by his agents outside the course of the employment, which he has neither commanded nor ratified. Obviously this must be so, because no principle of social justice could make one man liable for the torts of another where that other was acting in an affair in which the first had no interest and in which he did not participate either by prior counsel or subsequent acquiescence. But many nice distinctions are made in determining whether the agent was acting within the course of the employment.

§ 150. "The Course of the Employment."

The term 'the course of the employment,' like the term 'the scope of the authority' is hardly susceptible of accurate definition. In contract a principal is bound to concede that the agent is acting for him whenever a reasonably prudent man, in like circumstances with the third party, would conclude that the agent is so acting. In tort the doctrine is not so clear. Is the principal bound to concede that the agent is acting for him when the reasonable man would so conclude, or is it a question of absolute fact whether the agent is so acting or not? Does 'the course of the employment' mean the actual course of the employment or the apparent course of the employment? Upon the answer to these questions depends the solution of the difficulties presented by the case where the agent while apparently acting within the course of his employment is secretly accomplishing some benefit for himself.

If the appearance of being within the course of the employment leads a third person relying on the appearance to act in such a way as to imperil or involve his interests, as where he buys fictitious stock, there seems to be no reason why the principal should not be held on the same considerations as those which govern his liability for contracts.[1] In each case the agent violates his duty to the principal and to the third party; but the former and not the latter should bear the loss since he is responsible for that appearance of things upon which all reasonable men act. But how if the appearance of being within the course of the employment has no such causal relation to the injury because it does not induce any action or non-action on the part of the one injured, as where a ticket agent causes the arrest of a person on suspicion of passing counterfeit money,[2] or a locomotive engineer wantonly frightens horses by letting off steam and blowing the whistle?[3] Here, obviously, the ground of liability is shifted, if any liability at all exists. In such cases the liability, if any, depends on the fact that the principal has intrusted the agent with instrumentalities or powers the ordinary use of which is highly dangerous to the public generally, and he assumes thereby a liability in the nature of an insurance as to their proper use.[4] Again, how if neither the appearance of being within the course of the employment nor the possession of dangerous instrumentalities or powers, bears any such causal relation to the injury, as where a railway servant assaults a passenger for some end of his own?[5] Here the ground of liability, if any, shifts again, and the principal must be held, if at all, on the theory that he has undertaken a duty toward the one injured involving the utmost care and good faith, and that

[1] *Post*, § 155.

[2] Palmeri *v.* Manhattan Ry. Co., 133 N. Y. 261.

[3] Cobb *v.* Columbia, &c. R., 37 S. Car. 194.

[4] The analogy between this and the cases of "insuring safety" as to highly dangerous articles brought and kept on one's premises or sent into the market, will be apparent. See Pollock on Torts, (4th ed.) Ch. xii.; Bigelow on Torts, (4th ed.) Ch. xvi.

[5] As in Craker *v.* Chicago, &c. R. Co., 36 Wis. 657.

11

he warrants that his agent possesses and will exercise the qualities necessary for the discharge of this duty.

Obviously, the question as to the liability of the principal or master in such cases depends upon considerations of general public policy or social utility which escape any narrow construction of the term 'the course of the employment.'

2. *Liability for Fraud of Agent.*

§ 151. Fraud Generally.

Fraud, considered as a tort for which an action for deceit will lie, consists of a false representation of a material fact made without belief in its truth, or with a reckless disregard of whether it is true or false, with intent that it should be acted upon by another, who, reasonably relying on the representation, does act on it to his damage.[1] Whether all of these elements are necessary to constitute fraud for which rescission of contract may be had, we need not now inquire.[2]

Fraud is a wrong generally connected with contract, the representation being made as an inducement to the formation of the contractual relation. Consent being necessary to contract it follows that the third party whose consent has been induced by fraud may always rescind the contract on the ground of the unreality of consent.[3] It is, however, more than an element vitiating contract, like mistake or undue influence ; it is an independent wrong in and of itself for which an action *ex delicto* will lie. An action on the case for deceit is the appropriate remedy.

[1] Pollock on Torts, (4th ed.) p. 260; Derry *v.* Peek, L. R. 14 App. Cas. 337 ; Bigelow on Torts, (4th ed.) pp. 17–18.

[2] See Southern Development Co. *v.* Silva, 125 U. S. 247 ; Wilcox *v.* Iowa Wesleyan University, 32 Iowa, 367 ; School Directors *v.* Boomhour, 83 Ill. 17.

[3] 3 Anson on Const. (8th ed.) Pt. II., Ch. iv. § 3.

§ 152. Fraud in Relation to Agency.

In its relation to agency fraud presents some difficulties. Fraud requires as one of its essential elements that the representation should be made with knowledge of its falsity or with a reckless disregard of whether it be true or false. It requires as another that there should be an intent to deceive. How are these matters to be imputed to a personally innocent principal? The difficulty has given rise to much confusion in the decisions of the courts, and has been regarded by some of them as insurmountable.[1] But the difficulty and confusion have largely disappeared in the light of a clearer statement of the fundamental principles of the law of representation. Barwick *v.* English Joint Stock Bank[2] is regarded as the leading modern authority, although its conclusions had been anticipated by decisions in this country. "With respect to the question, whether a principal is answerable for the act of his agent in the course of his master's business, and for his master's benefit, no sensible distinction can be drawn between the case of fraud and the case of any other wrong."[3] "This rule of liability is not based upon any presumed authority in the agent to do the acts, but on the ground of public policy, and that it is more reasonable when one of two innocent persons must suffer from the wrongful act of a third person that the principal who has placed the agent in the position of trust and confidence should suffer, than a stranger."[4] "One who authorizes another to act for him, in a certain class of contracts, undertakes for the absence of fraud in the agent acting within the scope of his authority."[5] In

[1] Kennedy *v.* McKay, 43 N. J. L. 288; Udell *v.* Atherton, 7 H. & N. 172.

[2] L. R. 2 Ex. 259.

[3] *Ibid.*, p. 265.

[4] Erie City Iron Works *v.* Barber, 106 Pa. St. 125.

[5] McNeile *v.* Cridland, (Pa.) 31 Atl. Rep. 939.

short, this, like other cases of a constituent's liability for the act of his representative, is founded on "the great principle of social duty, that every man in the management of his own affairs, whether by himself or by his agents or servants, shall so conduct them as not to injure another."

§ 153. Fraud for Benefit of Principal.

In the case of fraud committed by the agent in the course of his employment, and for the benefit of the principal, it is now generally conceded that the principal is liable.[1] In the leading English case, where it appeared that the fraud had been committed by the manager of the defendant bank, the doctrine was announced that: "The master is answerable for every such wrong of the servant or agent as is committed in the course of the service, and for the master's benefit."

The English courts, however, seem to have recognized one exception to this rule. In a case where the agents of a corporation induce subscribers, by fraudulent representations, to purchase stock of the corporation, it is said that the subscribers cannot have an action for deceit against the corporation, but must seek their remedy by rescission of the contract.[2] And a few of our American courts, apparently misled by these cases and assuming the exception recognized in them to be the general rule, have denied altogether the liability of the principal for the unauthorized fraud of the agent, even though committed for the prin-

[1] Barwick *v.* Eng. Joint Stock Bank, L. R. 2 Ex. 259; Jeffrey *v.* Bigelow, 13 Wend. (N. Y.) 518; Peebles *v.* Patapsco Guano Co., 77 N. C. 233; Haskell *v.* Starbird, 152 Mass. 117; Busch *v.* Wilcox, 82 Mich. 315 s. c. 336; Griswold *v.* Gebbie, 126 Pa. St. 353; Wolfe *v.* Pugh, 101 Ind. 293; Rhoda *v.* Annis, 75 Me. 17; Smalley *v.* Morris, 157 Pa. St. 349.

[2] Western Bank of Scotland *v.* Addie, L. R. 1 H. L. (Sc.) 145; Houldsworth *v.* City of Glasgow Bank, L. R. 5 App. Cas. 317.

cipal's benefit. Thus in the case of Kennedy *v.* McKay,[1] this sweeping doctrine is announced: "In the light of such authorities it is clear that an innocent vendor cannot be sued in tort for the fraud of his agent in effecting a sale. In such a juncture the aggrieved vendee has, at law, two, and only two remedies; the first being a rescission of the contract of sale, and a reclamation of the money paid by him from the vendors, or a suit against the agent, founded on the deceit. But in such a posture of affairs, a suit based on the fraud will not lie against the innocent vendor, on account of the deceit practised without his authority or knowledge, by his agent."[2]

But the generally accepted rule in America is the same as that recognized by the English courts, and laid down in Barwick's case.[3] In a frequently cited New York case, it was held that where the defendant's agent, duly authorized to sell a flock of sheep, fraudulently sold a portion of the flock to the plaintiff, knowing at the time that they were diseased, the defendant was liable for the fraud.[4] And in a North Carolina case, in which the defendant was a corporation, the court said: "There is no reason that occurs to us why a different rule should be applicable to cases of deceit from what applies to other torts. A corporation can only act through its agents, and must be responsible for their acts. It is of the greatest public importance that it should be so. If a manufacturing and trading corporation is not responsible for the false and fraudulent representations of its agent, those who deal with it will be practically without redress and the corporation can commit fraud with impunity."[5]

[1] 43 N. J. L. 288, *citing* the two cases in the preceding note.

[2] See also Herring *v.* Skaggs, 62 Ala. 180.

[3] *Supra;* City Nat. Bk. *v.* Dun, 51 Fed. Rep. 160.

[4] Jeffrey *v.* Bigelow, 13 Wend. (N. Y.) 518.

[5] Peebles *v.* Patapsco Guano Co., 77 N. C. 233.

§ 154. Fraud for Benefit of Agent.

Where the fraud is committed in the apparent course of the employment, and under cover of the principal's name and business, but for the benefit of the agent, there is a sharp conflict of authority as to the liability of the principal.

In England it seems to be established that the principal is never liable under such circumstances. In the leading English case the statement was that, "The master is answerable for every such wrong of the servant or agent as is committed in the course of the service, and for the master's benefit." [1] In a later case it was expressly held that the limiting clause, "and for the master's benefit," is an essential element of the liability.[2]

In the United States two opposite views are taken. One class of cases follows the English holding;[3] another class of cases holds that, "where the principal has clothed his agent with power to do an act upon the existence of some extrinsic fact necessarily and peculiarly within the knowledge of the agent, and of the existence of which the act of executing the power is itself a representation, a third person dealing with such agent in entire good faith, pursuant to the apparent power, may rely upon the representation, and the principal is estopped from denying its truth to his prejudice." [4] "If his [the agent's] position and the confidence reposed in him were such as to enable him to escape detection for the while, then the consequences of his fraudulent acts should fall upon the bank, whose di-

[1] Barwick *v.* English Joint Stock Bank, *supra.* And see Houldsworth *v.* City of Glasgow Bank, L. R. 5 App. Cas. 317.

[2] British Mutual Banking Co. *v.* Charnwood Forest R. Co., L. R. 18 Q. B. Div. 714.

[3] Friedlander *v.* Texas, &c. Ry., 130 U. S. 416, and cases in succeeding sections.

[4] Bank of Batavia *v.* New York, &c. R., 106 N. Y. 195, 199.

rectors, by their misplaced confidence and gift of powers, made them possible, and not upon others who, themselves acting innocently and in good faith, were warranted in believing the transaction to have been one coming within the cashier's powers."[1]

This conflict of judicial opinion is well illustrated in two classes of cases: (1) where the agent fraudulently issues stock certificates and sells them for his own benefit; (2) where the agent fraudulently issues bills of lading and sells them for his own benefit.

§ 155. Fraud for Benefit of Agent. — Issue of Stock Certificate.

If a stock transfer agent fraudulently issues stock certificates in excess of the amount which the company may lawfully issue and, by collusion with the transferee of the stock, sells them to innocent purchasers for value for his own benefit, is the company liable in an action for deceit to the innocent purchasers of the stock ?

The English courts have answered this question in the negative. The purchasers called upon the transfer agent to inquire as to the validity of the stock, and were of course informed that the stock was valid. The Master of the Rolls (Lord Esher) said: "The secretary was held out by the defendants as a person to answer such questions as those put to him in the interest of the plaintiffs, and if he had answered them falsely *on behalf of the defendants*, he being then authorized by them to give answers for them, it may well be that they would be liable. But although what the secretary stated related to matters about which he was authorized to give answers, he did not make the statements for the defendant but for himself. . . . I know of no case where the employer has been held liable

[1] Phillips *v.* Mercantile Nat. Bk., 140 N. Y. 556, 563. And see cases in succeeding sections.

when his servant has made statements not for his employer, but in his own interest."[1] It has been thought that the United States Supreme Court has held the same doctrine, but the case in question may well be distinguished on the ground that the third party was buying the stock of the agent, and had therefore no right to rely on his representation where his interest was clearly adverse to that of his principal.[2] But it is clear that the tendency of that court is to follow the English doctrine.[3]

A considerable number of American courts have answered the question in the affirmative. The leading New York case[4] presents an exhaustive examination of the whole subject, after an argument by an array of eminent counsel rarely united in one proceeding, and in an opinion by Noah Davis, J., of singular ability and lucidity. The result is embodied in the doctrine that where the principal authorizes an act which necessarily involves in the doing of it a representation as to some extrinsic fact, that he assumes the risk that the representation will be true. "He knows that the person he authorizes to act for him, on condition of an extrinsic fact, which in its nature must be peculiarly within the knowledge of that person, cannot execute the power without as *res gestæ* making the representation that the fact exists. With this knowledge he trusts him to do the act, and consequently to make the representation which, if true, is of course binding on the principal. But the doctrine claimed is that he reserves the right to repudiate the act if the representation be false.

[1] British Mutual Banking Co. *v.* Charnwood Forest Ry., L. R. 18 Q. B. Div. 714, 716–717.

[2] Moores *v.* Citizens' Nat. Bk., 111 U. S. 156. Cf. Bank of New York, &c. *v.* American Dock & Trust Co., 143 N. Y. 559.

[3] Friedlander *v.* Texas, &c. Ry., 130 U. S. 416.

[4] New York & New Haven R. *v.* Schuyler, 34 N. Y. 30, especially pp. 65–75.

So he does as between himself and the agent, but not as to an innocent third party who is deceived by it. The latter may answer, you intrusted your agent with means effectually to deceive me by doing an act which in all respects compared with the authority you gave, and which act represented an extrinsic fact known to your agent or yourself, but unknown to me, existed, and you have thus enabled your agent, by falsehood, to deceive me, and must bear the consequences. The very power you gave, since it could not be executed without a representation, has led me into this position, and therefore you are estopped in justice to deny his authority in this case. By this I do not mean to argue that the principal authorizes the false representation. He only, in fact, authorizes the act which involves a representation, which, from his confidence in his agent, he assumes will be true; but it may be false, and the risk that it may he takes because he gives the confidence and credit which enables its falsity to prove injurious to an innocent party."[1] The doctrine thus established has been followed in many succeeding cases in New York and elsewhere.[2] But the doctrine of these cases is subject to the qualification that the purchaser must act in good faith and prudently; it is not good faith or prudence to trust to the representation where the agent is known to be acting for himself in the sale of the stock.[3]

[1] New York & New Haven R. *v.* Schuyler, 34 N. Y. 30, especially pp. 70–71.

[2] Fifth Ave. Bk. *v.* Forty-second Street, &c. R., 137 N. Y. 231; Tome *v.* Parkersburg Branch R., 39 Md. 36. See also Allen *v.* South Boston R., 150 Mass. 200; Farrington *v.* Same, 150 Mass. 406; American Wire & Nail Co. *v.* Bayless, 91 Ky. 94; Appeal of Kisterbock, 127 Pa. St. 601.

[3] Moores *v.* Citizens' N. B., *supra;* Allen *v.* South Boston R., *supra;* Farrington *v.* Same, *supra;* Bank of New York, &c. *v.* American Dock & Trust Co., *supra.* Cf. New York & New Haven R. *v.* Schuyler, *supra,* p. 64.

And, of course, the agent must be acting within the apparent scope of the powers intrusted to him; an unauthorized seizure of the powers as a means of fraud, where no authority to exercise them exists, will not render the principal liable.[1]

§ 156. Fraud for Benefit of Agent. — Issue of fictitious Bills of Lading.

A similar question arises where the agent, being authorized to issue bills of lading, issues fictitious bills of lading in the name of a confederate and sells them through the confederate to innocent purchasers.

In England it is held that the principal is not liable, the argument being that the agent is authorized to do what is usual in his agency and it is not usual to issue fictitious bills of lading.[2] This play upon words, if resorted to in other cases, would excuse the constituent for every tort of his representative. The English holding has been followed in the Federal courts and in some of the State courts in this country.[3]

In the United States many courts hold the principal liable. In a leading New York case,[4] the doctrine of the English courts is expressly disapproved and the doctrine of estoppel *in pais* applied. And this has been followed

[1] Manhattan Life Ins. Co. *v.* Forty-second Street, &c. R., 139 N. Y. 146.

[2] Grant *v.* Norway, 10 C. B. 665; Cox *v.* Bruce, L. R. 18 Q. B. Div. 147.

[3] Pollard *v.* Vinton, 105 U. S. 7; Friedlander *v.* Texas, &c., Ry., 130 U. S. 416; National Bank of Commerce *v.* Chicago, &c. R., 44 Minn. 224, and cases there cited. The artificial reasoning of this class of cases is illustrated by a comparison of the case last cited with McCord *v.* Western Union Tel. Co., 39 Minn. 181, where the same court went to an even questionable length in applying the doctrine of estoppel against the principal.

[4] Armour *v.* Michigan Central R., 65 N. Y. 111.

by subsequent cases in the same and other jurisdictions.[1] Even the courts which hold the other doctrine recognize the essential justice of this. "If the question was *res integra* we confess that it seems to us that this argument would be very cogent."[2] The doctrine is subject to the same qualifications as in its application to the issue of stock certificates.[3]

§ 157. Fraud for Benefit of Agent. — Other Illustrations. The doctrine above explained and illustrated may be invoked under other circumstances too various to be referred to in detail. Thus a bank cashier who employs his powers to draw checks, for the purpose of converting the funds of the bank to his own use, is using a trust and confidence reposed in him by the bank and the loss must fall on it rather than on innocent parties.[4] So an agent of a telegraph company who employs his power to send telegrams as an operator in the sending of forged telegrams requesting the transmission of money, is abusing a trust and confidence placed in him by the company, and the latter, rather than the innocent receiver of the telegram, should bear the loss.[5] "Persons receiving dispatches in the usual course of business, when there is nothing to excite suspicion, are entitled to rely upon the presumption that the agents intrusted with the performance of the business of the company have faithfully and honestly discharged the

[1] Bank of Batavia *v.* New York, &c. R., 106 N. Y. 195; Brooke *v.* N. Y., &c. R., 108 Pa. St. 529; St. Louis, &c. R. *v.* Larned, 103 Ill. 293; Wichita Bank *v.* Atchison, &c. R., 20 Kans. 519; Sioux City, &c. R. *v.* First Nat. Bk., 10 Neb. 556.

[2] National Bank of Commerce *v.* Chicago, &c. R., 44 Minn. 224, 235.

[3] Bank of New York, &c. *v.* American Dock & Trust Co., 143 N. Y. 559.

[4] Phillips *v.* Mercantile Nat. Bk., 140 N. Y. 556.

[5] McCord *v.* Western Union Tel. Co., 39 Minn. 181.

duty owed by it to its patrons, and that they would not knowingly send a false or forged message; and it would ordinarily be an unreasonable and impracticable rule to require the receiver of a dispatch to investigate the question of the integrity and fidelity of the defendant's agents in the performance of their duties, before acting."

3. *Liability for statutory Torts and Crimes.*

§ 158. Statutory Torts.

There seems to be no distinction between the liability of a constituent for the act of his representative amounting to a common law tort and an act amounting to a statutory tort. The question arises most frequently under the statutes giving a wife an action for a penalty, or for damages sustained, for the sale of intoxicating liquors to her husband. By these statutes, certain acts which may in themselves be innocent, are for reasons of public policy made torts, and prohibited under penalty. The agent's breach of a statutory prohibition of this nature, committed while acting within the scope of his employment, renders the principal liable in a civil action by the person aggrieved, for the prescribed penalty. Thus, in a Massachusetts case,[1] it is said: "We see no reason why the general principle which governs the responsibility of the master for the acts of his servant should not apply in the case at bar. The action is brought under a statute which makes that a tort which was not so before, and provides for the recovery of damages against the tort-feasor. The tort consists in selling intoxicating liquor to one who has the habit of using it to excess, after notice of his habit and a request from his wife not to sell such liquor to him. The defendant engages in the business of selling liquor voluntarily. He chooses to intrust the details of the business to a

[1] George *v.* Gobey, 128 Mass. 289.

servant. If he forbids the making of sales to the intemperate person, and his servant negligently, through forgetfulness of the instruction given him, or through a failure to recognize the person, continues to make sales to that person, there is no reason why the defendant should not be responsible for the wrongful act. The sale is his sale, made in the performance of his business, and is an act within the general scope of the servant's employment." [1]

§ 159. Crimes.

The criminal liability of the principal is not governed by the same rule as his civil liability. The presumption of authority which arises from the relation of the parties, and governs their civil responsibility, is counter-balanced in criminal law by the fundamental principle that every man is to be presumed innocent until he is proved guilty. From this presumption, the conclusion is natural, that a criminal act committed by the agent should be presumed to be committed contrary to, and not in obedience to the directions of the principal. Something more than the mere fact that the agent was acting within the scope of his employment, must therefore be shown in order to make the principal answerable in a criminal proceeding; — the crime must have been committed by the principal's direction and authority, or at least have resulted from his negligence. As was said in a Massachusetts case; [2] "Criminal responsibility on the part of the principal for the act of his agent or servant in the course of his employment, implies some degree of moral guilt or delinquency, manifested either by direct participation in or assent to the act, or by want of proper care and oversight or other negligence in reference to the business which he has thus

[1] See also Kreiter *v.* Nichols, 28 Mich. 496.

[2] Comm. *v.* Morgan, 107 Mass. 199.

intrusted to another."[1] However, there is one apparent exception to the rule. Where the agent, while acting within the course of his employment, violates a statutory enactment in the nature of a police regulation, such as those in regard to the speed of trains, the running of trains on Sunday, the sale of adulterated food, the doing of business without a license, &c., it is said that the principal is criminally answerable, even though the act was committed without his knowledge and consent, or indeed against his positive instructions. The statute arbitrarily imposes upon him the duty of seeing that its provisions are obeyed, and if he fail in that duty, he is answerable, irrespective of the question of actual criminality.[2]

4. *Liability for Torts of Sub-Agent.*

§ 160. — Torts of Sub-Agents.

Whether a principal is liable to third persons for the tort of a sub-agent depends upon whether the sub-agent was the agent of the principal or of the agent. While a servant has ordinarily no power to appoint assistants, there are circumstances under which he may have such authority, either from the implied assent of the principal or from the necessities of the case. We have already seen that railway servants may possess the power to appoint physicians or surgeons for the railway company in case of accident, and that a driver of a vehicle may possess power to appoint a substitute to take the necessary care of his employer's property in cases where he is suddenly incapacitated.[3] So there may arise an implied power to appoint helpers either from the nature of the duty to be performed

[1] See also Bishop's Crim. Law, § 649.

[2] People *v.* Roby, 52 Mich. 577; Comm. *v.* Kelly, 140 Mass. 441; State *v.* Baltimore, &c. Co., 13 Md. 181.

[3] *Ante*, § 59.

or from the course of conduct between the principal and agent.[1] If the power to appoint exist, then the appointee becomes the agent or servant of the principal and the latter is liable for his torts in the same way and to the same extent as if he had appointed him personally.[2] These cases are to be distinguished from those where an owner or occupier of real property is held liable for its defective condition, caused by a person not his agent or servant; in such cases the liability is independent of the question of agency.[3] Even where a servant has no power to appoint a helper, the act of the helper may be regarded as the act of the servant and bind the master.[4]

5. *Public Principals and Charities.*

§ 161. Exceptions to General Doctrine.

While the general doctrine of *respondeat superior* applies to principals who are represented by agents or servants, there are at least three exceptions of importance.

(1) *Public Officers.* Public officers are not generally liable in tort for the wrongful acts of their subordinates. The exception is based on considerations of public policy. Accordingly a postmaster is not liable for the loss of a letter occasioned by the negligence of his deputy.[5] A collector of customs is not liable for the negligence of his subordinate.[6] But each officer is liable for his own negli-

[1] Haluptzok *v.* Great Northern R. Co., 55 Minn. 446.

[2] Haluptzok *v.* Great Northern, *supra;* Althorf *v.* Wolfe, 22 N. Y. 355.

[3] Pollock on Torts, (4th ed.) pp. 459–464. Perhaps this may explain the much criticised case of Bush *v.* Steinman, 1 B. & P. 404; Bright *v.* Barnett, 88 Wis. 299.

[4] Booth *v.* Mister, 7 Car. & P. 66.

[5] Keenan *v.* Southworth, 110 Mass. 474; Hutchins *v.* Brackett, 22 N. H. 252; Conwell *v.* Voorhees, 13 Ohio, 523.

[6] Robertson *v.* Sichel, 127 U. S. 507.

gence or misconduct, and a superior may be held liable on the ground that his own negligence in the management of his office is a contributing cause with the default of the subordinate.[1]

(2) *Municipal Corporations.* Municipal and quasi-municipal corporations, so far as they are acting in a governmental or discretionary character for public ends are not liable for the negligent or wilful wrongs committed by their agents or servants.[2] But where distinct duties are imposed upon them, purely ministerial and involving no exercise of discretion, the same liability attaches as in the case of private persons doing the same duty.[3] Thus a city is not liable for the negligence of its officer in shooting at an unmuzzled dog,[4] nor for the negligent acts of members of its fire department,[5] or of any of the other of its agents or servants engaged in governmental or police duties.[6] But it is liable for failure to keep its streets in proper repair,[7] or properly to plan and construct its public works.[8]

(3) *Charities.* Where a corporation or trustees are conducting a charity with funds devotéd to that purpose, the charitable organization is not liable for the torts of its agents or servants, as "it would be against all law and

[1] Bishop *v.* Williamson, 11 Me. 495; Dunlop *v.* Munroe, 7 Cranch, (U. S.) 242.

[2] City of Richmond *v.* Long's Adm'r, 17 Gratt. (Va.) 375; City of Anderson *v.* East, 117 Ind. 126; Hines *v.* Charlotte, 72 Mich. 278.

[3] Seymour *v.* Cummins, 119 Ind. 148; Bates *v.* Westborough, 151 Mass. 174; Barron *v.* Detroit, 94 Mich. 601. But see Howard *v.* Worcester, 153 Mass. 426.

[4] Whitfield *v.* Paris, 84 Tex. 431; Culver *v.* Streator, 130 Ill. 238.

[5] Dodge *v.* Granger, 17 R. I. 664; Gillespie *v.* Lincoln, 35 Neb. 34.

[6] Robinson *v.* Rohr, 73 Wis. 436; O'Leary *v.* Marquette, 79 Mich. 281.

[7] Conrad *v.* Ithaca, 16 N. Y. 158.

[8] Barron *v.* Detroit, 94 Mich. 601; Seymour *v.* Cummins, 119 Ind. 148.

all equity to take those trust funds, so contributed for a special, charitable purpose, to compensate injuries inflicted or occasioned by the negligence of the agents or servants."[1]

[1] Fire Ins. Patrol *v.* Boyd, 120 Pa. St. 624; s. c. 113 Pa. St. 269; Feoffees of Heriot's Hospital *v.* Ross, 12 C. & F. 506. *Cf.* Newcomb *v.* Boston Protective Dept., 151 Mass. 215; Glavin *v.* Rhode Island Hosp. 12 R. I. 411.

CHAPTER XIV.

LIABILITY OF THIRD PERSON TO PRINCIPAL.

§ 162. Introductory.

We have thus far spoken in this part mainly of the liabilities of the principal for the acts of his agent. It now remains to consider briefly the rights which the principal may acquire from the acts of his agent, as against third persons with whom the agent deals. The liability of a third person to the principal may arise: (1) from a contract obligation of which the principal is entitled to avail himself; (2) from a quasi-contractual obligation of which the principal is entitled to avail himself; (3) from a tort obligation of which the principal is entitled to avail himself; (4) from a trust obligation of which the principal is entitled to avail himself in equity. Each of these classes of liabilities will be briefly discussed.

1. *Contract Obligations.*

§ 163. Contracts by Agent.

A contract made by an agent in behalf of his principal may be either: (1) made by the agent in the name of the principal within the scope of a prior authority; (2) made by the agent in the name of the principal outside the scope of a prior authority, but subsequently ratified; (3) made by the agent in the name of a foreign principal; (4) made by the agent in his own name. The rights of the principal vary in accordance with these variations in the manner of forming the contract.

§ 164. Contracts in the name of the Principal.

(1) *Authorized contracts.* It is too clear to need demonstration that a contract made by an agent within his authority, real or apparent, which would bind the principal will also bind the third party. This is in accordance with the established doctrines of the mutuality of contractual obligations. In such a case the principal is both the real and nominal party in interest and is the only one who can sue or be sued upon the contract.[1]

(2) *Ratified contracts.* An unauthorized contract made in the name of the principal and subsequently ratified stands upon the same footing as one previously authorized. The ratification exonerates the agent from liability, relates back to the time of the formation of the contract, and creates all the rights and obligations in favor of and against the principal, which would have sprung from an authorized contract. Accordingly after a binding ratification the principal is the only one who can sue or be sued upon such a contract.[2]

(3) *Contract for foreign principal.* It is a rule of the English law that *prima facie* a principal resident in one country is not a party to a contract made in another country, by his agent resident there, and that he can neither sue nor be sued upon it; but the presumption may be overcome by showing that the agent had authority to pledge his principal's credit and that the third party accepted the credit, thus establishing a privity of contract between the third party and the principal.[3] The rule of the American law is otherwise as will be seen hereafter.[4]

§ 165. Contracts in the name of the Agent.

An agent may contract in his own name either: (1) for

[1] Fairlie *v.* Fenton, L. R. 5 Ex. 169; Sharp *v.* Jones, 18 Ind. 314.
[2] *Ante*, § 45–49. [3] *Post*, § 187. [4] *Ibid.*

an undisclosed principal; (2) for a disclosed principal who, however, is not named in the formal contract. Each case presents features involving the rights and liabilities of the principal.

(1) *Undisclosed principals.* The rights and liabilities of an undisclosed principal have already been considered.[1] Subject to the exceptions there enumerated the third person is liable to the undisclosed principal in the same manner as if the latter had been disclosed.

(2) *Unnamed principal.* An agent may disclose his principal and intend to make a contract in his behalf, but fail of this purpose by an omission to name the principal in the formal instrument. In such a case if the instrument be a simple contract the omission may be supplied and the principal may both sue and be sued upon the contract;[2] but if the instrument be under seal or negotiable, parol evidence cannot, at common law, be received even to effectuate the intention of the parties.[3]

2. *Quasi-Contract Obligations.*

§ 166. Money paid by Mistake.

It is a general principle of the law that money paid under a mistake of material fact, in the belief that it is due, may be recovered back in an action for money had and received, where it would be against conscience for the payee to retain it.[4] The action is based on equitable principles and proceeds upon the fiction that the defendant promised to pay the money back. In this action it is immaterial whether the principal paid the money in person or through an agent; in either case he is entitled to proceed in quasi-contract for his remedy. Accordingly

[1] *Ante,* Ch. X.; *post,* § 196.

[2] *Post* § 197.

[3] *Post,* §§ 188, 189.

[4] Keener on Quasi-Cont. Ch. II.

a principal may maintain an action for money had and received against a third person to whom an agent has paid it under a mistake of fact,[1] or which is paid by him under a mistake originating with his agent,[2] or with a public or quasi-public officer, on the strength of whose certificate he relies.[3]

§ 167. Money paid under Duress or Fraud.

Where a third person obtains from an agent by duress or fraud moneys belonging to the principal, the latter may recover the moneys so paid by his agent in an action for money had and received.[4] Such actions may always be maintained by the real party in interest since they do not rest upon privity of contract, but upon the contract created by the law.[5] If an agent is compelled to pay illegal charges for the protection of his principal's interests, the latter cannot proceed against the agent but must proceed against the one making the unjust exaction.[6] The agent as well as the principal may, however, proceed against the third party for the amount so paid under duress.[7]

Where money belonging to the principal has been diverted by the agent into the hands of a third person who takes with notice of the breach of trust, the latter is liable to the principal in equity, and in some States in quasi-contract as for money had and received.[8]

[1] United States *v.* Bartlett, Daveis, (U. S. Dist. C.) 9, s. c. 2 Ware, 17.

[2] Lane *v.* Pere Marquette Boom Co., 62 Mich. 63.

[3] Talbot *v.* National Bank, 129 Mass. 67; Holmes *v.* Lucas Co., 53 Iowa, 211.

[4] Stevenson *v.* Mortimer, Cowp. 805; Demarest *v.* Barbadoes, 40 N. J. L. 604.

[5] Stevens *v.* Fitch, 11 Met. (Mass.) 248.

[6] Holman *v.* Frost, 26 So. Car. 290.

[7] Stevenson *v.* Mortimer, *supra.*

[8] *Post,* §§ 177–179.

3. *Tort Obligations.*

§ 168. Property diverted by Agent. — General Rule.

Where an agent disposes of his principal's property beyond the scope of the authority, the principal may recover it from any one into whose hands it has passed.[1] This doctrine rests upon the maxims that a buyer gets no better title than the seller had to give him, and that an owner cannot be divested of his title without his consent. The third party is therefore bound to show that the agent had the authority to transfer the title, or that the principal's conduct has been such as to work an estoppel. Authority may be shown in the usual ways; namely, by previous grant, by subsequent ratification, by necessity, and by estoppel.

To the general and sweeping rule as above stated there are two well recognized exceptions at the common law and a third which has been created by statute in some jurisdictions. The rule and the common law exceptions are well explained in the case of Saltus *v.* Everett,[2] and may be here briefly summarized.

§ 169. Exceptions. (1) Negotiable Instruments.

Where the property intrusted to the agent is currency, or negotiable paper transferable by delivery, then under the rules of the law merchant, a *bona fide* purchaser for value will take a title good against the principal even though the agent exceeds his powers or diverts the property to his own uses.[3] The doctrine is broader than the application to agency, since even a thief can give good title to money, or paper that passes like money. In agency,

[1] Thompson *v.* Barnum, 49 Iowa, 392; Barker *v.* Dinsmore, 72 Pa. St. 427; Jackson *v.* Bank, 92 Tenn. 154.

[2] 20 Wend. (N. Y.) 267.

[3] Goodwin *v.* Robarts, L. R. 1 App. Cas. 476; London Stock Bank *v.* Simmons, 1892, A. C. 201.

a principal can follow money or negotiable paper passing by transfer only where it is in the hands of one who took with notice of his rights or who did not give a valuable consideration for it. Purchase without notice and for value cuts off the owner's rights.

But if the money or notes come into the third party's hands *mala fide*, the principal may recover; in the case of money, or notes turned into money, the action may be in quasi-contract as for money had and received.[1]

§ 170. Exceptions. (2) Indicia of Ownership.

Where the principal not only entrusts his property to the agent but also clothes the agent with the documentary evidence of ownership of the property, and third persons have reason to believe from such documentary evidence that the agent is the owner, then a *bona fide* purchaser for value will be protected as against the principal.[2] Thus where the principal allows his property to stand on the books of a wharfinger in the name of his agent, he cannot set up his title as against a purchaser from the agent;[3] nor where he allows a vessel to be enrolled in the name of his agent;[4] nor where he allows his agent in purchasing goods to take a bill of sale in his own name;[5] nor where, under an ordinance which provides that licenses shall be taken out in the name of the owner, he allows his agent to take out a license for a public vehicle in his own name.[6] In all these and similar cases the true owner is estopped by his representation, or acquiescence in the representation, as to the agent's title, from setting up his own against one who purchases from the agent on the strength

[1] Clarke *v.* Shee, Cowp. 197.

[2] Nixon *v.* Brown, 57 N. H. 34; McNeil *v.* Tenth N. B., 46 N. Y. 325.

[3] Pickering *v.* Busk, 15 East, 38.

[4] Calais Steamboat Co. *v.* Van Pelt, 2 Black, (U. S.) 372.

[5] Nixon *v.* Brown, *supra.*

[6] McCauley *v.* Brown, 2 Daly, (N. Y. C. P.) 426.

of the representation. But the document must be a representation as to title in order to work an estoppel and the buyer must rely on it as such.[1]

This class of cases is often confused with the cases where the principal is estopped to deny the agent's authority to sell as agent. The confusion springs from the *dicta* or argument of Lord Ellenborough in Pickering *v.* Busk,[2] where it is argued interrogatively that if one sends goods to an auction room it must be inferred that they were sent there for sale. It is therefore sometimes said that possession of goods by one whose business it is to sell such goods, is evidence enough that he is authorized to sell them. But this is merely a question of the agent's authority to be solved in accordance with the tests already discussed.[3] Certainly there seems to be no adjudication that the rule has any broader or different significance.[4]

§ 171. Exceptions. (3) Factors Acts.

A factor is one whose business it is to receive consignments of goods and sell them for a commission.[5] He may sell in his own name, and it follows that an innocent purchaser may take the goods by barter, or for a pre-existing debt of the factor, or in pledge for a contemporaneous debt, in ignorance of the fact that they belong to an undisclosed principal. In any one of these cases the principal may reclaim his goods as against the innocent 'purchaser,' for the authority of the agent is only to sell and not to barter, or pledge.[6]

[1] Hentz *v.* Miller, 94 N. Y. 64.

[2] 15 East, 38.

[3] *Ante*, § 103 *et seq.*

[4] See Quinn *v.* Davis, 78 Pa. St. 15; Levi *v.* Booth, 58 Md. 305; Smith *v.* Clews, 105 N. Y. 283, s. c. 114 N. Y. 190; Biggs *v.* Evans, 1894, 1 Q. B. 88.

[5] *Ante*, § 111.

[6] Allen *v.* St. Louis Bank, 120 U. S. 20; Warner *v.* Martin, 11 How. (U. S.) 209.

Owing to the frauds made possible by this rule, and deeming it better that where one of two innocent persons must suffer he should bear the loss who reposed the trust in the wrong-doer, the legislatures in several jurisdictions have passed "Factors Acts" for the relief or protection of innocent third parties. The most sweeping is the English Factors Act of 1889 (52–53 Vict. c. 45) which supersedes earlier enactments beginning with 4 Geo. IV. c. 83. The New York Factors Act (1830 c. 179) is the beginning of similar legislation in this country.[1] These acts provide in substance that where the owner of goods intrusts a factor with the goods, or the documents of title to goods, for the purposes of sale,[2] or as security for advances to be made thereon, a person taking the goods or documents of title in good faith, under a contract for the sale or disposition or pledge of the goods (except as security for a pre-existing debt) shall acquire a title as complete as if such contract were expressly authorized by the owner, subject, however, to the right of the owner to redeem the goods or their proceeds upon the repayment of the money advanced, or the return of the securities given, and the satisfaction of any lien that may exist in favor of the agent. These statutes operate, therefore. as an exception to this extent to the general rule.

§ 172. Forms of action for property or its value.

When the principal's property has been converted by the third party, the principal may have his choice of several remedies. If the property is still in the hands of the third

[1] See Stimson's Am. Statute Law, §§ 4380–88. These acts will be found in the Appendix, *post*, pp. 229, 227.

[2] In England under the act of 1889 the factor need not be intrusted with the goods for purposes of sale; it is enough that he is in possession with the consent of the owner. This prevents the fraud made possible under the decision in Cole *v.* North Western Bk., L. R. 10 C. P. 354.

party an action of replevin will lie for its recovery or an action of trover for its value. If it has been sold by the third party, the tort may be waived and an action of assumpsit brought as for money had and received;[1] and in some jurisdictions when the goods have not been sold, but have been kept or consumed, the principal may waive the tort and sue in assumpsit as for goods sold and delivered.[2] If the third party took the property with notice of the principal's rights or without giving a valuable consideration, and has converted it into another form of property, equity will, in many cases, fasten a trust upon the property so obtained, and enforce the trust in favor of the principal.[3] In the case of money, an action for money had and received will lie against successive holders until it comes into the hands of a *bona fide* holder for value.[4]

§ 173. Wrongs of Fraud and Malice.

The third person may become liable to the principal in tort, aside from cases of conversion of property already noticed, either: (1) for a fraud connected with a contract entered into between the agent and the third person in behalf of the principal; (2) for a fraud committed on the principal by collusion between the agent and the third person; (3) for an unlawful interference with the agent in the discharge of his duties, or with the contract of agency. These classes of torts generally involve either fraud or malice, — fraud in inducing the principal to enter into a contract, or malice in unlawfully interfering with a contract which the principal has already made.

§ 174. Frauds in making Contract.

We have already seen that a principal is liable for the frauds of his agent committed while making contracts

[1] Keener on Quasi-Contracts, p. 170 *et seq.*

[2] *Ibid.*, pp. 192–195.

[3] *Post*, § 177.

[4] Keener on Quasi-Cont., pp. 183–188.

with third persons. Conversely the third person is liable to the principal for frauds practised on the agent while the latter is acting in behalf of the principal. This proposition needs no discussion. It extends to frauds for which an action for deceit will lie as well as to those for which the remedy is merely rescission of the contract.

§ 175. Collusive Fraud.

The third person and the agent may combine to commit a fraud upon the principal. In such a case they are joint tort feasors, and both are liable for the injury. Accordingly the principal may maintain an action against the third person, or the agent, or both jointly.[1] The fact that the agent may be held for his breach of trust does not prevent a recovery against the third person, since the agent is guilty of two wrongs: first, for his breach of trust as agent; and second, for the consummated conspiracy with the third person to injure the plaintiff.[2] If a contract has been made where the agent was in collusion with the third person, the principal may repudiate it[3] and recover damages either in tort or assumpsit.[4] So where the third person knows that the agent is committing a fraud on his principal, he becomes a party to the fraud by contracting with such knowledge, and the contract may be avoided by the principal.[5]

§ 176. Interference with Agency.

The third person is liable to the principal for unlawfully interfering with the agent or the agency. He is

[1] Boston *v.* Simmons, 150 Mass. 461; Mayor *v.* Lever, 1891, 1 Q. B. 168.

[2] Mayor *v.* Lever, *supra.*

[3] Panama, &c. Co. *v.* India Rubber Co., L. R. 10 Ch. App. 515; Miller *v.* R. R. Co., 83 Ala. 274.

[4] City of Findlay *v.* Pertz, 66 Fed. Rep. 427.

[5] Hegenmyer *v.* Marks, 37 Minn. 6.

liable if he unlawfully injures the agent, and thereby renders him unfit to perform the duties of the agency;[1] or if he unlawfully interferes with the agent in the performance of the duties of the agency.[2] He is also liable for unlawfully inducing the agent to break his contract of employment with the principal,[3] though some cases hold that he is liable only where he has used unlawful means, as force, threats or fraud.[4] Whether the act of the third person in inducing the breach can ever be justified, and if so on what grounds, seems not to be decided. The doctrine has become much broader in its application than inducing breach of contracts of employment, and extends to breach of contract generally.[5]

If the principal brings an action for the loss of the services of his agent occasioned by a negligent injury at the hands of a third party, it seems that the contributory negligence of the agent would be a bar to his recovery, though the principal is personally free from blame.[6]

4. *Trust Obligations.*

§ 177. Constructive Trusts.

Constructive trusts arise where one person has obtained money or property which does not equitably belong to him and which does equitably belong to another. Although the one so obtaining the property of another has never expressly or impliedly undertaken to hold it as trustee, yet equity fastens upon him the character of a trustee and

[1] Ames *v.* Union Ry. Co., 117 Mass. 541.

[2] St. Johnsbury, &c. R. Co. *v.* Hunt, 55 Vt. 570.

[3] Lumley *v.* Gye, 2 El. & Bl. 216; Walker *v.* Cronin, 107 Mass. 555; Haskins *v.* Royster, 70 N. C. 601.

[4] Bourlier *v.* Macauley, 91 Ky. 135.

[5] See Temperton *v.* Russell, 1893, 1 Q. B. 715; Angle *v.* Chicago, &c. Ry. 151 U. S. 1.

[6] Chicago, B. & Q. R. *v.* Honey, 63 Fed. Rep. 39.

compels him to account to the beneficial owner as such.[1] The trust so 'constructed' by equity is analogous to the contract 'constructed' by the common law in cases of quasi-contract.

§ 178. Following Trust Funds.

In accordance with this general doctrine, it is held that if a third person obtains from an agent the property of the principal under circumstances which give the third person no equitable claim to it, equity will fasten upon the property a trust for the benefit of the principal, and "will follow the fund through any number of transmutations and preserve it for the owner as long as it can be identified,"[2] or until it passes into the hands of a *bona fide* purchaser for value. It is not necessary that the trustee should be guilty of an intent to defraud the principal; he may intend no moral wrong, yet if he comes into the possession of the property with notice of the principal's rights, or as a volunteer not taking for value, he is declared to hold in trust for the principal.[3] It is only where the superior equity of a *bona fide* purchaser for value intervenes that the right of the principal to pursue the trust fund is cut off. It is under the application of this doctrine that banks are not allowed a banker's lien or right of set-off against funds deposited by the agent where the bank knows that the funds belong to the principal;[4] that attaching creditors of the agent are not allowed to reach the fund so deposited;[5] and that a donee of the fund, or property purchased with it, is declared to be a trustee for the benefit of the principal.[6]

[1] 2 Pomeroy's Eq. Jurisp. § 1047.

[2] Farmers, &c. Bank *v.* King, 57 Pa. St. 202.

[3] 2 Pomeroy's Eq. Jurisp. § 1048.

[4] National Bank *v.* Ins. Co., 104 U. S. 54; Baker *v.* New York N. B, 100 N. Y. 31; Union, &c. Bk. *v.* Gillespie, 137 U. S. 411.

[5] Farmers, &c. Bk. *v.* King, *supra.*

[6] Riehl *v.* Evansville Foundry Ass'n, 104 Ind. 70.

In order that the right to follow the fund should exist it is necessary that it be a fund to which title was in the principal before the diversion. Where an agent fraudulently took commissions from third persons and then invested the fund so received, it was held that the principal could not follow the fund into the investments, since it was not a fund previously belonging to him, but a debt due him from the agent for which an action for money had and received was an appropriate remedy.[1] It is further necessary that the fiduciary relationship of principal and agent should be established. If the relation is any other, as vendor and vendee, the fund is that of the independent operator and cannot be followed.[2]

§ 179. Legal Remedies for Diversion of Trust Fund.

The doctrine of following trust funds is a peculiarly equitable one, and it has been held that the only remedy in such cases is in equity.[3] But owing to the peculiarities of the history of equity jurisdiction in some of the States, legal remedies based on equitable principles are available.[4] In such jurisdictions actions for money had and received may be maintained by the principal against third parties into whose hands the fund had passed. And if the principal's *money* has been *converted* to the use of the third party, it may be followed until it reaches the hands of a *bona fide* holder for value, and recovered in an action as for money had and received.[5]

1 Lister *v.* Stubbs, L. R. 45 Ch. D. 1.

2 *Ex parte* White, L. R. 6 Ch. App. 397; *ante*, § 6.

3 National Bank *v.* Ins. Co., 104 U. S. 54.

4 Frazier *v.* Erie Bank, 8 Watts & Serg. (Pa.) 18; Sheffer *v.* Montgomery, 65 Pa. St. 329; Frue *v.* Loring, 120 Mass. 507.

5 Keener on Quasi-Contracts, pp. 183–188.

PART IV.

LEGAL EFFECT OF THE RELATION AS BETWEEN THE AGENT AND THIRD PARTIES.

§ 180. Introduction.

We must once more, and for the last time, shift our point of view. We have now to consider the mutual rights and obligations that may spring up between the agent and the third party in consequence of the manner in which the agent conducts himself toward the third party or the third party toward the agent. Obviously it is not the purpose of the agent or the third party to create obligations as between themselves, and yet through carelessness, ignorance, mistake, or fraud this may result. We will consider the subject under two heads: (1) mutual rights and obligations arising from contract; (2) mutual rights and obligations arising from tort.

CHAPTER XV.

CONTRACT RELATIONS BETWEEN AGENT AND THIRD PARTY.

§ 181. Questions to be considered.

Where an agent enters into a contract on behalf of his principal, he may bind the principal, or himself, or both, or neither; but different rules govern the liability of public agents. Where an agent has money equitably belonging to a third person but which he assumes to hold for his principal, he may be liable to the third person in quasi-contract. On the other hand, an agent who is under obligations to the third party may have rights commensurate with his obligations. This chapter deals therefore with the following topics: —

1. Where the principal alone is bound by the contract.
2. Where the agent alone is bound by the contract.
3. Where both principal and agent are bound by the contract.
4. Where neither principal nor agent is bound by the contract.
5. Special rules applicable to public agents as to liability upon contract.
6. Liability of agent in quasi-contract.
7. Liability of the third person to the agent upon the contract.

1. *Where the Principal alone is bound.*

§ 182. Authorized Contract.

Where the agent acts within the apparent scope of his authority for a disclosed principal, and contracts in the name of that principal, the latter alone is bound by the contract.[1] So where a principal, with full knowledge of the facts, ratifies an unauthorized contract entered into by his agent, the principal alone is bound by the contract.[2]

2. *Where the Agent alone is bound.*

§ 183. (I) Unauthorized Contract.

Where the agent knowingly, negligently, or mistakenly holds himself out, either expressly or impliedly, as having authority to act for a principal in a particular transaction, when in fact he has no such authority, he is liable to the third party with whom he deals for any damage the latter may suffer in consequence of such representation.[3] The question remains, in what kind of an action may the third party pursue his remedy?

(1). *Agent not liable upon the contract.* It is now generally agreed that the agent does not bind himself upon the contract. He does not bind his principal because he has no authority to do so; he does not bind himself because he is not a party to the contract, and the courts will not create a new contract either against or in favor of the agent.[4] Some early New York cases[5] which held that an action would lie upon the contract, must be regarded as overruled,[6] and other cases holding a similar doctrine[7] as opposed to the weight of authority.

[1] Bonynge *v.* Field, 81 N.Y. 159; Peters *v.* Farnsworth, 15 Vt. 155.

[2] *Ante*, §§ 46, 49, 101.

[3] Kroeger *v.* Pitcairn, 101 Pa. St. 311.

[4] McCurdy *v.* Rogers, 21 Wis. 199; Duncan *v.* Niles, 32 Ill. 532; Hall *v.* Crandall, 29 Cal. 568; Cole *v.* O'Brien, 34 Neb. 68; Lewis *v.* Nicholson, 18 Q. B. 503; Pollock on Cont. (6th ed.) 101–103.

[5] Dusenbury *v.* Ellis, 3 Johns. Cas. 70; White *v.* Skinner, 13 Johns. 307.

[6] Dung *v.* Parker, 52 N. Y. 494; Baltzen *v.* Nicolay, 53 N. Y. 467; Simmons *v.* More, 100 N. Y. 140.

[7] Dale *v.* Donaldson, 48 Ark. 188; Weare *v.* Gove, 44 N. H. 196.

(2). *Agent liable as for breach of warranty of authority.* Where the agent innocently exceeds his authority under circumstances not amounting to deceit, no action in tort can be maintained.[1] Yet clearly the third party has suffered as great an injury as if the representation had been made fraudulently. In order to provide a remedy in such an emergency, the courts have invented the fiction that the agent 'warrants' his authority whenever he makes a contract for his principal, and allow an action for damages for the breach of this warranty of authority.[2] The fiction is well enough, but it should not be allowed to disguise the fact that this is a plain exception to the rule that no action lies for an innocent misrepresentation.[3] It serves the additional purpose of giving an action against the estate of the agent after his death, whereas a tort action would not survive.[4]

(3). *Agent liable in tort for wilful deceit.* If the agent wilfully misrepresents his authority, by express declaration or by contract, he is liable to the injured party in an action of deceit.[5] The action *ex delicto* rests upon the wilful or reckless conduct of the agent. If, as suggested above, the fiction of implied warranty were rejected, and the action based upon the representation, whether innocent or guilty, an innocent misrepresentation by an agent would escape the general rule that deceit requires wilful or reckless representations. It is necessary that the other elements of deceit be present. The third party must actually be deceived. If he knows all the facts, the agent is not liable.[6]

[1] *Ante*, § 151.

[2] Collen *v.* Wright, 8 El. & Bl. 647; Baltzen *v.* Nicolay, 53 N. Y. 467; Kroeger *v.* Pitcairn, *supra.*

[3] Firbank's Ex'rs *v.* Humphreys, L. R. 18 Q. B. D. 54.

[4] Pollock on Torts (4th ed.), 58, note *k*, 489.

[5] Polhill *v.* Walter, 3 B. & Ad. 114; Noyes *v.* Loring, 55 Me. 408.

[6] Michael *v.* Jones, 84 Mo. 578; Hall *v.* Lauderdale, 46 N. Y. 70.

§ 184. (II) Incompetent Principal.

An agent is presumed to represent not only that he has authority but that his principal was competent to give such authority when it was given, and has not since, to the knowledge of the agent, become incompetent.[1] A breach of this representation resulting in damage gives the same remedies as a breach of the representation as to authority. But the damage must have been suffered. If the principal be one, as an infant,[2] who may ratify or disaffirm at his election, it must be shown that he has disaffirmed before an action will lie against the principal.[3]

§ 185. (III) Fictitious Principal.

Where an agent contracts for an alleged principal who is not in fact in existence at the time, he becomes personally liable on the contract as principal,[4] except that he is not liable where his principal dies without his knowledge.[5]

The commonest case of a fictitious principal is the case of a projected corporation whose promoters enter into contracts in anticipation of its formation, and sign "as agents" for the (named) corporation. Obviously there is no principal, as no corporation exists. If it should never exist there could be no question as to the sole liability of the promoters. But how if it is in fact incorporated and 'ratifies' the contract of the promoters? There can be no real ratification in such a case because it is the first essential of ratification that the principal should be an

[1] Drew *v.* Nunn, L. R. 4 Q. B. D. 661.

[2] In those jurisdictions where an infant's appointment of an agent is not void, but voidable. — *Ante*, § 15.

[3] Patterson *v.* Lippincott, 47 N. J. L. 457.

[4] Kelner *v.* Baxter, L. R. 2 C. P. 174; Patrick *v.* Bowman, 149 U. S. 411; Lewis *v.* Tilton, 64 Iowa, 220.

[5] Smout *v.* Ilbery, 10 M. & W. 1.

existing person at the time the contract was made.[1] Accordingly the agent remains liable unless, by agreement among the three parties, the corporation after it is in existence should be substituted in place of the promoters.[2] This, however, amounts to the discharge of the original contract and the formation of a new one.

Another common case is where A contracts with X in behalf of an unincorporated club or association. Here there is a body of more or less clearly identified persons who might jointly or severally be responsible principals, as individuals, but no legal entity composed of the members in the aggregate. There is not even a partnership.[3] In such case if the agent contracts in the name of a principal, which name conveys the idea of a corporate entity, the agent is clearly liable.[4] Whether the members of the club are also liable depends upon whether in fact they authorized A to make the contract. Such authority may be found in the constitution or by-laws of the club to which the members have assented,[5] or in the vote of a meeting at which the members were present and in the results of which they acquiesced.[6] If the credit was extended to the agent and not to the body he represents, the agent is liable.[7] But if the credit is extended to the club, or its members, and not to the agent, and the agent was authorized to procure such credit, then the club or its members, and not the agent, will be liable.[8]

[1] *Ante*, § 32.

[2] *Ibid.*

[3] Flemyng *v.* Hector, 2 M. & W. 172; Ash *v.* Guie, 97 Pa. St. 493.

[4] Lewis *v.* Tilton, 64 Iowa, 220; Blakely *v.* Bennecke, 59 Mo. 193; Comfort *v.* Graham, 87 Iowa, 295.

[5] Flemyng *v.* Hector, *supra;* Todd *v.* Emly, 7 M. & W. 427.

[6] Willcox *v.* Arnold, 162 Mass. 577; Heath *v.* Goslin, 80 Mo. 310.

[7] Eichbaum *v.* Irons, 6 Watts & Serg. (Pa.) 67.

[8] Pain *v.* Sample, 158 Pa. St. 428.

§ 186. (IV) Exclusive credit to Agent.

Where an agent expressly pledges his own personal credit in a contract made for the benefit of his principal, and the third party, knowing the principal, elects to give exclusive credit to the agent, the latter alone is liable on the contract.[1] The third party must actually know the principal and understand that the buyer is his agent; it is not enough that he has means of knowledge, nor that he knows that the agent is representing some unknown person. In such cases the third party may hold either the agent or the principal, since he has not made a final election between them. It has been held that accepting a written contract in the name of the agent when the principal is known, is conclusive evidence of an intent to look to the agent alone;[2] but this is doubtful.[3]

§ 187. (V) Foreign Principal.

Where the agent contracts in behalf of a foreign principal, that is one residing out of the jurisdiction, it is the rule of the English law that the agent is presumed to pledge his own credit, and that the third party does not rely upon the credit of the principal, but exclusively upon the credit of the agent, although the contract discloses the principal and the fact of the agency.[4] But there is nothing to prevent one foreign merchant from contracting with another through the instrumentality of an agent, and if he does so, he is, of course, bound by his contract.[5]

[1] Thomson *v.* Davenport, 9 B. & C. 78, 89; Raymond *v.* Eagle Mills, 2 Met. (Mass.) 319; Kelly *v.* Thuey, 102 Mo. 522.

[2] Chandler *v.* Coe, 54 N. H. 561.

[3] *Post*, § 197.

[4] Leake on Cont. (3d ed.) p. 417; Pollock on Cont. (6th ed.) p. 95. But in a recent English work on Agency it is said that, "it now seems that there is no presumption either way, and that it is always a question as to what was the intention of the parties." — Wright on Agency, pp. 296–7.

[5] Flinn & Co. *v.* Hoyle, 63 L. J. Q. B. 1 (1894).

And the agent may contract exclusively for the foreign principal without recourse to himself.[1]

In the United States, this rule as to foreign principals has been generally disapproved. It is held that there is no presumption that one dealing with an agent of a foreign principal gives exclusive credit to the agent; that it is in each case a question of fact; and that the fact that the principal resides in a foreign jurisdiction has merely an evidential force.[2] In reaching this conclusion the courts have probably been influenced by the consideration that the States of the Union are, as to the law merchant, foreign to each other, and that the English rule would work serious inconvenience to trade among the States.[3] Even if the rule were admitted as to principals resident in foreign countries generally, it would probably be denied as to those resident in two different States of the Union.[4]

§ 188. (VI) Contract under Seal.

Where an agent makes a contract under seal in his own name (the seal not being merely superfluous) the agent alone is liable on the contract whether his principal be known or unknown. It is a technical rule of the common law that only those parties can be charged upon a sealed instrument who appear by name or description upon the face of it.[5] Nor is there any remedy against the principal even in equity.[6] But if the seal is superfluous it may be

[1] Green *v.* Kopke, 18 C. B. 549.

[2] Kirkpatrick *v.* Stainer, 22 Wend. (N. Y.) 244; Oelricks *v.* Ford, 23 How. (U. S.) 49, 64–5; Barry *v.* Page, 10 Gray, (Mass.) 398; Kaulback *v.* Churchill, 59 N. H. 296.

[3] See Wharton on Agency, §§ 791–3.

[4] Vawter *v.* Baker, 23 Ind. 63; Barry *v.* Page, *supra;* Barham *v.* Bell, 112 N. C. 131.

[5] Briggs *v.* Partridge, 64 N. Y. 357; Kiersted *v.* R. R. Co., 69 N. Y. 343; Sanders *v.* Partridge, 108 Mass. 556.

[6] Borcherling *v.* Katz, 37 N. J. Eq. 150.

disregarded.[1] If the instrument be unsealed the principal may be held, even though it be on a contract required by the statute of frauds to be in writing.[2]

§ 189. (VII) Negotiable Instruments. — General Rules. Only the parties who are named or described in a negotiable instrument can sue or be sued upon it. For our present purpose we may state the rule to be that only the person who signs a negotiable instrument is liable upon it, and that parol evidence is inadmissible to prove that he signed in behalf of an undisclosed principal, or of a principal disclosed but unnamed in the instrument.[3]

We have already seen that in the case of simple contracts generally, parol evidence is admissible to show that an instrument signed by A. B. was in fact signed by him in behalf of P. Q., and that thereupon P. Q. may be held, though A. B. will not be discharged.[4] But in the case of sealed instruments and negotiable instruments the rule is otherwise; — the first because of the technical rules of the common law governing sealed instruments; the second because of the technical rules of the law merchant governing negotiable instruments. As to either no parol evidence is admissible to change the legal effect of what appears upon the face of the instrument.[5]

But the face of the negotiable instrument may disclose an ambiguity or doubt as to who is the real maker and in such a case parol evidence is admitted to remove the ambiguity. At one extreme are cases where clearly the instrument is upon its face the obligation of the principal. At the other extreme are cases where clearly the obligation

[1] Lancaster *v.* Knickerbocker Ice Co., 153 Pa. St. 427.

[2] Beckham *v.* Drake, 9 M. & W. 79, 91; Briggs *v.* Partridge, *supra;* Byington *v.* Simpson, 134 Mass. 169.

[3] *Ante,* § 128.

[4] *Ante,* § 123. See Leake on Cont. (6th ed.) pp. 441–2.

[5] Briggs *v.* Partridge, 64 N. Y. 357.

is that of the agent. Between these extremes, and shading into them by imperceptible degrees, are cases of ambiguity or doubt. Some of these ambiguous cases are resolved by the court as cases for interpretation upon an examination of the instrument. Some are resolved by the aid of parol evidence introduced to remove the ambiguity. Almost hopeless confusion arises from the fact that practically the same instrument will be resolved by one court by interpretation as the obligation of the principal, by another as the obligation of the agent, and by a third in accordance with the fact as established by parol evidence.[1]

Under such circumstances it is impossible to formulate settled rules as to the interpretation of these intermediate cases. Perhaps the most useful course will be to take up the general classes of cases and ascertain the trend of judicial opinion. The cases for construction fall first into three classes: (1) where the construction rests upon the signature alone; (2) where the construction rests upon the signature aided by recitals in the body of the instrument; (3) where the construction rests upon the signature aided by marginal recitals, memoranda, or headings. These will be considered in the order named.

The parties upon a negotiable instrument may be the maker of a promissory note or the drawer of a bill of exchange, or the acceptor of a bill of exchange, or the indorser of a bill or note. And first of the maker or drawer.

§ 190. Same. — (I) Construction from Signature alone.

1. The signature written by the agent as maker or drawer may be unequivocally that of the principal, and

[1] Compare, for example, Carpenter *v.* Farnsworth, 106 Mass. 561; Casco National Bank *v.* Clark, 139 N. Y. 307; and Frankland *v.* Johnson, 147 Ill. 520. And compare Liebscher *v.* Kraus, 74 Wis. 387; Matthews *v.* Dubuque Mattress Co., 87 Iowa, 246; and Reeve *v.* First National Bank, 54 N. J. L. 208.

the sole inquiry will be as to the authority of the agent to sign. The following are such signatures. (1) P. Q.; (2) P. Q. by his agent A. B., or by A. B., agent, — or by A. B.; (3) A. B. agent for P. Q.; or A. B. for P. Q.; (4) Pro. P. Q. — A. B.[1]

2. The signature written by the agent as maker or drawer may be unequivocally the signature of the agent alone, and the agent alone will be bound. The following are such signatures: (1) A. B.; (2) A. B. agent; (3) A. B. agent of P. Q.;[2] (4) A. B. president, or treasurer, etc.;[3] (5) A. B. president, or treasurer, etc., of the P. Q. Co.[4]

It has been thought that the signature "A. B. cashier," stands upon a different footing, but this is questionable.[5] It has also been thought that there is a distinction between suits brought by a party to the instrument, or one who stands in his shoes, and suits by a *bona fide* holder for value;[6] but this seems unwarranted, since an ambiguity which is obvious to a judge ought certainly to be obvious to a merchant, who would therefore take with actual notice of the doubt regarding the personality of the principal. The rule is applicable to negotiable instru-

[1] 1 Daniel on Neg. Inst. § 298; Long *v.* Colburn, 11 Mass. 97. Cf. Tannatt *v.* Rocky Mt. Nat. Bk., 1 Colo. 278.

[2] Sparks *v.* Dispatch Trans. Co., 104 Mo. 531; Pentz *v.* Stanton, 10 Wend. (N. Y.) 271; Williams *v.* Robbins, 16 Gray, (Mass.) 77; Bank *v.* Cook, 38 Ohio St. 442; Tarver *v.* Garlington, 27 So. Car. 107; Cragin *v.* Lovell, 109 U. S. 194.

[3] Davis *v.* England, 141 Mass. 587; Hobson *v.* Hassett, 76 Calif. 203. Cf. Metcalf *v.* Williams, 104 U. S. 93, which seems difficult to sustain on principle or authority, and Devendorf *v.* West Virginia, &c., Co., 17 W. Va. 135, which seems to proceed upon the theory that the principal had 'adopted' the agent's name.

[4] Rendell *v.* Harriman, 75 Me. 497; Tucker Mfg. Co. *v.* Fairbanks, 98 Mass. 101; Burlingame *v.* Brewster, 79 Ill. 515; Bank *v.* Cook, 38 Oh. St. 442.

[5] See *post*, § 194.

[6] Metcalf *v.* Williams, *supra*.

ments, not to negotiable instruments in the hands of *bona fide* holders, and rests on doctrines peculiar to those instruments as the rule regarding contracts under seal rests on doctrines peculiar to specialties. The only case which should admit parol evidence is a case of ambiguity, and that is as obvious to a *bona fide* holder as to the original party.

3. The signature written by the agent as maker or drawer may be the signature of his principal followed by his own signature with the descriptive words, "agent," "president," "treasurer," etc., added, as, for example, "The P. Q. Co., A. B. President." In such a case there are three holdings on practically the same state of facts: (*a*) that it is the signature of the principal alone; [1] (*b*) that it is the signature of both the principal and agent; [2] (*c*) that it is an ambiguous signature and parol evidence is admissible to explain it.[3]

Two other auxiliary holdings may be noted. First, the seal of the corporation is to be given the same effect as the written name of the corporation.[4] Second, in a jurisdiction where parol evidence would not be admitted to discharge the agent, the instrument may be reformed in equity to work his discharge.[5]

4. The principal may adopt the name of the agent as his trading name, and in such cases the signature A. B. is the signature of P. Q. Thus a corporation may trade under a partnership name,[6] or the name of an officer,[7] or a

[1] Liebscher *v.* Kraus, 74 Wis. 387.

[2] Matthews *v.* Dubuque Mattress Co., 87 Iowa, 246.

[3] Reeve *v.* First Nat. Bk., 54 N. J. L. 208; Bean *v.* Pioneer Mining Co., 66 Calif. 451.

[4] Means *v.* Swormstedt, 32 Ind. 87; Scanlan *v.* Keith, 102 Ill. 634; Miller *v.* Roach, 150 Mass. 140.

[5] Lee *v.* Percival, 85 Iowa, 639.

[6] Melledge *v.* Boston Iron Co., 5 Cush. (Mass.) 158.

[7] Devendorf *v.* West Virginia, &c. Co., 17 W. Va. 135.

partnership under the name of an individual.[1] This presents one case, therefore, where parol proof may always be given to charge a person whose (true) name does not appear upon the negotiable instrument; and, as this exception exists, it seems it would be improper to sustain a demurrer to a complaint alleging the agency, since "*non constat* but the plaintiff may be able to bring his case under that exception."[2] At common law a husband may adopt as his own the indorsement made by his wife in her name upon a bill or note payable to her order, and in such a case her signature is his signature.[3] It has been suggested that a bank adopts the name of its cashier as its trading name in the drawing and indorsing of negotiable paper, but the cases are easily explainable without resorting to this assumption.[4]

§ 191. Same. — Construction from Signature aided by Recitals in the Instrument.

5. The body of the instrument may contain recitals as to the identity of the principal or the fact of the agency which, taken with the signature of the maker or drawer, will either, — (*a*) render the obligation clearly that of the principal, or (*b*) render the instrument so ambiguous as to raise a case for interpretation or construction by the court, or (*c*) render the instrument so ambiguous as to let in parol evidence to explain it. It is in the treatment of this class of instruments that the greatest diversity of views prevails. A few illustrations are given to show the nature of the problem.

[1] Rumsey *v.* Briggs, 139 N. Y. 323; Bank *v.* Monteath, 1 Denio, (N. Y.) 402.

[2] Tarver *v.* Garlington, 27 So. Car. 107.

[3] Hancock Bank *v.* Joy, 41 Me. 568.

[4] *Post*, § 194. Cf. *dictum* in Robinson *v.* Kanawha Valley Bank, 44 Oh. St. 441, 448.

(*a*) The following has been said to be clearly the obligation of the principal: "We, as trustees (or we, trustees) of the P. Q. Co., promise," etc., (signed) "A. B., C. D., trustees of the P. Q. Co."[1] But the same recital with the signature "A. B., C. D., trustees," was held to be the individual obligation of the signers.[2] This is a very refined distinction, and of doubtful utility. In another case it was held that a like recital signed "A. B., C. D.," with no official description, was clearly the obligation of the principal, but this construction was, perhaps, aided by statute;[3] and is not in accordance with the general holding.[4] (*b*) Cases falling under this head are only a phase of those just considered. But that the obligation is not clearly that of either the principal or the agent is shown by the fact that one court will hold practically the same instrument to bind the principal while another court will hold it to bind the agent, and a third to be so ambiguous as to admit parol evidence.[5] (*c*) The following have been said to be so ambiguous as to let in parol evidence: "The P. Q. Co. promises," etc., (signed) "A. B. Gen. Supt.;"[6] "The directors of the P. Q. Co. promise," etc. (signed) "A. B., C. D.," with no additional words indicating agency;[7] "Pay to the order of the P. Q. Co." etc., (signed) "A. B., President P. Q. Co."[8]

[1] Blanchard *v.* Kaull, 44 Calif. 440; New Market Savings Bank *v.* Gillet, 100 Ill. 254.

[2] Powers *v.* Briggs, 79 Ill. 493.

[3] Simpson *v.* Garland, 72 Me. 40.

[4] Bradlee *v.* Boston Glass Manufactory, 16 Pick. (Mass.) 347.

[5] Compare, for example, Simpson *v.* Garland, *supra*, with Pack *v.* White, 78 Ky. 243, and McKensey *v.* Edwards, 88 Ky. 272.

[6] Frankland *v.* Johnson, 147 Ill. 520.

[7] McKensey *v.* Edwards, 88 Ky. 272.

[8] Kean *v.* Davis, 21 N. J. L. 683.

§ 192. Same. — Construction from Signature aided by marginal Heading or Memoranda.

6. The margin of the instrument may contain headings or memoranda disclosing the identity of the principal, or the fact of the agency, which, taken with the signature of the maker or drawer, will raise a case for interpretation. But there is the widest divergence in the decisions as to the effect of the interpretation.

(*a.*) *Headings.* It has been held that negotiable instruments headed with the name and, possibly, address of the principal and signed "A. B., agent," or "president," "secretary," etc., is the obligation of the principal whose name is thus disclosed upon the instrument.[1] But other cases are to the contrary.[2] And where one agent of the principal so named draws upon another signing "A. B., agent" and the latter accepts, signing "C. D., agent," the acceptor is personally bound since the force of the heading is exhausted in qualifying the liability of the drawer.[3] In the leading case of Mechanics' Bank *v.* Bank of Columbia,[4] the instrument was headed "Mechanics' Bank of Alexandria" and signed "Wm. Paton, Jr.," with no words indicative of agency. The court held the instrument ambiguous and admitted parol evidence to explain it. Had signature been followed by the word "cashier," it would have been held unequivocally the obligation of the bank.[5] This case is the origin of a vague doctrine that the signature of a cashier stands upon a different footing from that of other agents, but clearly it is to be explained in accordance with the rule governing an ambiguity appearing on the face of the instrument.

[1] Hitchcock *v.* Buchanan, 105 U. S. 416; Olcott *v.* Tioga R. R. Co., 27 N. Y. 546.

[2] Cf. Casco Nat. Bk. *v.* Clark, 139 N. Y. 305.

[3] Slawson *v.* Loring, 5 Allen, (Mass.) 340.

[4] 5 Wheat. (U. S.) 326.

[5] Mr. Justice Lamar in Falk *v.* Moebs, 127 U. S. 597, 606.

(*b*) *Marginal Memoranda.* It has been held that negotiable instruments with the name of the principal across the end, and signed "A. B., agent," or "president," "treasurer," etc., are the obligations of the principal whose name is thus disclosed upon the instrument.[1] But the contrary decision has been reached in other cases,[2] though with a suggestion that the result might have been otherwise had the action been between the original parties; this qualification seems to be unwarranted.[3]

§ 193. Same. — Acceptors of Bills of Exchange.

The above illustrations cover mainly the cases of makers of promissory notes and drawers of bills of exchange, as to whom, in these matters, there is no distinction.[4] We have yet to consider the cases of acceptors of bills of exchange and indorsers of bills or notes.

A bill of exchange is drawn upon some designated person, known as the drawee. If he accepts the bill he is bound as acceptor, and the mere fact that he adds "agent" or "president," "treasurer," etc., after his signature will not render his unnamed principal liable. The following will illustrate the phases of this question:

(1) The bill may be drawn on "A. B." and accepted by "A. B.;" or drawn on "A. B., agent," and accepted by "A. B., agent;" or drawn on "A. B., agent of P. Q.," and accepted by "A. B., agent of P. Q." In the first two cases there is general agreement that, in the absence of recitals or other indications of the identity of the principal, A. B. alone is bound.[5] In the third case there is disagreement, one case holding the obligation clearly

[1] Carpenter *v.* Farnsworth, 106 Mass. 561; Chipman *v.* Foster, 119 Mass. 189.

[2] Casco National Bank *v.* Clark, 139 N. Y. 305.

[3] *Ante*, § 190, sub-sec. 2.

[4] Tucker Mfg. Co. *v.* Fairbanks, 98 Mass. 101.

[5] Slawson *v.* Loring, 5 Allen, (Mass.) 340.

that of the agent,[1] and another holding parol evidence admissible to explain it.[2] But there seems to be no more reason for giving the term "agent of P. Q." any different construction here than when added to the signature of a maker or drawer.

(2) The bill may be drawn on "A. B." and accepted by "P. Q. by A. B. agent." Here clearly A. B. is not bound. But neither is P. Q., because P. Q. is not the drawee, and only the drawee can accept.[3]

(3) The bill may be drawn on "P. Q." and accepted by "A. B. agent." Here it would seem that only P. Q. is liable, for as only the drawee can accept it is clear that "A. B. agent" is to be read "A. B. agent for the drawee."[4]

(4) The bill may be drawn on "A. B. agent," etc., but may bear other marks indicating that A. B. is the agent of the drawer. This is held to be the case where a bill is drawn by "The P. Q. Co., by C. D. Pres't," upon "A. B. Treas.," with a direction to charge to the account of the company.[5] But it is difficult to reconcile the cases upon this point.[6]

§ 194. Same. — Indorsers of Bills and Notes.

In the case of indorsers of bills and notes the whole doctrine of terms *descriptio personæ* seems to have broken down. The indorsement of the payee or subsequent holder is necessary to transfer the title to the paper; the addition of the term "agent" is indicative that the indorsement is in a representative capacity for that purpose;

[1] Moss *v.* Livingston, 4 Comst. (4 N. Y.) 208.

[2] Shelton *v.* Darling, 2 Conn. 435; Laflin, &c. Co. *v.* Sinsheimer, 48 Md. 411.

[3] Walker *v.* Bank, 9 N. Y. 582.

[4] Soughegan Nat. Bk. *v.* Boardman, 46 Minn. 293, 296 (*dictum*).

[5] Hager *v.* Rice, 4 Colo. 90.

[6] Robinson *v.* Kanawha Valley Bank, 44 Oh. St. 441.

and the courts have practically arrived at the conclusion that where the instrument is payable to "A. B., agent" and indorsed "A. B., agent," that it may be shown that A. B. was acting as agent for an unnamed principal: for example, "A. B. treasurer;"[1] "A. B. agent of the P. Q. Co.;"[2] "A. B. cashier."[3] And some cases have gone to the length of holding that in a note payable to "A. B., sec. and treas." signed "P. Q. Co., A. B. sec. and treas.," and indorsed "A. B. sec. and treas.," the indorsement was conclusively that of the P. Q. Co.[4]

The courts have not always distinguished between cases involving the liability of a maker or drawer or acceptor, and cases involving the liability of a payee indorser, and needless "anarchy" has resulted from the confusion.[5] The distinction is, however, a valid one and is supported by the decisions. Indeed, the supposed distinction between "A. B. cashier" and "A. B. agent," is largely if not wholly explained by the fact that most of the cases holding the signature "A. B. cashier" to be the signature of the bank of which A. B. is shown to be cashier, are cases of indorsement;[6] where this was not the case the instrument bore the name of the bank upon the margin;[7] or it was a case in which the bank brought suit upon a bill or note in which "A. B. cashier" was named as payee.[8]

[1] Babcock *v.* Beman, 1 E. D. Smith (N. Y. C. P.) 593; Soughegan National Bank *v.* Boardman, 46 Minn. 293.

[2] Vater *v.* Lewis, 36 Ind. 288; Nichols *v.* Frothingham, 45 Me. 220.

[3] First Nat. Bk. *v.* Hall, 44 N. Y. 395.

[4] Falk *v.* Moebs, 127 U. S. 597.

[5] See Falk *v.* Moebs, 127 U. S. 597, 606.

[6] Bank of Genesee *v.* Patchin, 13 N. Y. 309, s. c. 19 N. Y. 312; Folger *v.* Chase, 18 Pick. (Mass.) 63; Garland *v.* Dover, 19 Me. 441; Houghton *v.* First Nat. Bk., 26 Wis. 663; Bank of the State *v.* Wheeler, 21 Ind. 90.

[7] Mechanics' Bank *v.* Bank of Columbia, 5 Wheat. (U. S.) 326.

[8] Baldwin *v.* Bank, 1 Wall. (U. S.) 234; Nave *v.* First Nat. Bk., 87 Ind. 204; *ante,* § 135.

§ 195. Same. — Summary.

It will be seen that the vexed question is, what creates an ambiguity on the face of an instrument? In their desire to render negotiable instruments certain, and to avoid deciding that an ambiguity exists, the courts have reached exactly opposite conclusions as to the legal effect of practically identical instruments. No stronger evidence is needed to prove that such an instrument is ambiguous. If reasonable men may differ as to the meaning of an instrument, a case of ambiguity is raised which should be determined by the aid of extrinsic evidence. The following rules seem to be justified by an examination and comparison of the cases: —

(1) An ambiguity is not created merely by words descriptive of agency added to the signature, *except* (*a*) where there are two signatures and the one with the descriptive words follows the other, and (*b*) in cases of indorsement.

(2) An ambiguity may be created by recitals or marginal memoranda, disclosing the name of the principal, which, if read with the signature and its descriptive words, would leave a reasonable doubt as to which party is intended to be charged.

(3) An ambiguity is created by merely descriptive words following an indorsement.

(4) Parol evidence is always admissible to show that the principal does business under the name of the agent.

3. *Where both Principal and Agent are bound.*

§ 196. (I) Undisclosed Principal.

Where an agent contracts in his own name, whether by parol or in writing (other than sealed or negotiable instruments), for an undisclosed principal, both the agent and the principal are liable, and the third party may elect which he will hold.[1] Even where a negotiable instrument is given signed by the agent, the third party may by disregarding the instrument, proceed against the principal upon the original contract.[2] But a principal is not undisclosed merely because he is not named, if the third party knew or ought to have known that the agent was acting for another person.[3]

§ 197. (II) Simple Contract signed by Agent.

Where an agent contracts in writing (other than sealed or negotiable instruments) in his own name for a disclosed principal not named or described in the writing, both the agent and the principal are liable, and the third party may elect which he will hold,[4] unless exclusive credit has been given to the agent. This rule rests upon two considerations: (1) parol evidence may be admitted to charge the unnamed principal, (2) parol evidence may not be admitted to discharge the named agent: the first because such evidence does not contradict the written agreement, but shows that such agreement also binds another; the second because such evidence does contradict the written agreement by seeking to establish that the agreement does not bind him whom it purports to bind.[5]

"A principal may be charged upon a written parol executory contract entered into by an agent in his own name, within his authority, although the name of the principal does not appear in the instrument, and was not disclosed, and the party dealing with the agent supposed that he was acting for himself, and this doctrine obtains as well in re-

[1] See *ante*, § 123; suing the agent before discovering the principal is not an election. Remmel *v.* Townsend, 83 Hun, (N. Y.) 353.

[2] Pentz *v.* Stanton, 10 Wend. (N. Y.) 271.

[3] Johnson *v.* Armstrong, 83 Tex. 325.

[4] *Ante*, § 123; but see Chandler *v.* Coe, 54 N. H. 561.

[5] Cream City Glass Co. *v.* Friedlander, 84 Wis. 53; Higgins *v.* Senior, 8 M. & W. 834; Leake on Cont. (3d ed.), p. 413.

spect to contracts which are required to be in writing, as to those where a writing is not essential to their validity. It is, doubtless, somewhat difficult to reconcile the doctrine here stated with the rule that parol evidence is inadmissible to change, enlarge or vary a written contract, and the argument upon which it is supported savors of subtlety and refinement. . . . Whatever ground there may have been originally to question the legal soundness of the doctrine referred to, it is now too firmly established to be overthrown, and I am of the opinion that the practical effect of the rule as now declared is to promote justice and fair dealing."[1]

It has been thought, however, that if the principal is known to the third party, and he accepts the written obligation of the agent, he cannot sue the principal; this on the ground that he is conclusively presumed to have given exclusive credit to the agent. "Where there is a written contract not under seal, executed in the name of the agent, parol evidence is admissible for the purpose of charging an unknown principal, but not for the purpose of charging a known principal, and . . . is inadmissible for the purpose of discharging the agent whether the principal was known or unknown."[2] But this is not in accordance with the general statement of the rule,[3] nor, it would seem, with the weight of authority.[4]

If the contract is signed by the agent in his principal's name, as "P. Q. per A. B.," parol evidence is inadmissible to charge the agent (A. B.) upon the instrument, since the contract clearly shows the relations of all the parties to it, who was to be bound, and who was not to be bound, and its legal effect cannot be varied by parol.[5]

[1] Andrews, J., in Briggs *v.* Partridge, 64 N. Y. 357; Waddill *v.* Sebree, 88 Va. 1012.

[2] Chandler *v.* Coe, 54 N. H. 561, 576.

[3] Story on Agency, § 160 *a*.

[4] Byington *v.* Simpson, 134 Mass. 169.

[5] Heffron *v.* Pollard, 73 Tex. 96.

§ 198. (III) Effect of Custom.

Where an agent contracts, though as agent, in a capacity or business where, by custom, the agent is usually liable, the agent and the principal are both presumptively liable and the third party may elect which he will hold. The clearest case of this kind is that of the master of a ship who, when contracting within his authority, binds both himself and the owner according to the custom of the maritime law,[1] though the effect of the custom may be overcome by proof of contrary intent.[2] The custom of trade may be shown in other cases to impose liability upon the agent.[3]

§ 199. (IV.) Interest in Subject-matter.

Where an agent has an interest in the subject-matter of the contract, the agent and the principal are both liable, and the third party may elect which he will hold.[4] Such is the case where an auctioneer sells goods, for he has a special property in the goods and could maintain an action for the price. It follows that he is liable personally on the contract.

4. *Where neither Principal nor Agent is bound.*

§ 200. (I) Revocation of Authority by Death.

Where the agent's authority, unknown to him, has been revoked by the death of his principal, and subsequent to such revocation he makes a contract in behalf of the former principal, no one is bound by the contract: not the estate of the principal, because the agency is revoked; not the agent, because there is a presumption that those

1 Sydnor *v.* Hurd, 8 Tex. 98.

2 James *v.* Bixby, 11 Mass. 34.

3 Fairlie *v.* Fenton, L. R. 5 Ex. 169; Pike *v.* Ongley, 18 Q. B. D. 708.

4 Woolfe *v.* Horne, L. R. 2 Q. B. D. 355.

who deal with an agent assume the risk that the authority may be terminated by death.[1]

§ 201. (II) Disclosure of Facts affecting Authority.

Where an agent discloses to a third party all the material facts affecting the scope of his authority, and with full knowledge of such facts the third party enters into a contract with the principal through the agent, which contract is in excess of the agent's authority, no one is bound; neither the principal for he never authorized the contract, nor the agent for he never warranted his authority.[2] An agent's liability on a contract executed in the name of his principal rests on the implied warranties as to the existence and competence of his principal, and the sufficiency of the authority.[3] But clearly no such warranty can be implied when the third party is as fully informed of all the facts as is the agent himself.

§ 202. (III) Insufficiency of Form.

Where the agent contracts in the name of his principal and within the scope of his authority but employs an insufficient form of contract, probably no one is bound; certainly not the principal for the contract cannot be enforced, and probably not the agent for he can hardly be said to warrant the sufficiency of the form of the contract.[4]

5. *Special case of Public Agents.*

§ 203. Public Agents.

The rules governing the liabilities of a private agent are not generally applicable to public agents. There is a strong presumption that a public agent does not intend to

[1] Farmers', &c., Co. *v.* Wilson, 139 N. Y. 284.

[2] Lilly *v.* Smales, 1892, 1 Q. B. 456; Michael *v.* Jones, 84 Mo. 578; Ware *v.* Morgan, 67 Ala. 461; Newman *v.* Sylvester, 42 Ind. 106.

[3] See *ante*, § 183.

[4] See Beattie *v.* Lord Ebury, L. R. 7 Ch. App. 777.

bind himself personally, or to become a party to the contract. Even a contract under seal, made in the name of a public agent, will be construed to be the contract of the government and not of the agent, where, in case of a private agency, such a result would be impossible;[1] *a fortiori* if the contract be not under seal.[2] But the presumption in the agent's favor may be overcome by clear proof of an intent to render himself personally liable.[3]

There seems to be no good reason why the same indulgence should not be granted to public officers who sign negotiable instruments, adding words descriptive of their office, and several cases have distinctly decided that such officers are entitled to the usual presumption.[4] But the doctrine is overlooked or questioned in other cases.[5]

Some cases make a further distinction to the effect that the presumption does not extend in any case to the officers of a municipality or town which is capable of making contracts for itself and is liable to be sued thereon.[6]

6. *Liability of Agent in quasi-contract.*

§ 204. Money paid to Agent by Mistake or Fraud.

An agent is liable to a third party in quasi-contract under the following circumstances: —

(1) Where the third party has paid money to the agent, as agent, from a mistake of fact, and notice is given the agent before he pays the money over to his principal or

[1] Hodgson *v.* Dexter, 1 Cranch, (U. S.) 343; Knight *v.* Clark, 48 N. J. L. 22.

[2] Walker *v.* Swartwout, 12 Johns. (N. Y.) 443; Savage *v.* Gibbs, 4 Gray, (Mass.) 601; Parks *v.* Ross, 11 How. (U. S.) 362.

[3] Simonds *v.* Heard, 23 Pick. (Mass.) 120; Brown *v.* Bradlee, 156 Mass. 28.

[4] Monticello *v.* Kendall, 72 Ind. 91; Sanborn *v.* Neal, 4 Minn. 126; McClellan *v.* Reynolds, 49 Mo. 312.

[5] Cahokia *v.* Rautenberg, 88 Ill. 219; Wing *v.* Glick, 56 Ia. 473.

[6] Providence *v.* Miller, 11 R. I. 272; Brown *v.* Bradlee, *supra.*

otherwise changes his legal position on the strength of such payment.[1] But there must be a mistake of fact; other circumstances, as failure of consideration, would not bring the case within the rule.[2] If the agent has not acted as agent, but for an undisclosed principal, the case escapes the doctrines of agency and is treated like any case of payment of money by mistake.[3]

(2) Where the third party is induced by the fraud of the agent or his principal to pay money to the agent, he may recover the money from the agent, — certainly before the agent has changed his legal situation, since the payment of the money, and upon the faith of such payment.[4] If the fraud be that of the agent, it would seem that the money could be recovered at any time. The same result follows if an agent receives for his principal money which the law forbids him to receive, as from an insolvent debtor.[5]

(3) Where the third party pays the money to the agent through compulsion or extortion, even though no notice has been given and the agent has paid the money to the principal, an action may be brought against the agent for its recovery.[6] But where the third party pays the money voluntarily, or where an innocent agent has before notice paid the money over to the principal, the agent is not liable.[7]

[1] Cox *v.* Prentice, 3 M. & Sel. 344; La Farge *v.* Kneeland, 7 Cow. (N. Y.) 456; O'Connor *v.* Clopton, 60 Miss. 349; Smith *v.* Binder, 75 Ill. 492.

[2] Ellis *v.* Goulton, 1893, 1 Q. B. 350.

[3] Newall *v.* Tomlinson, L. R. 6 C. P. 405; Smith *v.* Kelly, 43 Mich. 390.

[4] Herrick *v.* Gallagher, 60 Barb. (N. Y.) 566; Buller *v.* Harrison, 2 Cowp. 568.

[5] Larkin *v.* Hapgood, 56 Vt. 597.

[6] Elliott *v.* Swartwout, 10 Pet. (U. S.) 137.

[7] Ellis *v.* Goulton, *supra;* Buller *v.* Harrison, 2 Cowp. 568.

§ 205. Money received to the use of the Third Party.

(4) Where the agent has received money from his principal to be paid to the third party, and undertakes so to pay it, but instead converts it to his own use, the third party may, at his election, proceed against the agent as for money had and received to his use.[1] And it has been held that if the third party requests the agent to pay it to X, that X may maintain an action against the agent. "An action for 'money had and received' is a most liberal action, and may be as comprehensive as a bill in equity."[2] But an election to hold the agent is final and discharges the principal from further liability.[3] If the agent after receiving the money promises to pay the third party, he is liable upon his promise. "No consideration need pass as between the agent and the creditor. The funds in his hands are a sufficient consideration for his agreement."[4] This falls under the doctrine of a "promise for the benefit of a third person," and escapes the general doctrine as to privity of contract.[5]

7. *Liability of Third Person to Agent.*

§ 206. Introduction.

Since the agent may be liable, either solely, or in common with the principal, on contracts entered into in behalf of the latter, it should follow that the contractual obligation is reciprocal and that the third person is also liable to the agent. Such is found to be the case. The right of the agent to sue the third person may be treated under the following classes: —

[1] Keene *v.* Sage, 75 Me. 138; Beach *v.* Ficke, (Iowa), 62 N. W. Rep. 753, 756.

[2] Keene *v.* Sage, *supra.*

[3] Beach *v.* Ficke, *supra.*

[4] Goodwin *v.* Bowden, 54 Me. 424.

[5] *Ante,* § 118.

1. Where the agent alone may sue.
2. Where the agent or principal may sue, but the principal may control the suit.
3. Where the agent or principal may sue, but the principal cannot control the suit.

§ 207. (I) Where the Agent alone may sue.

Where the agent alone is bound on a contract made by him with a third party [1] (other than on the warranty of authority), the agent alone can maintain an action on the contract against the third party; [2] but the principal may, perhaps, control the action in the name of the agent. And where the action is brought in the agent's name for the benefit of the principal, the defendant may avail himself of any defence or set-off that would be good against either, for he is entitled to defend against the party of record, and he is entitled equally to defend against the one for whose use the action is brought.[3]

In the following cases the agent alone can sue: (1) where he contracts in his own name by deed; [4] (2) where he is solely named as payee of a negotiable instrument; [5] (3) where by the terms of the instrument the rights under it are expressly restricted to the agent; [6] (4) where the plaintiff contracts as agent for an unnamed principal, but is in fact the principal himself.[7] In the last case the third party cannot be presumed to have contracted in reliance on the credit of a principal who is not named, but on that of the agent who is named, and the doctrine that "every man has a right to elect what parties he will deal

[1] *Ante*, § 183 *et seq.*
[2] Colburn *v.* Phillips, 13 Gray, (Mass.) 64.
[3] Bliss *v.* Sneath, 103 Cal. 43.
[4] *Ante*, §§ 134, 188.
[5] *Ante*, §§ 135, 194.
[6] *Ante*, § 133; Humble *v.* Hunter, 12 Q. B. 310.
[7] Schmaltz *v.* Avery, 16 Q. B. 655.

with," seems to have no application. If, however, the agent contracts for a named principal, but is in fact the principal himself, it seems he cannot sue as plaintiff, at least unless the third party has subsequently recognized him as principal.[1]

§ 208. (II) Where both Agent and Principal may sue.

Where the agent and principal are both bound on the contract,[2] the primary right to maintain an action against the third party is in the principal, but, subject to his assent express or tacit,[3] the agent may maintain an action wherever an action could be maintained against the agent.[4] "It is a well-established rule of law that when a contract not under seal, is made with an agent in his own name for an undisclosed principal, either the agent or the principal may sue. If the agent sues, it is no ground of defence that the beneficial interest is in another, or that the plaintiff, when he recovers will be bound to account to another. . . . The agent's right is, of course, subordinate to and liable to the control of the principal, to the extent of his interest. He may supersede it by suing in his own name, or otherwise suspend or extinguish it, subject only to the special right or lien which the agent may have acquired."[5] The right of the agent to sue ceases with the termination of the agency, whether the agency is terminated by the act of the parties or by operation of law.[6]

These cases are those in which the agent contracts in

[1] Dicey on Parties (Am. ed. 1879), 165; Rayner *v.* Grote, 15 M. & W. 359.

[2] *Ante*, § 196 *et seq.*

[3] Sadler *v.* Leigh, 4 Camp. 194.

[4] Rowe *v.* Rand, 111 Ind. 206; Albany, &c. Co., *v.* Lundberg, 121 U. S. 451.

[5] Rhoades *v.* Blackiston, 106 Mass. 334.

[6] Miller *v.* State Bank of Duluth, (Minn.) 59 N. W. Rep. 309.

his own name, but in behalf of his principal, the contract not being under seal, or a negotiable instrument, or expressly restricted to the agent.[1]

§ 209. (III) Where Principal cannot control the Suit.

Where the agent has a beneficial interest in the contract,[2] he may maintain an action in his own name free from the control of the principal,[3] at least to the extent of his interest. But such an interest must exist in order to give the agent a right of action;[4] though this will be presumed where the agent is one who usually has such an interest, as an auctioneer.[5] The measure of damages is the same whether the suit be brought in the name of the agent or in that of the principal.[6]

§ 210. Liability in Quasi-contract.

Where the agent has paid money by mistake to the third party, he may maintain an action for its recovery. It seems either the principal or the agent may sue,[7] and as the agent is liable to the principal for negligence in the conduct of the business, this may be the only way in which the agent can protect himself against loss.[8]

[1] *Ante*, §§ 123, 196–199.

[2] *Ante*, § 199.

[3] Chitty on Pleading, p. 8; Rowe *v.* Rand, 111 Ind. 206; Thompson *v.* Kelly, 101 Mass. 291.

[4] Fairlie *v.* Fenton, L. R. 5 Ex. 169.

[5] Minturn *v.* Main, 7 N. Y. 220.

[6] Evrit *v.* Bancroft, 22 Oh. St. 172.

[7] Stevenson *v.* Mortimer, Comp. 805; Oom *v.* Bruce, 12 East, 225.

[8] Kent *v.* Bornstein, 12 Allen, (Mass.) 342.

CHAPTER XVI.

TORTS BETWEEN AGENT AND THIRD PARTY.

§ 211. Principles of Liability.

It is a fundamental proposition that every man is liable personally for all the wrongs committed by him to the damage of another, and that he cannot shield himself behind the plea that he was acting under the direction and for the benefit of an employer. So far as the rights of third persons are concerned the agent acts at his own peril, whether he act wilfully, negligently, or mistakenly.[1]

But the law makes a distinction, sometimes very subtle, between what is termed misfeasance on the part of the agent and what is termed non-feasance, holding that the agent is personally liable for the first but not for the second. It becomes necessary therefore to examine these two concepts of the law as bearing upon the liability of an agent for his torts.

§ 212. Meaning of Non-feasance.

Strictly, as applied to this subject, non-feasance means the not doing at all by an agent of the thing which by his contract with the principal he has agreed to do. Strictly, it does not extend to a case where an agent has once entered upon the performance of the contractual obligation and then neglected to do something which by his contract or promise he has undertaken to do. This is the view

[1] Weber *v.* Weber, 47 Mich. 569; McEntire *v.* Potter, L. R. 22 Q. B. D. 438.

taken of the distinction between non-feasance and misfeasance in cases of gratuitous agencies where the question arises between principal and agent,[1] and it is the view taken by the best considered authorities in cases of negligence arising between an agent and third persons. "It is often said in the books that an agent is responsible to third persons for misfeasance only, and not for non-feasance. And it is doubtless true that if an agent never does anything toward carrying out his contract with his principal, but wholly omits or neglects to do so, the principal is the only person who can maintain any action against him for the non-feasance. But if the agent once actually undertakes and enters upon the execution of a particular work, it is his duty to use reasonable care in the manner of executing it, so as not to cause any injury to third persons which may be the natural consequence of his acts; and he cannot, by abandoning its execution midway and leaving things in a dangerous condition, exempt himself from liability to any person who suffers injury by reason of his having so left them without proper safeguards. This is not non-feasance, or doing nothing; but it is misfeasance, doing improperly."[2]

Suppose that an agent undertakes the general management of real estate, agreeing to lease it, collect the rents, pay the taxes, keep it insured, repair it when necessary, and so on, and that he enters upon the performance of his duties, all of which he faithfully performs except as to the repairs, and that, as to those, he allows the premises to be so dangerously out of repair that X is injured in consequence of their defective condition; can X recover for his injuries against the agent? The question has been answered in the negative on the same state of facts by the

[1] Thorne *v.* Deas, 4 Johns. (N. Y.) 84.

[2] Osborne *v.* Morgan, 130 Mass. 102. And see Bell *v.* Josselyn, 3 Gray, (Mass.) 309.

Federal courts and the courts of the State of Louisiana,[1] and these cases are now regarded as the leading American authorities. Another court has reached the same conclusion where it was alleged that the omission of the agent was malicious and with the intent to injure the plaintiff.[2] Other courts, however, have taken the opposite view, holding that the agent is liable for his own personal negligence in the management of his principal's premises, where he has once entered upon the discharge of his duties.[3]

The latter view seems more consonant with sound principles, for it distinguishes between negligence and non-feasance. Had the agent entered upon the repair of the premises and done his work ill, he would undoubtedly have been liable.[4] Why not also when he enters upon the care of the premises by taking 'possession' of them for his principal and doing all that a possessor should except repair ? If non-feasance were confined to cases where the agent simply fails to enter upon the performance of his duties at all, much confusion would be avoided and a fundamental principle of personal obligation for one's own acts and omissions would be vindicated.[5]

§ 213. Liability for Misfeasance.

For misfeasance an agent is unquestionably liable. The two torts which an agent may most easily commit in the conduct of his agency are fraud and conversion. The first is always wilful, or at least reckless; the second may be wholly free from moral turpitude.

[1] Delaney *v.* Rochereau, 34 La. Ann. 1123; Carey *v.* Rochereau, 16 Fed. Rep. 87.

[2] Feltus *v.* Swan, 62 Miss. 415.

[3] Baird *v.* Shipman, 132 Ill. 16; Campbell *v.* Portland Sugar Co., 62 Me. 552, 566.

[4] Harriman *v.* Stowe, 57 Mo. 93.

[5] See Kelly *v.* Metropolitan Ry., 1895, 1 Q. B. 944.

(1) *Fraud.* An agent is personally liable for his own frauds committed in the course of the agency, although committed for the principal's benefit. "A person cannot avoid responsibility merely because he gets no personal advantage from his fraud. All persons who are active in defrauding others are liable for what they do, whether they act in one capacity or another. . . . While it may be true that the principal is often liable for the fraud of his agent though himself honest, his own fraud will not exonerate his fraudulent agent."[1] It is, of course, necessary that the essential elements of deceit should be present in order to found an action in tort. Therefore if the agent makes the representation believing it to be true, he is not guilty of fraud, although his principal may have known it to be false.[2]

(2) *Conversion.* "Any person who, however innocently, obtains possession of goods of a person who has been fraudulently deprived of them, and disposes of them, whether for his own benefit or that of any other person, is guilty of conversion."[3] Accordingly an agent is bound to know that his principal has title to the goods which form the subject matter of the agency. "He who assumes to deal or intermeddle with personal property which is not his own must see to it that he has a warrant therefor from some one who is authorized to give it."[4] If an agent sells stolen bonds for the thief and pays the proceeds over to his principal, he is liable to the true owner for conversion and it is no defence that he acted innocently or that the bonds were negotiable.[5] So if one act innocently as the agent of one of two joint owners of a chattel and sell

[1] Weber *v.* Weber, 47 Mich. 569.

[2] Pollock on Torts, (4th ed.) 280.

[3] Hollins *v.* Fowler, L. R. 7 H. L. 757.

[4] Spraights *v.* Hawley, 39 N. Y. 441.

[5] Kimball *v.* Billings, 55 Me. 147; Swim *v.* Wilson, 90 Cal. 126.

the entire chattel without the consent of the other joint owner, he is liable for conversion.[1]

A doubt was expressed by some of the judges in the case of Hollins *v.* Fowler[2] whether the rule was as broad as is above stated, and one American case at least has held that a factor is not liable for selling stolen goods unless after demand or notice.[3] But the weight of authority sustains the rule.[4]

214. Whether Principal and Agent are liable jointly.

The question as to whether the principal and agent may be sued jointly has given rise to some discussion. Two classes of cases are distinguishable:

(1) Where the principal and agent are in fact joint tort-feasors, as where the principal commands the wrong to be done and therefore purposely participates in it, the two may be sued jointly.[5] They are in no different position than any other joint tort-feasors. In trespass all participants are regarded as joint tort-feasors.[6] If there are two or more principals, one or all or any number may be joined.[7]

(2) Where the principal and agent are not in fact joint wrong-doers, but the principal's liability rests upon the ground of public policy heretofore explained,[8] there is a difference of opinion as to whether the two are liable jointly. As stated above, if both are liable in trespass,

[1] Perminter *v.* Kelly, 18 Ala. 716.

[2] L. R. 7 H. L. 757.

[3] Roach *v.* Turk, 9 Heisk. (Tenn.) 708. And see Leuthold *v.* Fairchild, 35 Minn. 99, 111.

[4] Hoffman *v.* Carow, 20 Wend. 21, s. c. 22 Wend. 285; Rice *v.* Yocum, 155 Pa. St. 538; Robinson *v.* Bird, 158 Mass. 357.

[5] Moore *v.* Fitchburg R., 4 Gray, (Mass.) 465.

[6] Hewett *v.* Swift, 3 Allen, (Mass.) 420.

[7] Roberts *v.* Johnson, 58 N. Y. 613.

[8] *Ante*, §§ 148–150.

they are regarded as joint wrong-doers; but if the principal is liable in an action on the case, simply because of his position as principal, it has been held that a joint action would not lie.[1] But it is believed that the weight of authority is otherwise, and that in any case where an action would lie against the two severally it will lie against them jointly.[2]

215. Liability of Third Person to Agent for Torts.

The third person is liable to the agent for torts committed against him; but the torts that may be committed against him as agent are not numerous.

(1) Where the agent has a special property in the goods which form the subject-matter of the agency, he may maintain an action for an injury to the goods or for their conversion. In such cases he is both bailee and agent, and it is a general rule of law that a bailee, or a possessor having a special property in the goods, may maintain an action against such as injure or take away the chattel.[3] Indeed it is not clear that anything more than possession is necessary to sustain the action.[4]

(2) Where the agent is engaged in the sale of a specific article, his compensation being by way of commission on his sales, a false and libellous statement concerning such articles which diminishes his sales and profits, will found an action against the one making the statement.[5]

(3) We have already seen that the principal may main-

[1] Parsons *v.* Winchell, 5 Cush. (Mass.) 592; Campbell *v.* Portland Sugar Co., 62 Me. 552, 566.

[2] Dicey on Parties, (Am. ed. 1879) 490; Phelps *v.* Wait, 30 N. Y. 78; Shearer *v.* Evans, 89 Ind. 400. Cf. White *v.* Sawyer, 16 Gray, (Mass.) 586.

[3] Moore *v.* Robinson, 2 B. & Ad. 817; Fitzhugh *v.* Wiman, 9 N. Y. 559, 567; Robinson *v.* Webb, 11 Bush, (Ky.) 464, 483.

[4] Pollock on Torts, (4th ed.) 303–5.

[5] Weiss *v.* Whittemore, 28 Mich. 366.

tain an action against any one who unjustifiably induces the agent to quit the employment.[1] In the same way, and for the same reasons, the agent may maintain an action against any one who induces the principal to dismiss him from the employment.[2]

[1] *Ante*, § 176.

[2] Chipley *v.* Atkinson, 23 Fla. 206.

APPENDIX.

NEW YORK FACTORS ACT, 1830.

L. 1830, c. 179.

An Act for the Amendment of the Law Relative to Principals and Factors or Agents.

§ 1. After this Act shall take effect, every person in whose name any merchandise shall be shipped, shall be deemed the true owner thereof, so far as to entitle the consignee of such merchandise to a lien thereon,

1. For any money advanced, or negotiable security given by such consignee, to or for the use of the person in whose name such shipment shall have been made; and,

2. For any money or negotiable security received by the person in whose name such shipment shall have been made, to or for the use of such consignee.

§ 2. The lien provided for in the preceding section, shall not exist where such consignee shall have notice, by the bill of lading or otherwise, at or before the advancing of any money or security by him, or at or before the receiving of such money or security by the person in whose name the shipment shall have been made, that such person is not the actual and *bona fide* owner thereof.

§ 3. Every factor or other agent, entrusted with the possession of any bill of lading, custom-house permit, or warehouse-keeper's receipt for the delivery of any such merchandise, and every such factor or agent not having the documentary evidence of title, who shall be entrusted with the possession of any merchandise for the purpose of sale, or as a security for any advances to be made or obtained thereon, shall be deemed to be the true owner thereof, so far as to give validity to any contract made by such agent with any other person, for the sale or disposition of the whole or any part of such merchandise, for any money advanced, or negotiable instrument or other obligation in writing given by such other person upon the faith thereof.

§ 4. Every person who shall hereafter accept or take any such merchandise in deposit for any such agent, as a security for any antecedent debt or demand, shall not acquire thereby, or enforce any right or interest in or to such merchandise or document, other than was possessed or might have been enforced by such agent at the time of such deposit.

§ 5. Nothing contained in the two last preceding sections of this act, shall be construed to prevent the true owner of any merchandise so deposited, from demanding or receiving the same, upon repayment of the money advanced, or on restoration of the security given, on the deposit of such merchandise, and upon satisfying such lien as may exist thereon in favor of the agent who may have deposited the same; nor from recovering any balance which may remain in the hands of the person with whom such merchandise shall have been deposited, as the produce of the sale thereof, after satisfying the amount justly due to such person by reason of such deposit.

§ 6. Nothing contained in this Act shall authorize a common carrier, warehouse-keeper, or other person to whom merchandise or other property may be committed for transportation or storage only, to sell or hypothecate the same.

§ 7. [Repealed by L. 1886, ch. 593.]

§ 8. Nothing contained in the last preceding section, shall be construed to prevent the Court of Chancery from compelling discovery, or granting relief upon any bill to be filed in that court by the owner of any merchandise so entrusted or consigned, against the factor or agent by whom such merchandise shall have been applied or sold contrary to the provisions of the said section, or against any person who shall have been knowingly a party to such fraudulent application or sale thereof; but no answer to any such bill shall be read in evidence against the defendant making the same, on the trial of any indictment for the fraud charged in the bill.

ENGLISH FACTORS ACT, 1889.

52 & 53 Vict. c. 45.

An Act to Amend and Consolidate the Factors Acts.
[26th August, 1889.]

Be it enacted by the Queen's most Excellent Majesty, by and with the advice and consent of the Lords Spiritual and Temporal, and Commons, in this present Parliament assembled, and by the authority of the same, as follows:—

Preliminary.

1. For the Purposes of this Act — (1.) The expression "mercantile agent" shall mean a mercantile agent having in the customary course of his business as such agent authority either to sell goods, or to consign goods for the purpose of sale, or to buy goods, or to raise money on the security of goods: (2.) A person shall be deemed to be in possession of goods or of the documents of title to goods, where the goods or documents are in his actual custody or are held by any other person subject to his control or for him or on his behalf: (3.) The expression "goods" shall include wares and merchandise: (4.) The expression "document of title" shall include any bill of lading, dock warrant, warehouse-keeper's certificate, and warrant or order for the delivery of goods, and any other document used in the ordinary course of business as proof of the possession or control of goods, or authorizing or purporting to authorize, either by endorsement or by delivery, the possessor of the document to transfer or receive goods thereby represented: (5.) The expression "pledge" shall include any contract pledging, or giving lien or security on, goods, whether in consideration of an original advance or of any further or continuing advance or of any pecuniary liability: (6.) The expression "person" shall include any body of persons corporate or unincorporate.

Disposition by Mercantile Agents.

2. — (1.) Where a mercantile agent is, with the consent of the owner, in possession of goods or of the documents of title to goods, any sale, pledge, or other disposition of the goods, made by him when acting in the ordinary course of business of a mercantile agent, shall, subject to the provisions of this Act, be as valid as if he were expressly authorized by the owner of the goods to make the same; provided that the person taking under the disposition acts in good faith, and has not at the time of the disposition notice that the person making the disposition has not the authority to make the same. (2.) Where a mercantile agent has, with the consent of the owner, been in possession of goods or of the documents of title to goods, any sale, pledge, or other disposition, which would have been valid if the consent had continued, shall be valid notwithstanding the determination of the consent: provided that the person taking under the disposition has not at the time thereof notice that the consent has been determined. (3.) Where a mercantile agent has obtained possession of any documents of title to goods by reason of his being or having been, with the consent of the owner, in possession of the goods represented thereby, or of any other documents of title to the goods, his possession of the first-mentioned documents shall, for the purposes of this Act, be deemed to be the consent of the owner. (4.) For the purposes of this Act the consent of the owner shall be presumed in the absence of evidence to the contrary.

3. A pledge of the documents of title to goods shall be deemed to be a pledge of the goods.

4. Where a mercantile agent pledges goods as security for a debt or liability due from the pledgor to the pledgee before the time of the pledge, the pledgee shall acquire no further right to the goods than could have been enforced by the pledgor at the time of the pledge.

5. The consideration necessary for the validity of a sale, pledge, or other disposition, of goods, in pursuance of this Act, may be either a payment in cash, or the delivery or transfer of other goods, or of a document of title to goods, or of a negotiable security, or any other valuable consideration; but where goods are pledged by a mercantile agent in consideration of the delivery or transfer of other goods, or of a document of title to goods, or of a negotiable security, the pledgee shall acquire no right or interest in the goods so pledged in excess of the value of the goods, documents, or security when so delivered or transferred in exchange.

6. For the purposes of this Act an agreement made with a mercantile agent through a clerk or other person authorized in the ordinary course of business to make contracts of sale or pledge on his behalf shall be deemed to be an agreement with the agent.

7. — (1.) Where the owner of goods has given possession of the goods to another person for the purpose of consignment or sale, or has shipped the goods in the name of another person, and the consignee of the goods has not had notice that such person is not the owner of the goods, the consignee shall, in respect of advances made to or for the use of such person, have the same lien on the goods as if such person were the owner of the goods, and may transfer any such lien to another person. (2.) Nothing in this section shall limit or affect the validity of any sale, pledge, or disposition by a mercantile agent.

Dispositions by Sellers and Buyers of Goods.

8. Where a person, having sold goods, continues, or is, in possession of the goods or of the documents of title to the goods, the delivery or transfer by that person, or by a mercantile agent acting for him, of the goods or documents of title under any sale, pledge, or other disposition thereof, or under any agreement for sale, pledge, or other disposition thereof, to any person receiving the same in good faith and without notice of the previous sale, shall have the same effect as if the person making the delivery or transfer were expressly authorized by the owner of the goods to make the same.

9. Where a person, having bought or agreed to buy goods, obtains with the consent of the seller possession of the goods or the documents of title to the goods, the delivery or transfer, by that person or by a mercantile agent acting for him, of the goods or documents of title, under any sale, pledge, or other disposition thereof, or under any agreement for sale, pledge, or other disposition thereof, to any person receiving the same in good faith and without notice of any lien or other right of the original seller in respect of the goods, shall have the same effect as if the person making the delivery or transfer were a mercantile agent in possession of the goods or documents of title with the consent of the owner.

10. Where a document of title to goods has been lawfully transferred to a person as a buyer or owner of the goods, and that person transfers the document to a person who takes the document in good faith and for valuable consideration, the last-mentioned transfer shall have the same effect for defeating any vendor's lien or right of stoppage in transitu as the transfer of a bill of lading has for defeating the right of stoppage in transitu.

Supplemental.

11. For the purposes of this Act, the transfer of a docu ment may be by endorsement, or, where the document is by custom or by its express terms transferable by delivery, or makes the goods deliverable to the bearer, then by delivery.

12. — (1.) Nothing in this Act shall authorize an agent to exceed or depart from his authority as between himself and his principal, or exempt him from any liability, civil or criminal, for so doing. (2.) Nothing in this Act shall prevent the owner of goods from recovering the goods from an agent or his trustee in bankruptcy at any time before the sale or pledge thereof, or shall prevent the owner of goods pledged by an agent from having the right to redeem the goods at any time before the sale thereof, on satisfying the claim for which the goods were pledged, and paying to the agent, if by him required, any money in respect of which the agent would by law be entitled to retain the goods or the documents of title thereto, or any of them, by way of lien as against the owner, or from recovering from any person with whom the goods have been pledged any balance of money remaining in his hands as the produce of the sale of the goods after deducting the amount of his lien. (3.) Nothing in this Act shall prevent the owner of goods sold by an agent from recover ing from the buyer the price agreed to be paid for the same, or any part of that price, subject to any right of set-off on the part of the buyer against the agent.

13. The provisions of this Act shall be construed in amplification and not in derogation of the powers exercisable by an agent independently of this Act.

14. The enactments mentioned in the schedule to this Act are hereby repealed as from the commencement of this Act, but this repeal shall not affect any right acquired or liability incurred before the commencement of this Act under any enactment hereby repealed.[1]

15. This Act shall commence and come into operation on the first day of January one thousand eight hundred and ninety.

16. This Act shall not extend to Scotland.[2]

17. This Act may be cited as the Factors Act, 1889.

[1] Repeals 4 Geo. 4. c. 83; 6 Geo. 4. c. 94; 5 & 6 Vict. c. 39; 40 & 41 Vict. c. 39.

[2] Extended to Scotland with slight modifications by 53 & 54 Vict. c. 40.

INDEX.

www.ingramcontent.com/pod-product-compliance
Lightning Source LLC
Chambersburg PA
CBHW030717250326
R18027900001B/R180279PG41599CBX00018B/27

* 9 7 8 1 8 9 3 1 2 2 2 3 9 *